# DUSTY BOB

Manchester University Press

# Dusty Bob

## A cultural history of dustmen, 1780–1870

BRIAN MAIDMENT

Manchester University Press
Manchester and New York

*distributed exclusively in the USA by Palgrave*

*Published by* Manchester University Press

Oxford Road, Manchester M13 9NR, UK
*and* Room 400, 175 Fifth Avenue, New York, NY 10010, USA

www.manchesteruniversitypress.co.uk

*Distributed exclusively in the USA by*
Palgrave, 175 Fifth Avenue, New York,
NY 10010, USA

*Distributed exclusively in Canada by*
UBC Press, University of British Columbia, 2029 West Mall,
Vancouver, BC, Canada V6T 1Z2

*British Library Cataloguing-in-Publication Data*
A catalogue record for this book is available from the British Library

*Library of Congress Cataloging-in-Publication Data applied for*

ISBN 978 0 7190 5283 5 *hardback*

First published 2007

16 15 14 13 12 11 10 09 08 07 10 9 8 7 6 5 4 3 2 1

Typeset by Carnegie Book Production, Lancaster
Printed in Great Britain
by Biddles Ltd, King's Lynn

It is necessary to respect what we discard.

(Dan DeLillo, *Underworld*, 1998)

My lords and gentlemen and honourable boards,… you in the course of your dust-shovelling and cinder-raking have piled up a mountain of pretentious failure.

(Charles Dickens on Parliament, *Hard Times*, 1859/60)

Indeed much of the class system of European and American life up until the present century, rested upon the distinction between those who dealt habitually with human detritus and those who did not.

(Robertson Davies, *The Cunning Man*, 1994)

[Mass culture is]
… transformational work on social anxieties and fantasies, which must then have some effective presence in order to be managed or repressed.

(Fredric Jameson, *Signatures of the Visible*, 1992)

The refined are drawn to the unrefined, whose coarseness deceptively promises what their own culture denies …

(Adorno, Minima Moralia)

If thou art a Londoner, gentle reader, thou well knowest what a *dustman* is, but if, peradventure, thou art a dweller in the provinces, and thy business or pleasure never bid thee to sojourn in that wilderness of human nests that extendeth from Brentford, in Middlesex, unto Stratford-le-Bow, in Essex, and from Camberwell, in Surrey, even unto merry Islington, it is more than probable that thou knowest nothing about the matter; and therefore I will endeavour to inform thee, in order that thou may'st fully comprehend the dusty demerits of the subjoined case – shoulds't thou think proper to read it. If, on the other hand thou deems't it derogatory to thy dignity to read of dust and dustmen, why, shut the book and go thy way – but remember that thou thyself art dust, and unto dust shalt thou return, indeed, as all *men* are *dust*, thou art thyself, in some sort, a *dust-man*; and the very dust of which thy particular manhood is compounded, may, as the Lord Hamlet saith, be found some day or other stopping the bung-hole of a beer-barrel! – But go thy way, with thy dignified dust for the present, whilst I pursue my dusty record in peace.

John Wight
*More Mornings in Bow Street*
(London: J. Robinson, 1827), 261–2

# Contents

# Note on citation of images

Where possible, images have been cited from the two easiest available sources, the British Museum Catalogue and the Lewis Walpole Library Digital Collection. References to F. G. Stephens and M. D. George's *British Museum Catalogue of Political and Personal Satires* (11 vols, British Museum, 1874–1950), which is available in many scholarly libraries often with the accompanying microfilm of the images, are abbreviated to *BMC*. References to the Lewis Walpole Library are abbreviated to LWL followed by the call number for the relevant print.

# Acknowledgements

One of the pleasures of scholarly research is that, far from being solitary and unhealthily obsessional, it requires high levels of human contact. Human contact is always fraught with risks, but in the case of this book, all my many necessary dealings with others – librarians, curators, scholars, booksellers, print dealers – have been at worst courteous and efficient, and at best a genuinely creative pooling of knowledge, knowledge offered not as part of an economy of exchange and mart, but as something interesting, valuable and worthwhile for its own sake – in short, a gift of knowledge. To all those many who have anonymously written this book, I offer thanks, even if I have misrepresented their knowledge or ideas.

More pragmatically, I owe considerable debts to many libraries, most obviously those at the Universities of Huddersfield, Salford, Liverpool, Manchester Metropolitan University, Liverpool John Moores University and the University of Central Lancashire. For the more metropolitan and obscure parts of my work I have used the resources in the British Library, the Theatre Museum in Covent Garden, the Guildhall Library, The Museum of London, The Wellcome Institute, The Bodleian Library, Oxford (the John Johnson Collection in particular), The Museum of Labour History, Manchester and the Library of the Working Class Movement in Salford. This book owes a particular debt to the Lewis Walpole Library of Yale University in Farmington, Connecticut, which awarded me a Charles Cole Fellowship in the spring of 2001. I have had the good fortune to be invited back to Farmington on several subsequent occasions to teach amidst its astonishing collections. These visits have also allowed me to use the Beinecke and Sterling Libraries in New Haven as well as the Yale Centre for British Art. The knowledge and help of Joan Sussler, Cindy Roman, Sue Walker and Maggie Powell in particular have made my time at the Library as productive as it has been pleasurable. I am also grateful to Scott Wilcox and Gillian Forrester for offering me much help in using the Centre's magnificent collections. Print sellers have shown gusto, ingenuity and retentive memories in furthering my interests. Barbara Cavanagh of Motley Books, Grosvenor Prints in Covent Garden and Michael Finney (formerly The Print Room) in Bloomsbury have provided me with obscure prints and much information as well as many hours of productive rummaging. Catalogues from G. J. Saville have also offered me much information. Among booksellers, Laurie Hardman of Broadhursts, Bryan Kernaghan, Gibbs of Manchester and George Kelsall in Littleborough have all been crucial allies.

Most valuable of all has been the practical and financial support offered to me in the recent past. The University of Huddersfield funded sabbatical leave in 1998, and the University of Salford in 2004. The Wellcome Trust provided me with the resources to spend time working in London, which proved a vital part of the preliminary research on which this book is based. Salford University generously allowed me time to take up the Lewis Walpole Fellowship just at the moment I took up post there, and later supported a semester's study leave, which allowed me to finish the manuscript. My debts to the Lewis Walpole Library have already been acknowledged. Its generosity in allowing me to reprint material held in their collections in this book has been of great service.

The debts to individual friends and colleagues are even more obvious, and they can only be briefly acknowledged here. Trefor Thomas generously gave me a copy of Moncrieff's playtext of *Life in London*. Among many individuals who have helped through their interest, knowledge and enthusiasm are Diana Donald, Vic Gattrell, Louis James, Janice Allan, Ian Rogerson, John Simons, David Taylor and Bill Stafford as well as those many who have asked questions, made comments and offered information at conferences, seminars and events where I have talked of dustmen.

Matthew Frost has been a particularly agreeable and companionable publisher, as patient as he has been enthusiastic, and I thank him and his colleagues at Manchester University Press for seeing this lengthy project into print in a far better form than it deserves.

I have written on dustmen elsewhere, and parts of this book in different form have appeared as chapter 3 in *Reading Popular Prints* (Manchester: Manchester University Press, 1996); 'One Hundred and One Things To Do with a Fantail Hat: Dustmen, Dirt and Dandyism 1820–1860', *Textile History* 33 (spring 2002), 79–97; and '*Penny* Wise, *Penny* Foolish? – Representations of Mass Circulation Periodicals and "The March of Intellect" in the 1820s and 1830s', in Laurel Bell, Bill Brake and David Finkelstein (eds), *The Nineteenth Century Media and the Construction of Identity* (Macmillan, 2000).

To Maxine Melling, who has, besides mocking this project into perspective, contributed much to my understanding of dustmen, my debts remain incalculable.

# Preface

One of my childhood family holidays in the 1950s – I think spent in Swanage – was haunted by the promenade jukebox hit 'My Old Man's A Dustman', sung by Lonnie Donegan's skiffle group. I don't suppose I gave much thought to the social and ideological implications of the song – it was a comic 'novelty' number with a catchy refrain interspersed with deliberately childish jokes related in cod proletarian accents. 'My old man's a dustman,' the refrain runs, 'He wears a dustman's hat, He wears Gor-blimey trousers, And he lives in a council flat.' I am sure as a teenager I regarded the song as an affectionate music-hall turn which positioned the dustman in a celebratory way as a comic eccentric. I still do. I am equally sure that I didn't have much sense of what 'a dustman's hat' was (remember that Donegan's song was issued well before the film of 'My Fair Lady'), and even less idea of what 'gor-blimey trousers' might be. I certainly didn't connect this vernacular street hero with the rather alarming, boisterous, dirty bin men of my suburban childhood, who had to be tipped at Christmas – failure to do so would lead to terrible but unspecified consequences, involving, I guessed, the vengeful bestrewing of waste on neat beds of flowers. I suspect my respectable, anxious childhood self regarded dustmen as a vulgar, possibly even dangerous, intrusion of my worst imaginings of proletarian culture into our deferential, orderly, rather retiring social life.

I now know, to my own satisfaction at least, what a 'dustman's hat' was, and what it represented. I have constructed a history for it out of its remarkably prominent representation in prints, caricatures, plays, fiction and reportage. I think I know what 'gor-blimey' trousers were, though I leave the reader of this book to put together his or her own favoured version from the illustrations reproduced here. This book is the narrative of my construction of the history of the nineteenth-century dustman through such literary, dramatic and graphic evidence as I have been able to assemble. Accordingly, it is a history of acts of representation and their implications as much as it is a history of dustmen. It forms a record of how dustmen have been perceived and understood rather than a definition of who, and how, they were. Any history of representation must situate its chosen artefacts at the intersection between social history, the history of ideology and the history of the chosen means of representation. Thus, as well as offering a narrative of perceptions, beliefs and assumptions, this book also offers some sense of changes within the genres of print-making, caricature, journalism, fiction, song and the popular theatre between the Regency and the mid-Victorian era, changes which crucially affected the nature of the meanings produced by individual texts. As such it offers a modest contribution to an as yet unwritten history of representation in this period.

# Illustrations

## Figures

1

# Dustmen real and imagined

## What do dustmen mean?

The study of Victorian ideas of waste, dirt, dust and mess has become an important strand of recent scholarly work on the nineteenth century. For the Victorians dust was, of course, both a symbolic and physical presence that resonated far beyond its narrower meaning of a particular if complex form of household waste. It was, at one level, a quotidian reality along with its close companion, mud. 'Walking in the streets of London is almost at all times disagreeable. There is rarely any alternative between dust and mud', as one observer put it in 1839.[1] Dust was an integral part of the fabric of everyday life, normal enough to provide a stock subject for whimsical but nonetheless knowing articles in the weekly journals. *Leigh Hunt's London Journal*, for example, devotes an 1835 lead article to 'A Dusty Day', drawing every last literary possibility from the topic. 'The reader knows what sort of a day we speak of. It is all dusty; – the windows are dusty; the people are dusty; the hedges in the road are horribly dusty, – pitiably – you think they must feel it; ... men on horseback eat and drink dust; coachmen sit screwing up their eyes' – the article runs on and on with its list of familiar banalities, legitimated by the literary and graphic idea of 'the miseries of human life' tradition.[2] But if Leigh Hunt here, doubtless oppressed by deadlines and the need for immediate copy, fails to transform the literal into symbolic or emblematic significance on this occasion, there were many other Victorian commentators who recognised the huge symbolic importance of the topic. One spectacular single-plate comic etching, William Heath's 'Dust O', also from 1835, seems at first merely a comic representation of the grotesque transformation of ordinary social life caused by a high wind. An assortment of mainly genteel and fashionable pedestrians is shown as they try to negotiate the wind and its dusty consequences.[3] But lurking under the main image of bent trees, immodestly billowing dresses, hats whirling away on the wind, and tornado-like columns and spouts of wind-driven dust, almost as a caption, is a tiny image of dustman bellowing out his call of 'Dust O' and vigorously ringing his bell in the middle of two hovering clouds of dust (fig. 1). The suggestion seems to be that, in some

1 William Heath, *Dust O*

unspecified way, the dustman is implicated in, perhaps even responsible for, the chaotic scene depicted above his head. The dustman emerges from this image as some kind of impish representative of elemental energy, confusion and mischief, thus binding together the literal and incommoding presence of dust on the streets of the metropolis with deeper meanings, meanings which figure dust as the symbolic fabric of life and death themselves. As the epigraph to this book reminds us, however mockingly, 'remember thou thyself art dust, and unto dust shalt thou return, indeed, as all *men* are *dust*, thou art thyself, in some sort, a *dust-man*'.[4] This remark comes not from an earnest devotional manual but rather from a witty and picaresque book of urban incidents that, although it describes human misdemeanours and follies, is more interested in vibrant life than redemptive death. But obviously dust was, for the Victorians, a memento mori of the most dramatic kind.

But it has perhaps been the psycho-social implications of dust which have drawn critics to the topic in such enthusiastic numbers. Novels like *Our Mutual Friend* (1864–65) or Wilkie Collins's *Law and the Lady* (1875), in which the authors imagistically link powerful psychological ideas about the hidden, the repressed and the unspeakable to the social experience of ordure, dust and waste disposal, have obvious attractions for the contemporary critics. The imperatives of psychoanalytically orientated criticism have obviously found an alluring subject in dirt and the disorder it represents. Beginning with Nancy Aycock Metz's 1979 article 'The Artistic Reclamation of Waste in *Our Mutual Friend*' in *Nineteenth-Century Fiction*, a number of critics have pursued an interest in waste and excrement, driven by the wish to re-interpret major mid- and late-Victorian texts in the light of both contextual awareness of Victorian science, social theory and economic practice and psychoanalytic theory.[5] Kate Flint, for example, discusses the scientific understanding of dust that was becoming increasingly available to the Victorians through the use of the microscope and the development of climate theory among many other advances. She notes that '[to] focus on dust raises certain questions about the Victorian fascination with the relationship between the visible and the invisible, and with techniques of seeing, both technological and physiological'.[6] David Trotter's *Cooking with Mud – The Idea of Mess in Nineteenth Century Art and Fiction* theorises mess in relation to its near neighbour, waste:

> Waste remains for ever potentially in circulation because circulation is its defining characteristic. Waste is the measure of an organism's ability to renew itself by excluding whatever it does not require for its own immediate purposes. However foul it may have become, it gleams with efficiency … Moreover, because the purpose which both created and discarded it shows inexorably through, because the discarding is the negative image of the creation, it is condemned to meaning … Mess, I would suggest, is waste that has not yet become, and may never become, either symptom or symbol. The difference between mess and waste is partly a difference of scale and point of view, and partly a difference in the imaginative uses to which they have consistently been put … Waste is a condition, mess is an event.[7]

Such conceptualisations of waste as a Victorian preoccupation have been extremely valuable in the writing of this book, but one central aim of this book is to consider pre-Victorian constructions of waste and their emissaries, managers and entrepreneurs, and suggest the ways in which this cultural inheritance affected Victorian perceptions of dust and dustmen. The idea that the invention of the idea of waste was something newly and uniquely Victorian seems to me an inaccurate one. Indeed, it is the pre-figuring of Victorian concepts of waste in the prints, plays and fiction of the Regency period that gave the Victorians a vast repertoire of assumptions and stereotypes of the dustman through which to frame – and against which to test – their own ideas of what dustmen represented. The writers and social theorists of the Regency and the early Victorian period were, however, equally clear that dustmen were figures of outstanding interest and importance, with a distinctive cultural history of their own which was distinct from other trades.

Similarly, this book draws on, but is not constrained by, those many scholarly accounts of the representation of the urban street as a site of both social contest and visual complexity. The narrative of a perceptual shift in the first half of the nineteenth century – from an inherited eighteenth-century idea of the street as an essentially theatrical space in which difference was acknowledged but largely accommodated, to an early Victorian vision of the street as the site of a bitter contest over order and differentiation – is clearly central to the argument. Fortunately, this complex narrative of the changing cultural understanding of metropolitan urban space between 1780 and 1870 has been extensively and perceptively explored in recent scholarship. Drawing on excellent overviews of the cultural history of the eighteenth century by John Brewer, Roy Porter and Linda Colley[8] among others, scholars have begun to write a full history of London street culture in the first two or three decades of the nineteenth century. Such a project has been underpinned by extremely useful reprints of rare texts, especially John Marriott's six-volume and polemically titled *Unknown London – Early Modernist Visions of the Metropolis 1815–1845*.[9] One of the many virtues of Marriott's project – which, as its title suggests, seeks to identify the roots of urban Modernism not just in the work of writers like Pierce Egan and John Bee but also in graphic artists like George Cruikshank and Robert Seymour – has been his defence of Pierce Egan's extremely well-known but little-studied picaresque novel *Life in London* as a seminal text. Beloved by Thackeray but dismissed as an influence by Dickens, Egan has at last begun to attract serious and informed scholarly interest.[10] *Life in London* is a central text for the study of dustmen, immensely far reaching in its definition of the figure of 'Dusty Bob' as a popular cultural stereotype.

A sequence of studies of the street culture of nineteenth-century London, derived to a considerable extent from the interests of feminist critics in locating and describing women's experiences of a metropolis which had been previously largely constructed as a masculine public domain, have provided an extremely helpful way into the urban culture of the nineteenth century. A collection of essays on *Victorian Artists and the City* and Dana Arnold's *Re-presenting the Metropolis* have added an art-historical dimension to Deborah Epstein Nord's immensely suggestive *Walking the Victorian Streets: Women, Representation, and the City*.[11] Nord's book itself sits alongside the well-known work of Carol Bernstein, Celina Fox, Lynda Nead and Judith Walkowitz, which has traced the history of the representation of London streets through the Victorian period.[12] Underpinning all this work has been a desire to use important analytical concepts derived from cultural theorists like Bakhtin, Foucault, Kristeva and, in particular, Stallybrass and White to locate the roots of modernist ideas of, for instance, alienation, marginality and spectatorship within the emergent Victorian metropolis. Inevitably, this book is concerned with the low, though I have tended to use pragmatic definitions of 'lowness', like Kathleen Tillotson's list of 'every-day vulgar, shabby genteel or downright low' rather than the more theorised ones offered by White and Stallybrass.[13] Due attention will be paid to these ideas in the course of what follows, but it is fair to say that this project partly derives from a similar impulse, with the proviso that it is the pre-modern dustman rather than his modernised successor who dominates the bulk of this book.

The main starting place for this book is not primarily, however, a wish to engage in theoretical debates, important as they are, but rather a growing sense that the *representational* history of nineteenth-century dustmen was, especially between 1820 and 1850, at a level of density and complexity out of all proportion to their literal history during this period, a density and complexity only similarly devoted to chimney sweeps among the other urban or street trades. The cultural preoccupation with dustmen in these years is largely manifested by the figuring of dustmen in a range of popular media as a series of interrelated, complex and essentially comic stereotypes. Stereotypes can be linked closely to social anxiety. As Sander Gilman has put it:

> The complexity of the stereotype results from the social context in which it is to be found. This context parallels, but is not identical to, the earlier symbiotic context in which the child begins to differentiate himself from the world. The deep structure of the stereotype reappears in the adult as a response to an anxiety having

its roots in the potential disintegration of the mental representations the individual has created and internalised.[14]

This book is certainly about two of the key elements that comprise Gilman's definition of stereotypes: difference and anxiety. Once negotiated and established, the stereotype of the dustman was used by Regency and early Victorian society as a means of exploring and, in a limited way, of rendering less troublesome some of its deepest anxieties and fears. Such a process of 'rendering less troublesome' is crucially ascribed to popular culture by Frederick Jameson in his essay on 'Mass Culture and Modernism' in *Signatures of the Visible*, where he describes the kinds of popular cultural texts and images that form the substance of this book as 'transformational work on social and political anxieties and fantasies, which must then have some effective presence in order to be managed or repressed.'[15] By representing the dustman in popular culture as an emblematic, non-naturalistic (or, more often, a not entirely naturalistic) figure, society provided itself with the means to articulate and publicise a normally repressed sense of threat, contamination and upheaval. This only half-conscious attempt to define and debate potential challenges to the social and psychic order in the 1830s and 1840s created for the dustman, in representational terms at least, a prominence and controversiality way beyond his literal importance in the social history of the period.

The emblematic burden of social anxieties and possibilities carried by the represented figure of the dustman was varied and complex. One issue was primarily economic. Were dustmen representative of the newly alienated urban proletariat, the just working or non-working classes described later in Mayhew's *London Labour and the London Poor*, and thus liable to initiate street violence through drunkenness and social aggression? Or were they rather spritely proponents of a new 'penny capitalism', willing to use their own labour as a form of capital, and to work (or not) according to a self-determined pattern? My argument is that it is probably the latter of these two interpretations which troubled early Victorian, if not Regency, society the most. A second issue concerned popular education and the 'march of intellect', which formed important sites of ideological contest in the first half of the nineteenth century. Dustmen became inextricably connected in popular figuration with the social challenges offered by the advance of mass education and debates concerning the desirability of self-advancement.[16] If even dustmen could be redeemed into a wide and accommodating vision of social progress through the march of intellect, then why should society resist the spread of literacy, wealth and class mobility? Was mass education, or mass self-improvement, less dangerous, less absurd, less divisive than the conservatives had believed? A close reading of the image of the 'educated dustman', constructed primarily in graphic satire in the 1820s and 1830s, takes us to the central issues of these debates, and suggests a perhaps more liberal and tolerant awareness of the mechanisms of social progress among urban working people than might be supposed. But these images also show contradictions and ambiguities within social interpretations of the march of intellect. If the educated dustman was sometimes represented as a cultural hero, he was also present as a dirty, threatening, uncivilised, irredeemable proletarian vulgarian.[17]

Dustmen, too, were crucially associated with the streets. To study dustmen is almost exclusively to study London during this period, and to study London as represented within popular culture is to study the streets. Streets were where dustmen defined their identity. They worked there, spectated there, and spent much of their leisure time there. The endlessly repeated representation of dustmen as spectators makes them particularly important in the many discussions of the 'flaneur' or the leisured observer as a proto-Modernist idea. Much of their eating and drinking was undertaken at street stalls and tea bars. To be off the streets, except possibly to be in beerhouses or taverns, was to lose control of their own lives, to become unmanned, intrusive, awkward and ill at ease. So inevitably dustmen partake of, or even represent, the changing repertoire of social attitudes towards, and cultural analyses of, street life across thirty crucial years between 1820 and 1850, attitudes which ranged from reading the streets as pleasurable theatre to reading them as dangerous, violent and disfigured emblems of enforced contiguity and contaminating proximity. Accordingly, the individual chapters of this study look at the various representation codes through which the urban streets might be constructed visually and verbally on a continuum ranging from the rural picturesque (exemplified, for example, in Wheatley's famous coloured engravings of 'The Cries of London') through the morally corrupt but animalistically vivid emblematic London enacted in Hogarth's prints to the semi-naturalistic black dreamscapes of Doré's and Jerrold's *London* or 'Phiz's' 'dark' plates for *Bleak House*. And where there were streets, there also were dustmen.

Discussions of this kind raise further themes which might be described as 'psycho-social' ones. Dustmen were dirty, and they did a dirty job. Their constant presence on the streets was a reminder of what precisely 'dust' was in Regency and early Victorian London, an issue much debated by literary critics in relation to *Our Mutual Friend*. Dust was of course everywhere, but could seldom be named, certainly not in later respectable literature. Yet it was visibly omnipresent not just on the streets, but on dustmen themselves. Accordingly, dustmen posed a threat of both literal and metaphorical contamination, and, as we shall see, the metaphors were extended on out to include not just disease but also vulgarity, violence and even miscegeny. Dustmen, as represented in popular culture, were notoriously amorous. Their sexuality might be read as comic, a vigorous manifestation of their soft-heartedness or even gallantry as much as their brawniness or their social aggressiveness. But if comic lust, magnificently rendered and ridiculed in Gillray's truly terrifying caricature *Love and Dust*, was one possibility, so was the more obvious reading of their sexual vigour as threat and nuisance. This connection between lust and dirt is an important one, both implicitly and explicitly rendered in caricature, and even more prominently represented in the clumsy but unmistakably sexual 'pas de deux' danced not just on the stage but widely in popular prints and songs but the archetypal dustman 'Dusty Bob' and his theatrical partner, a black domestic servant variously called 'African Sal', 'Black Sal' or just 'Sal'. Given that on the stage Sal was nearly always played by a man, cross-dressed and blacked up, the number of transgressive possibilities opened up by this strange, comic but unsettling pair can only be guessed at. Luckily, though, a considerable body of evidence can be accumulated to help to decode the ultimately positive and celebratory rendering of this famous couple in the discourses of mass-produced popular culture.

To read the coupled Bob and Sal as a celebration of an instinctual good nature and legitimate passion associated with vulgarity and social repudiation is to raise further issues about the cultural significance of the dustman not so much as a figure of fun but as a figure *having* fun. And this would be to articulate the most subversive possibility of all in relation to genteel decorum – the possibility that down there, on the streets, in the beerhouses and among the rotting heaps of ordure, the dustman was living a life of pleasure and gratification, based on his social marginality and powers of economic self-determination, way beyond the reach of the repressed and anxious genteel or professional spectator. As Theodor Adorno aptly remarked in *Minima Moralia*: 'The refined are drawn to the unrefined, whose coarseness promises what their own culture denies'.[18] Such ideas clearly touch on the idea of 'abjection' put forward by Julia Kristeva and further theorised by White and Stallybrass: 'differentiation is dependent on disgust. The division of the social into high and low, the polite and vulgar ... maps out divisions between the civilized and the grotesque body'.[19] Or again, 'in the slum, the bourgeois spectator surveyed and classified *his own antithesis*'.[20] But it is not entirely clear that dustmen were 'low' in the terms that White and Stallybrass use, and certainly they fail to list dustmen among the many trades that comprise Mayhew's 'carnivalised picturesque' and to which his 'scopophilia' draws him.[21] Indeed, the problematic 'lowness' of dustmen provides one of the central themes of this book. If their work was filthy and degraded, and their social habits animalistic and barbaric in the middle-class imagination at least, nonetheless dustmen took a pride in their appearance, were frequently represented as socially ambitious as well as socially disruptive, and, in their more entrepreneurial manifestations at least, shown to be financially successful. It is ultimately the negotiation between the polite and the low or, to put it another way, the genteel attempt to accommodate the vernacular and render it culturally comprehensible that gives the history of the dustman such particular and intense resonance.

In providing a carnivalesque but fictional low-life 'other' for genteel readers and audiences to experience through novels like Pierce Egan's *Life in London* and its many imitations or through the vast numbers of stage explorations of low-life London, the danger was that of producing envy rather than the mocking reductiveness and safe distances of comedy or the repulsion of disgust. This complex of attitudes towards pleasure, carnival and transgression is thoroughly examined within the images, texts, performances, and occasions discussed in this book. Dustmen once again take us to central social, imaginative and ideological concerns within an urban culture trying to find new ways of representing its own anxieties in creative and socially cohesive forms.

Dustmen, in the representations assembled here at least, were also *consumers*, consumers especially of the new luxury products that the development of mass markets were beginning to make available – a further way in which their 'lowness' is rendered complex. They ate well and drank a lot. If the images are to be believed, they discussed the price of opera tickets. They went, at least in the imagination of comic artists, to lectures, read newspapers and magazines, and bought classical statues. Some caricaturists even imagined them by the 1840s discussing the state of the stock market – penny capitalists indeed. In many ways, dustmen in caricatures acted like the lottery-winners of modern Europe – their patterns of consumption were described in caricature in the 1820s and 1830s as a grotesque parody of genteel spending, concentrated on pointless luxuries, garish vulgarities or ostentatious and socially pretentious forms of cultural commodities. These commodities, and their emblematic significance will be discussed in detail in Chapter 4.

But again it is through the represented figure of the dustman that social change is depicted and explored.

Finally, at least within the scope of this book, dustmen articulated a complex connection between dirt and wealth. At one level they expounded the theme that wealth *is* dirt, or at least dirty. 'Filthy lucre' is a term that only the Victorians could have invented.[22] But beyond even this complex of Christian and social confusion over whether money was a form of moral contamination, – an issue explored with obvious profundity but considerable ambiguity in Dickens's *Our Mutual Friend* – there lies a literal recognition that there was money to be earned from dirt. A licence to collect dust was also a licence to keep the spoils of the dust collected (and think of the complexities of meaning resonating between 'spoils' and 'spoilt'). Dust was intrinsically valuable. Sorted and sifted, and with any lurking valuables, scrap or resaleable objects removed, it could be marketed at very least as manure. This connection between dirt, wealth and moral health (and to some extent, especially to Mayhew, literal health) was one which exercised later Victorian writers, most obviously Dickens as editor of *Household Words* as well as more famously in *Our Mutual Friend*. Only a mid-Victorian journalist could have stated, without any apparent irony, when observing the sifters in a dustyard that 'I never yet met a body of female labourers looking so thoroughly healthy and jolly.'[23] Several of Mayhew's informants similarly went out of their way to stress the healthiness and longevity of those engaged in the dust trade, and Mayhew himself regarded dustmen as 'tall stalwart fellows' with 'healthy and strong' children.[24] Mr Boffin, the 'golden dustman' of *Our Mutual Friend*, remains the single most powerfully imagined exposition of the complex interdependence between dust, wealth, health, happiness, contamination and redemption. Characteristically, Dickens draws on a massively wrought tradition of popular cultural tropes, refrains and stereotypes to create something of true profundity. This is not to deny the importance of his 'low' sources, but rather to celebrate their creativity, suggestiveness and longevity.

These brilliantly realised literary responses drew also on a more literal, documentary exploration of the connection between work, industry and the moral economy which was being undertaken by the likes of G. A. Sala, James Grant, Henry Mayhew, James Greenwood and other mid-Victorian writers of urban sketches, interests that seal off the later Victorian commentators from their Regency predecessors. All of these versions of the dustman as a socially suggestive figure are explored in Chapters 5 and 6, which takes the representational history of the dustman on up to the turn of the nineteenth and twentieth centuries.

## Historical dustmen

The issue of what Victorian dustmen actually did flared into a moment of brief but energetic scholarly controversy in 1971 and 1972. The controversy concerned the most famous literary dustman of all, Mr Boffin, the Golden Dustman in Dickens's novel *Our Mutual Friend*, first published in volume form in 1865. The issue of whether dustmen were involved in the disposal of human ordure as well as household waste was at the centre of the discussion, a discussion that had been initiated by a footnote in Stephen Gill's 1971 Penguin edition of the novel. Gill, seeking both to inform and help the non-specialist reader, acknowledged that it would be 'obviously attractive in view of the symbolic significance of the dust in the novel' if Boffin's Mounds 'included human excrement'.[25] While Humphrey House had previously provided scholarly legitimacy for the idea that dustheaps contained ordure, Gill, despite Mayhew's categorical statement in *London Labour and the London Poor* that 'The dustmen, scavengers, and nightmen are, to a certain extent, the same people',[26] drew on articles in Dickens's own periodical *Household Words* from 1850 and pointed to evidence of the clear separation out of dust and ordure within the organisation and practices of the street cleansing trades. Gill's revisionist view was acknowledged by another critic Stephen Wall who somewhat reluctantly admitted that the 'irresistably attractive ... equation between money and ordure' may be more a post-Freudian fantasy of modern literary interpretation than a connection imaginatively available to Victorian readers.[27] But the matter (if you will excuse the pun) did not rest there. Another eminent Dickens scholar, H. P. Sucksmith, brought to the discussion both further textual details which associated ordure and dust and the evidence of legislation introduced in the late 1840s which, in banning the dumping of night-soil in dust yards, seemed to imply that this had been previously happening on a widespread basis.[28] Sucksmith, in concluding that there remained compelling and legitimating evidence within both the novel and Victorian society more generally to sustain a link between wealth and dirt, nonetheless warned of the dangers of crude Freudian reductionism, and argued that 'if the Freudian equation is present and functioning in *Our Mutual Friend*, it succeeds precisely because it does reduce money to filthy lucre, and thus plays a legitimately scatological role of depreciation, whether conscious or subconscious, in Dickens's satirical vision.'[29]

I begin this chapter with this small-scale and apparently trivial critical joust from thirty years ago because it poses important questions (as Sucksmith implies) to do with the relationship between information and interpretation. This book advertises itself as both a *cultural* and a *representational* history of dustmen, which is to say that the main focus is on the ways in which meanings and understandings are constructed in society through cultural exchange. Such a focus is not meant to deny fact but rather to delegate the project of a documentary history of dustmen to a properly qualified historian. It is in default of such a history, rather than in dialogue with it, that this book is written. The way in which 'facts' may interact with or operate against interpretation is clearly illustrated by the combined activities of House, Gill, Wall and Sucksmith quoted above. In many ways, this critical episode serves as a model for my own project which, although it aims methodologically to combine information with interpretative desire, is nonetheless driven overall by an aspiration to delineate broad symbolic socio-economic meanings. Such a debate raises a variety of key issues which this chapter wants to begin to address – the ways in which the precise details of how trades operate and function becomes confused and mythologised in the popular imagination, the ways in which the representation of such trades is itself compromised by the representational modes employed, and, most substantial of all, the psycho-social complexity that attaches itself to trades which deal with dirt, excrement, waste and dust. It is the larger purpose of this book to pursue these issues through the mass of material pertaining to the history of dustmen between 1790 and 1870, and to deal, chapter by chapter, with the varied representation codes, social discourses and potential meanings constructed in this evidence. But this chapter, in the absence of any solid documentary history of the trade, and acknowledging that even key issues such as the composition of the dust that they handled are unlikely to be entirely resolved, seeks to offer some account of the nature and history of dustmen and their work.

*Our Mutual Friend* was written in the 1860s so it hardly surprising that Gill, Wall and Sucksmith should have drawn on the most prominent available evidence of dustmen: Mayhew's famous detailed survey *London Labour and the London Poor* (1851),[30] the several articles in *Household Words* about waste, re-cycling and the utility of dust (especially R. H. Horne's 'Dust; or Ugliness Redeemed' from 1850) which suggested something of the informed preoccupation Dickens may have had with dust,[31] and the Nuisances Removal and Diseases Prevention Act of 1848. Mayhew has remained a key source for Dickens, and indeed all other Victorian scholars. One obvious answer to the question 'what did dustmen do?' is to invite readers to go and read the relevant section of *London Labour and the London Poor*, which proves to be one of the most extended and elaborated of Mayhew's investigations,[32] and thus one which has been extensively reprinted at length in popularisations of Mayhew, most notably Peter Quennell's *Mayhew's London*.[33] Additionally, dustmen are accorded two illustrations in *London Labour*, one of which shows a dust yard with assembled sifters and the other a somewhat heroicised single dustman calling out his trade.[34] Certainly no other single source contains the same density and extent of information about the dustman trade, and Mayhew remains a crucial source. But this book is concerned, just as Dickens scholars have been concerned, to situate Mayhew within the wide range of available discussions and depictions of dustmen, most of which pre-date Victorian social investigators. The Dickens' critics cited above were keen to dispute the ways in which Mayhew's evidence might be used to favour psycho-social readings of fiction despite Mayhew's apparently authoritative statements. In similar ways, this book seek will seek in chapter 6 to challenge some of Mayhew's conclusions, which were structured not just by his evidence but also by the preoccupations of the author and his contemporaries. Mayhew's conclusions come from a moment when dustmen had begun to be re-situated within the socio-economic landscape of London. His conclusions about their ignorance, their illiteracy, their drunkenness and their profligacy, for example, seem at odds with much other admittedly less avowedly documentary evidence.

In summarising the available evidence for Dickens's knowledge of dustmen for *The Companion to Our Mutual Friend*,[35] Michael Cotsell rehearses the same familiar sources of Mayhew and *Household Words*, but adds in an important illustrated article on 'Mr Dodd's Dustyard' which had appeared anonymously in the *Penny Illustrated Paper* in 1866,[36] too late to be a direct source for Dickens's novel, but nonetheless highly suggestive of Dickens's knowledge of Dodd as a possible model for Nicodemus Boffin. But it is important to recognise that all these sources, despite their documentary aspirations, derive from a particular set of mid-Victorian imperatives which included the wish to celebrate the technological feats and collective responsibility shown by Victorian management and re-use of waste, the desire to manage poverty and social disorder through the investigation, categorisation and deeper understanding of the 'Modern Babylon', especially the urban poor, and, not least, the persistence of the urban picturesque, in which the 'other England', for all the social dangers it represented, nonetheless remained an ever-absorbing street theatre. The prominence of these mid-Victorian accounts of dustmen have tended to obscure the broader and longer literary and graphic traditions through which they had been previously represented. By the 1850s, indeed, dustmen had largely become municipalised by being directly employed as waste-removal contractors by parishes, thus losing the economic independence that had crucially determined their previous behaviour. Thus, despite critical efforts to relate Dickens's text precisely to contemporary concerns through the use of supporting documentary evidence, it is important to recognise that the status of the 'documentary' remains uncertain. Nor is it clear that Dickens's main sources of imaginative energy in *Our Mutual Friend* were related to precise and immediate factual knowledge of the kind made available by Mayhew. Indeed, Nicodemus Boffin, as I shall argue in Chapter 7, was at least as much a construct of Dickens's fascination with Regency urban myths, popular cultural stereotypes and a nostalgic attraction to the urban picturesque as he was the product of contemporary investigative journalism and middle-class social concern. The delineation of Boffin was also highly dependent on cross-textual references, especially to the popular theatre. Boffin, it might be argued, is essentially a cultural anachronism characteristic of a mid-Victorian regret for the loss of the picturesque and the triumph of urban anxiety. Yet he also represents an extraordinary, and highly intelligent, synthesis of nearly a century of varied cultural clutter that had assembled itself around dustmen and their social significance.

This cultural clutter manifests itself in a staggering variety of forms ranging from legislation concerning waste disposal, street noise and municipal responsibility, parish records, documentary evidence of trade practices (flyers, advertisements, trade cards and the like), 'documentary' accounts drawn from a variety of genres as diverse as children's school books and primers, 'cries of London' sequences, investigative journalism, reformist literature and on through less obviously 'reliable' material such as picaresque fiction, the popular theatre, comic verse, song, prints and, especially, caricature. Much of this material is derived from, and seeks to perpetuate, stereotypes rather than offer an accurate documentary account of dustmen. Subsequent chapters seek to order this material both chronologically and in terms of the history of representational practices and genres. The remainder of this chapter seeks, however, to offer a brief historical account of the trade without straying too far into the detail of the cultural contests over meanings which form the substance of subsequent chapters.

Dustmen were a London phenomenon, and they belonged to a group of trades that collectively took responsibility for public cleanliness and convenience. Along with crossing sweepers, scavengers, sweeps and night-soil men, they operated in a highly visible fashion on the London streets. Unlike sweeps and night-soil men, however, they were never afforded access to the domestic interior. Their contact with genteel households at least was entirely mediated through servants, and the very few occasions when dustmen actually met their real clients (when asking for their Christmas boxes, for example) were fraught ones. The trade emerged into being as a recognisable one as a consequence of increasing parochial interventions on behalf of public health in the 1780s and 1790s and flourished until the 1840s and 1850s, by which time regulatory legislation, changing methods of domestic heating and waste disposal, and the recognition of the potential nuisance value of an unregulated trade changed the ways in which public cleansing took place. While dustmen persisted on after 1850, they became increasingly and more obviously public employees, directly managed by the parish and waged rather than being free to keep the rewards of their own labours, or else specialised in the re-cycling of waste materials rather than street cleansing. Until these transformations dustmen were – unlike scavengers and sweeps, who operated on their own behalf – organised on a franchise basis, buying yearly licences from a parish that gave them both the right and the obligation to clear dust from the streets of that parish on a regular basis. Thus, although they were in some senses parish employees, they were nonetheless remarkably free to organise their working practices to suit their own needs.

Existing evidence, which is not plentiful, largely confirms the notion that the separate elements within the public cleansing spectrum preserved a considerable distance from each other. Street sweepers, the least stable of these groups, operated on their own behalf and were entirely dependent on the donations of those whose path they cleared of street mess. Scavengers, beyond those unfortunates who merely turned muck over in the hope of finding something of value, were employed to clear streets directly by the parish authorities, and patrolled the streets in high-wheeled and high-sided carts. Sweeps combined a number of functions to do not just with cleansing sooty chimneys but also with night-soil removal and fire fighting (where their knowledge of the consequences of soot was useful).[37] Trade cards from the late eighteenth century onwards give clear evidence of this combination of activities, and also suggest how businesses, together with their profitable and carefully nurtured list of customers, were handed on within families, often through the female line.[38] As Mayhew was later to note, 'the dustmen are, generally speaking, an hereditary race' with children, 'reared in the dust-yard' becoming 'born-and-bred dustmen'.[39]

The declared interest of sweeps in night-soil disposal is a major reason for thinking that dustmen on the whole did not deal with ordure. Dustmen rather cleared household dust and ashes ('ashes & c.' as T. L. Busby put it[40]) and the narrow focus of their activities can be gauged from the parallel existence of specialist brick-dust dealers in the late eighteenth century at least.[41] Persuaded, perhaps, by its simplicity, I am inclined to believe the summary of dustman activities offered in a *Cries of London* reprinted by Hindley:

> Dust or ash this chap calls out
> With all his might and main
> He's got a mighty cinder heap
> Somewhere near Gray's Inn Lane.[42]

While, presumably as a result of the franchise system, dustmen never became unionised, there appears to have been considerable *esprit de corps* among them, and they chose, seemingly voluntarily, to dress in similar fashion.

Two descriptions from the early phase of the trade, when it had been established but not yet subject to either sustained social opprobrium or legislative and municipal control, which have no particular reason to be unreliable, and both of which contain considerable goodwill towards the dustmen, give the key facts and are worth quoting at length. The first comes from T. L. Busby's *Costume of the Lower Orders of London*, primarily a book of plates of individual street characters depicted against a sketched or blank background, but also containing a considerable amount of text, and first published in about 1819. Busby's work is poised in mode between what he described as depictions of 'rural picturesque character' (that is to say, the application of the tradition of the rural picturesque to the urban streets mainly within the 'Cries of London series and other costume books)[43] and the emergent sociological and categorising impulse of Victorian accounts of the streets, with both modes modified by Busby's evident sense of humanitarian concern and desire to make his readers think:

> [The dustman] is represented carrying the dust, by resting his basket on a flapped hat slouched over the neck and shoulders. They carry with them a large bell, the sound of which is well understood by the inhabitants. The commissioners of the parishes of the metropolis dispose of the ashes, &c, to individuals by yearly contract, which gives the contractors the exclusive right to the dust of the respective parishes. At convenient places the ashes are sifted, by which process the bones, rags, nails, &c, are separated, and of course disposed

of to the best advantage. The breeze is sold for brick making and manure, and the cinders for heating kilns, the bones to make china and hartshorn, and the rags to the manufacturers of paper. Thus we find every part of that which appears rubbish to the housekeeper, is property of no little value to the Dustman.

It is not unusual for the sifters to find, through the negligence of servants, & c, silver spoons, and other valuables; when this happens, some contractors allow one half to their sifters, the other part they consider their right.[44]

The second comes from John Wight's *Mornings in Bow Street*, published in 1824 as a series of sketches and anecdotes of the teeming comic urban variety that flooded through a London magistrate's court on the morning after a lively night's activity. Wight's text, drawing on the traditions of comic almanacs and song books, is illustrated by the 'new' mode of vignette wood engravings dropped into the text and, in this case, brilliantly drawn by George Cruikshank. The final section of Wight's picaresque collection comprises an elaborate anecdote, so elaborate that it aspires to becoming an urban myth, concerning the aggression and brazenness of 'flying dustmen'. Concerned that his readers will have neither the specialised knowledge to understand the full significance of his tale of urban street contest nor the courage to flout genteel taste by reading about dustmen, Wight offers an elaborate and informative peroration to his anecdote, opening with the baroque meditation on dustmen that forms the epigraph to this book, and then continuing by way of explanation for his provincial readers:

Dust is of divers kind. In London the term *dust* is understood to signify the ashes – not of the *great* but of the *grate*; that is to say *coal*-ashes. Dust-*men* are two legged animals who go about with horse and cart, or with horses and carts, to carry away this dust from the houses of the inhabitants; and these dustmen are divided into two kinds – legitimate and illegitimate. The *legitimate* dustmen are those who collect it for the contractors – persons who, under the authority of special Act of Parliament, contract with their high mightinesses the parochial authorities for the dust of their respective parishes; and give, in some instances, more than a thousand pounds for the dust of a single parish. The *illegitimate* dustmen are those who collect the dust for their own particular benefit; and thereby defraud the contractors. Your legitimate dustman is tintinnabulary; slow in his movements; careless and somewhat saucy in his demeanour – like

> most other official personages: the illegitimate is silent, obsequious, vigilant and nimble; hence those of his species are designated *flying* dustmen; and so active are they, that though Mr Michael Angelo Taylor, in his care for the cleanliness of this metropolis, procured the enacting of a Statute subjecting them to a penalty of ten pounds, or three months imprisonment, for every offence; yet the contractors find it necessary to keep a number of *inspectors* constantly prowling about the streets as a check on their dusty depredations ...[45]

Busby and Wight here touch on a wide range of issues concerning the trade in dust, to which I want to return in a moment. But it may be useful to preface that discussion with a few comments on the nature of the documentary record.

The visual evidence that describes the work practices of dustmen concentrates on their widely visible street presence. According to such evidence, what dustmen centrally did was extremely simple. As Mayhew put it, 'As the operation of emptying a dust-bin requires only the ability to handle a shovel, which every labouring man can manage, all workmen, however unskilled, can at once engage in the occupation'.[46] One elaborately drawn caricature, a dramatic single plate caricature by Henry Heath (Plate VI) entitled 'No Genius' renders the dustman's job as laughably simple. Two old hands, working newly lit streets on the edge of London, discuss the merits of an apprentice dustman sweeping in the background. 'Vot do you think of our new man Bill eh?' asks one. His companion replies authoritatively, 'Vy he's a werry good un on a strait road – but if he comes to a bit of fancy work sich as scraping round a post or anythink with a of that ere sort – he's nothing – heny body can see he vosent edicated at Westminster'.[47] To make sure the point is taken, Heath has included the towers of Westminster Abbey in the background. The laughably simple activities of dustmen involved announcing their presence by the vigorous ringing of their bells and cries of 'Dust Hoa' or 'Dust Ho', followed by sweeping up with brooms the heaps of ash and domestic refuse left out for them by scullery maids, transferring the gathered dust into large wicker baskets by means of shovels, and loading the contents of the baskets into high-sided, large-wheeled and lumbering horse-drawn carts reached by means of a short ladder. If the caricaturists are to be believed, the dustmen were so clumsy and careless in their activities that much of the dust missed the cart and fell on passers-by. The dust was then taken off to be added to mounds situated initially in quite central locations but increasingly, as the century progressed, in the suburbs.[48]

The graphic and journalistic evidence for the visible working practices of dustmen, simple as they were, is curiously uneven. The caricature record in fact seldom showed dustmen working – part of the 'joke' about dustmen concerned their supposed idleness in a society where socially and economically useful activity was rapidly becoming fetishised. Yet the equipment dustmen used is very much part of the caricature record – they are seldom depicted in caricature without at least one item out of their kit of bell, broom, basket or cart. In caricature, however, dustmen are centrally depicted as proximate to their work rather than actually doing it, and often their work equipment is transformed into the accoutrements of leisure – baskets upturned as seats, bells stowed in capacious pockets, brooms turned into useful poles to lean on (fig. 2).

**2** George Cruikshank, 'February' from *Comic Almanack* (1838)

The reasons for such a particular version of dustmen activity will be fully discussed in Chapter 4. A number of graphic and verbal discourses were, however, more interested in dustmen at work, notably the many series of 'Cries of London', children's primers and chapbooks, and the increasingly documentary strands of urban description in the journalism published in the periodicals of the 1840s and 1850s. These discourses were on the whole as optimistic and celebratory as the caricatures were knowing and disillusioned – how far the couplet 'His noisy bell the dustman rings/ Her dust the housemaid gladly brings'[49] describes the feelings of those involved in the dust collection process is a matter for some conjecture – but at least they offer some details of the social exchanges involved in clearing household waste. Again, detailed examination of these kinds of evidence will follow in later chapters.

More complex is the work that dustmen did less visibly, bur clearly central to Busby and Wight's understanding of the trade. Such work was partly financial (tendering for licences, estimating the value of accumulated dust,[50] ensuring that the dust be sold on or disposed of in the most profitable way and – in the case of contractors – employing and supervising the workforce necessary for both the street operations and picking through and sorting the dustheaps), partly organisational (the management of the dustheaps, the maintenance of the carts and ensuring the welfare of the horses), and partly defensive (ensuring that the licensed territory was not invaded by flying dustmen or privateers, protecting Christmas boxes, and so on). The trade thus involved a number of activities which might be split between contractors, collectors and sifters even though the vast weight of the graphic evidence before the 1840s is concentrated on the street collection of dust. Often, however, it seems likely that all these activities would be undertaken by a single individual with some hired help – dustmen are almost always shown working in pairs. While there is occasional mention of the financial underpinning and contractual complexity of the trade – Nicodemus Boffin is away 'on a country contract which was to be sifted before carted' at one moment in *Our Mutual Friend*, for example[51] – very little reference is made in the graphic and journalistic record to the relationships between dustmen and parochial authority, and none at all to the inspectorate described by Wight. Indeed, it is the absence of surveillance or control before 1840 at least that characterises the vast mass of evidence.

More evidence is available for a number of other characteristic activities of dustmen. A range of caricatures show dustheaps in what Busby calls 'convenient places' in the suburbs. A number of Henry Heath's series of *Scenes in London* show really quite large heaps surrounded by housing – one in particular shows a hot-potato seller and his clients dwarfed by an alpine dust mound sketched in the square beyond. The top of the mound is being picked over by three sifters, while another dustman leans on the fence below and a disembodied fantail moves off to the right[52] (fig. 3). A sly and beautifully drawn coloured lithograph shows a characteristically brutalised dustman admiring his image in a

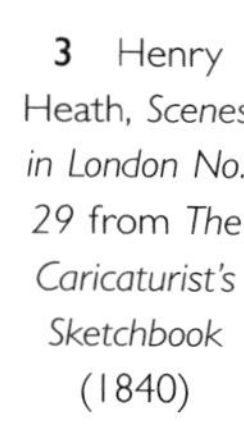

Vot have you von all they? Vy blow your luck!!


**3** Henry Heath, *Scenes in London No. 29* from *The Caricaturist's Sketchbook* (1840)

stagnant pool while behind him a rounded dust mound towers above (Plate XIV). As we shall see, although dust was increasingly taken out of London for tipping and traditional sites for dumping waste like Tothill Fields changed their use, even as late as Mayhew's survey of *London Labour and the London Poor* from the early 1860s, dustheaps remained a feature of the London streetscape. Mayhew visited a dust yard described only as 'at the east end of London' but remarked that dustheaps could be 'found all round London, ... generally situated in the suburbs' and 'scattered' 'as near as possible to the river, or to some canal communicating therewith'.[53] The lowest and filthiest aspect of the trade – sifting the dust – is also sometimes represented, especially in later Victorian publications, with three defining and much reprinted images – Rowlandson's brutalised sifters in *Love and Dust* (1788),[54] Mayhew's 'View of a Dust Yard' (fig. 50),[55] and the anonymous illustration to James Greenwood's urban sketch of *Mr. Dodd's Dust Yard*, first published in 1866 (fig. 51), both discussed in Chapter 6 – acting as something like prologue and epilogue to this study. Greenwood's article in particular stressed the precarious and poverty-stricken existence of the dust-sifters, who are certainly less picturesque than their street collecting associates.

One of Busby's key observations was that concerning the elaborate disposal and re-use of the various constituent elements of dust – 'Thus we find every part of that which appears rubbish to the housekeeper, is property of no little value to the Dustman.' While today we might see such re-cycling largely in environmental or ethical terms, for the Victorians the re-disposable nature of matter was predominantly an economic phenomenon, and, in the 1850s and 1860s at least, formed part of a celebratory narrative of financial success. To Busby's list of the re-usable contents of dust as breeze, cinders, bones and rags, later Victorian entrepreneurs added many additional elements. The dust-sifters in Mr Dodd's dustyard, according to James Greenwood's informants in the trade, were sorting through hard-core, fine-core, rags, bread, bones, bits of metal, cabbage-stumps, offal, bits of iron, old tin pots, boots and shoes, paper, wood and broken glass. When these had been identified and separated out, the sifters could move on to 'breeze and ashes straightforward'.[56] Even breeze and ashes proved not to be entirely straightforward, as they could be further classified as 'the breeze, the ashes, the manure, and the 'core' (broken crockery, oyster shells, broken bottles, &c., used for the foundation of new roads)'.[57] Greenwood's detailed journalistic account of his visit to a dust yard dates from the mid-1860s and plays off a deliberately understated but nonetheless shocking humanitarian concern against a sense of economic triumph – there were fortunes to be found in rags, but only at a terrible human cost. Other journalists from the mid-Victorian period were equally fascinated by the detailed processes of re-cycling and their economic implications. R. H. Horne's celebrated article 'Dust; or Ugliness Redeemed' was included in the first volume of *Household Words* and contains a revealing combination of fascination and disgust.[58] Like Greenwood, Horne compulsively lists and categorises the precise constituent elements that comprise 'dust', and repeatedly enumerates the re-cycling opportunities available to contractors. Both writers show an interest in the immense wealth represented by dustheaps, an idea that is of course central to *Our Mutual Friend.* As Ellen Handy has put it, with proper caution: 'The actual monetary value of the waste so collected has not yet been charted accurately by historians ... Whether or not collection efforts were profitable in practice, however, the belief in the economic value of this waste was widespread.'[59] The socio-economic vision that drove writers like Horne, Dickens, Mayhew and Greenwood will be examined in detail in Chapter 6, but the key point to make here is that these mid-Victorian writers were only re-iterating what everyone either knew or believed – that dust was both disgusting and valuable, as fascinating in its commercial potential as it was troubling in its psychic implications and social consequences. Mid-Victorian journalists and social theorists, in making public and specific the implicit social narrative of waste and its disposal, were attempting to give documentary weight and socio-economic context to a set of beliefs, urban myths, and largely unacknowledged processes that had already been widely examined in the popular culture of several generations. It was the combination of documentary intensity, economic buoyancy and the will to social change rather than any fundamentally new information that transformed the established social discourses concerning dust into something new in the 1850s and beyond.

Leaving aside for the moment the wealth of detailed information offered by Victorian documentary and journalistic writing from the middle decades of the century, and using Wight and Busby as guideposts, what then can confidently be said in relation to the dust trade in its popular cultural heyday between 1790 and 1840? First, I believe it is clear that in this period dustmen generally dealt in ashes and household waste, but did not usually clear night-soil or other forms of human ordure. This distinction is important to bear mind when trying to evaluate the extent to which dustmen were associated with excrement in the popular imagination. Second, it is not easy to categorise dustmen as part of the London poor. Their business required considerable capitalisation – the licence fees, the need for a horse and cart, and the employment of sifters all required some capital. Dust heaps were extremely valuable commodities, and their management required shrewdness if not education. While the sifters and street collectors of dust may have been economically at the bottom end of the economic scale, the dust contractors must have been men and women of substance. Furthermore, the economic independence of dustmen under the franchise system through which they were employed was exceptional. The financial success of dustmen, as well as their status as venture capitalists, was underscored in the popular imagination by the belief that the refuse they collected offered dustmen hidden treasure in the form of mistakenly discarded silver, jewellery or other valuables, including documents. While there is considerable evidence that dustmen did occasionally find extremely valuable items among their dust, the popular belief that they were wealthy beyond imagination as a result of chance finds was something of an urban myth. The sources and meanings of this myth will be analysed in later chapters. Third, the trade privileges of dustmen, however well they may have been legally encoded, were subject to considerable amounts of sometimes violent negotiation on the street. Fourth, while there was no trade organisation specifically for dustmen and they retained a fierce sense of individualism, there was strong sense of pride in the trade. One outcome of this pride was the more or less universal adoption of something close to a trade uniform. It is these issues about the dialogue between independence and municipal reform, between economic self-determinism and increasing legislation, between sometimes violent self-protection and the need to adapt to a more regulated and docile urban order, that dominate the history of dustmen after 1840.

Perversely, it was a piece of legislation that deliberately privileged dustmen – the Metropolitan Police Act of 1839 – that, in the popular imagination at least, began to spell out the end of the dustman trade as a private-sector enterprise except in the specialist role of re-cycling agents as described by Greenwood and his contemporaries. The Metropolitan Police Act was centrally concerned with the regulation of street noise, especially street cries and street music. The banning of trade calls was an essential element in its legislation, although dustmen, as an integral element in public cleanliness and as, by implication, municipal employees, were allowed to continue using their bells to announce their presence. It was well understood that although the focus of the new legislation was on noise, much wider issues were at stake. The Bill came during an early phase of what was to be a major preoccupation of Victorian society, the management of urban public space in order to impose a vision of civic order on a potentially volatile urban mob. Implicit in this process was an attack on traditional rights and privileges in the name of civic improvement. However, the street cries of traders, as Blake had so brilliantly recognised in *Songs of Innocence and Experience* forty years before, had combined a commercial with a socio-cultural meaning. Advertising aloud your trade presence also proclaimed your social and economic vulnerability – the linguistic shift from an economic to a humanitarian register managed by Blake in metamorphosing 'sweep' into 'weep' was entirely typical of the way in which the New Police Act was perceived in the popular mind. Here, for example, is the opening verse of a comic song 'sung at the London concerts' and written by C. P. Thompson that even draws on Blake's energetic punning, admittedly in a somewhat debased form:

SWEEPING REFORMATION
Oh, the days are all gone when the sweeps were the first men
    Who peeped out of doors when the morn did appear,
But – alas! They're debar'd, though the vagabond dustman,
    Are free, and the law with 'em don't interfere.
Such vagabond fellows of course make us jealous
    They ring their loud bells, and they laugh us to scorn –
We mustn't cry sweep, so the parliament tell us,
    So, we're nearly cleaned out by this sweeping reform.[60]

While this song was published late in the 1830s and written by a professional songwriter who was doubtless pandering to the sentiments of his supper-room audiences, there is a considerable amount of confirmatory evidence that the issues raised by Thompson's lyrics were of widespread concern. A song purportedly written from the point of view of a dustman in the same songbook, with the elegiac title of *The Werry Last of Dustmen* summarises the perceived situation:

Poor chimbley sweeps, for whom I veeps'
    Mustn't soot be bawling;
So them you see, as well as we
    Are hungered in their calling.
And vot's the cause? Them precious laws –
    Made by, they say, the first men;
I tells you vot, an idea I've got,
    That they're nothing more than dustmen.[61]

While concert-hall songs might be tonally ambiguous, and offer a mocking version of traditional proletarian grumbles as much as a complaint on behalf of newly disempowered street traders, similar combinations of the elegiac and the mocking can be found in other media too. There are, for instance, two strange multi-image plates by George Cruikshank, dated 1 June 1841 and initially published in a characteristic monthy part-issue miscellany edited by Laman Blanchard called *George Cruikshank's Omnibus* (fig. 4).[62] At first the two plates seem unequivocally opposed to the New Police Act. In the first plate the title – 'COMMENTARY upon the late – "New Police Act" by which it appears that …' – introduces a sequence of images that conclude this remark by depicting a broad variety of 'fun' that has been proscribed by the act,

**4** Two plates from *George Cruikshank's Omnibus* (1842)

including such apparently harmless activities as children trundling hoops and flying kites to say nothing of obviously socially useful ones like ringing a dustman's bell. However, much more socially ambiguous kinds of fun are also shown, including lamp smashing, letting off fireworks and lighting bonfires. Is Cruikshank suggesting that the Bill is a mixed

blessing that fails by including innocent pleasures amongst the genuine nuisances that are its real target? The issue is further complicated by Cruikshank's choice of an exuberant and whimsical mode of representation in which individuals are drawn without torsos so that their massively elongated legs lead directly into grinning and slightly enlarged heads. While Cruikshank is doubtless both celebrating and satirising a fad in caricature at this time by using such grotesquerie, the result is that his depiction of 'fun' is overlaid by the rather disturbing physical presences of his chosen subjects.

The second plate again seems initially entirely hostile to the Act, as the images depend on a concluding caption which states that, in all the depicted events, 'Somebody gets punished'. Again the activities depicted, and thus proscribed by the Act, seem to comprise, indiscriminately, the harmless (sweeps crying out their trade, for instance), the harmful (yobbos wrenching knockers off doors or 'mangling' policemen) and the ambiguous (small boys riding precariously on the tails of coaches). Again the mode of representation depends on the physical peculiarity of the protagonists. Whatever Cruikshank's purpose, however, his images are useful in suggesting the depth of feeling provoked, and range of activities rendered illegal, by the Metropolitan Police Act. The narrowness of the line between 'fun' and socially unacceptable behaviour is something that the caricaturist has seized upon here, and certainly his images seem to defend the carnivalesque and the grotesque against the implied rationality and 'good sense' of legislation and prohibition. Cruikshank, too, recognises in these two images that noise emblematically stands for a whole range of highly contested social activity.

In his fascinating recent work on what he calls 'Victorian soundscapes', John Picker has linked the contests over street noise to two major areas of social change. The first is the contest over urban space: 'It follows that the anti-street music movement can be considered an urban territorial campaign, a conflict for control between regions of harmony and dissonance. That conflict often manifests itself in legal action, for "the institutionalization of the silence of others assure[s] the durability of power"'.[63] Elsewhere, Picker notes that *Punch* 'transforms a controversy about offensive sounds into one of invaded spaces'.[64] As the following chapters will show, the noisiness of dustmen is part of their wider assumption of public space and part of their perceived threat to social order.

But if the territorial wars over noise were primarily about the management of urban space, they were also crucially about the hegemonic will of the rapidly developing professional middle classes. The growth of the social influence of these classes, which began to include artists and caricaturists, is one of the key narratives that underpin this book. In a chapter entitled 'The Soundproof Study – Victorian Professional Identity and Urban Noise', Picker convincingly and unequivocally links the legislation about street noise to the working practices and ideological imperatives of those new urban professionals who had begun to use their own houses and studies as their work place – writers and artists in particular. He cites as the main example of his thesis the later career and death of the caricaturist John Leech, who many contemporaries believed had been hurried to the grave by the persistent noisiness of the streets surrounding his house. That a caricaturist features as a central protagonist in debates concerning the emergence of a class of workers for whom silence was imperative and for whom the domestic interior became the site that gave them the space to depict the rowdy world outside their windows has particular resonance for this book. As Picker notes, 'advocates for silence on the streets waged a battle to impose the quiet tenor of interior middle class domesticity upon the rowdy terrain outside'.[65]

By the early 1840s, then, dustmen were beginning to be represented in an essentially elegiac way, and Chapter 6 contains a detailed account both of the many songs, novels and journalistic accounts of the disappearing or metamorphosing dustman and of the centrality of the dustman to an urban reformist agenda that centred on public space. But it was, of course, not just his noisiness that had begun to outmode the traditional figure of the dustman during this period. Legislation had attempted to purify the famously contaminated atmosphere of the metropolis by limiting the use of domestic coal fires, in the process hastening the introduction of steam heating systems which consumed their own smoke. As Frederick Farmer's popular song 'The Werry Last of Dustmen' put it, 'A precious joke, they burn the smoke/ and heats the room by steam, sir, …'.[66] Dust and soot thus became considerably less available commodities. Further legislation specifically concerning dustmen was less concerned with protecting their rights, as previous Acts had been, but more interested in ensuring the separation out of dirt and ordure from residential areas by regulating the storage and disposal of waste. The Nuisances Removal and Diseases Prevention Act of 1848 has already been mentioned, and it was this act that finally ensured that the disposal of ordure and the removal of dust became entirely separate activities in the eyes of the law. But the key shift had been a recognition by parish and metropolitan authorities that the removal of dust, now no longer as important as it had been given the smaller production of soot and ashes, might be increasingly combined with street cleansing more generally. Increased horse-drawn traffic, in particular, had led to the streets often being turned into a morass of filthy straw, ordure and mud, and the old system of entrepreneurial crossing-sweepers and scavengers could no longer cope. Accordingly, local authorities increasingly began to use dust contractors in a wider combined role of both street cleaning and dust collection. The scope of these new activities is clearly illustrated by the Schedule of Rakers' Duties for the City of London in 1838.

> CLEANSING
> 'By cleansing is to be understood to mean, that not only mud, dust, filth & rubbish, but all animal and vegetable matter, and everything that is offensive or injurious shall be properly swept up into the middle of all streets which exceed sixteen feet in width from curb to curb (but not within ten feet of any sewer grating,) and carted away therefrom within one hour after it shall have been so swept up, and in cleansing all places, the iron gutters laid across or along the footways shall be raked out and made clear for the water to run off, and all the straw, litter & c., laid before the houses of sick persons, is to be removed by the Contractors when notice has been given by the Inspector of the district so to do.
>
> DUST
> The Contractors are to take away from every house or building, at least twice in every week, or oftener, if required by the householders or their servants, the dust, ashes, dirt, rubbish, and refuse vegetable and animal matter, and all other, the usual refuse of a house, and to give notice of their being in the street or place, by constantly ringing a hand bell of the usual kind; and the same is to be taken away by the Contractors, respectively, from the Prison of Newgate, the Fleet Prison, the Giltspur-Street Compter, the Prison in White-Cross-street, the Hospital of St. Batholomew, the Mansion-House, the Bank of England, the east India Company's-house, the Custom-house and the Excise Office, every day, (Sundays excepted) before ten'o clock in the forenoon.
>
> The contents of all public dustbins wherever situate, shall be cleaned out and carted away twice in every week, or oftener if need be, whatever may be the nature of their contents.
>
> ALL THE REFUSE from the houses of the inhabitants, AND ALL THE SWEEPINGS OF THE STREETS, as afore described, ARE TO BE TAKEN ENTIRELY AWAY FROM THE CITY OF

> LONDON, and not be carted to, shot, or deposited at any place within this City and liberties, upon any pretence WHATEVER.[67]

Thus, even well before the 1848 Act, the dumping of rubbish within densely populated areas had been under attack. By 1838, if this Schedule is characteristic, dustmen's contracts had become formalised and specific, with the range of duties more related to civic cleanliness than the individual household.

Even more dramatic evidence not just of the major shift from a franchise to a contract system but also of the increasingly broad responsibility for public cleansing activities being undertaken by London civic authorities comes from a series of meetings held in 1846 and sponsored by the National Philanthropic Association. The papers for a meeting of 4 May laid out the financial arguments for a more inclusive 'improved system' of waste collection and street management.[68] According to the Association, 'scavengers' had been paid £6,040 in the preceding year to keep the streets clean. It calculated £5,500 to be 'the value of Ashes and Dust of the City of London, given gratis to the above Contractors' – an interesting set of figures suggesting, apart from the large sums of money involved, that dustmen had already combined their interest in dust with a wider responsibility for street cleansing, that they were paid on a contractual basis, but were additionally allowed to keep any profits they made from re-cycling what they had collected. When the costs of street watering were added in (£4,000) along with the salaries of 'Surveyors, Inspectors, Beadles and Clerks' (£2,485), the total cost of a year's street cleansing was reckoned to be £18,025 and involved the employment of 58 men. The improved system put forward by the association was to municipalise street cleansing, including the collection of dust, through the introduction of a unitary body with a clear hierarchy of Director, Superintendent, and Foreman who would manage a massive labour force of 520 men drawn directly from the able-bodied poor. Their numbers would mean that streets would be cleaner because the causes of dirt, especially animal droppings, would be removed sooner.

The 4 May meeting was prominently reported in the press, most spectacularly in the *Pictorial Times*, which gave it a full page, including two dramatic illustrations (fig. 5).[69] The article begins by expressing concern over the state of London Streets, exemplified by the state of the steep steps leading off London Bridge into Thames Street. The report continues by applauding the work of the National Philanthropic Association before launching into a fairly detailed account of the Association's meeting, listing the three resolutions that were carried. The

# IMPROVED STREET CLEANING IN THE METROPOLIS.

## IMPROVED STREET CLEANING.

There cannot be a doubt that the cleanly state of the streets in such a metropolis as London must be conducive to the health and comfort of its residents and visitors, and we may add our tribute of approbation for what was effected on this point during the last winter by the association formed for the purpose. We have endeavoured to illustrate this subject by pictorial representations: — 1st. A group of the National Society's men engaged in keeping a great thoroughfare clean from impurity; and 2dly. The flight of stone stairs on the Billingsgate side of London Bridge descending into Thames Street — a place that is always in a dangerous condition, but more especially on what may be called a "greasy day," when accidents are constantly occurring from the muddy state of the steps and the superabundant supply of orange peel, that not only threatens to overthrow the passenger, but frequently does introduce them from one landing place to another in much quicker time than is convenient or expected, to the great detriment of limbs and clothes. Our engraving represents an affair of this kind, and indeed almost every part of London evidences the immense number of oranges that must be consumed by the peel which is so plentifully strewed upon the pavements by the individuals who carelessly throw the pieces about, though they themselves are liable to be affected by the abominable practice. A public meeting took place on Monday at the Guildhall, London, in accordance with a numerously signed requisition, convened by the National Philanthropic Association for the employment of the poor in an improved system of street cleansing, and for the purposes of considering the advantages to be derived by the citizens of London and the public at large from carrying out the object contemplated.

THE "NATIONAL" STREET SWEEPERS AT WORK.

Lord R. Grosvenor, M.P., was, on the motion of Mr. Pattison, M.P., at 1 o'clock called to the chair. The hall was about one-third full, and upon the platform were observed Mr. R. L. Jones, Mr. Deputy Peacock (chairman of the court of sewers), Mr. Deputy Corney, Mr. C. Cochrane, Mr. Eagleton, Dr. Lynch, and several other members of the court of common council.

The noble chairman opened the business of the meeting by offering a few observations on the objects and the circumstances which had led to the formation of the association by which the present meeting had been convened.

The Rev. Mr. Harris, rector of Mile End New Town, moved the first resolution.

"That as uncleanliness and ungodliness are akin, so must the moral and spiritual as well as social and physical condition of the people be improved in proportion to the extension of habits of cleanliness among them — advantages which cannot fail to attend on the maintenance of greater cleanliness in the dwellings and surrounding localities of the community at large."

The Rev. Mr. Lusignan seconded the resolution, which was put from the chair and carried unanimously.

Mr. Eagleton moved the second resolution —

"That the system of street cleansing benevolently demonstrated in the city by the National Philanthropic Association during the winter months, the principle of which consists in keeping the streets clean by the continuous employment of men throughout the day as fast as the streets became dirty, has met with the general approbation of the citizens of London."

This resolution having also been seconded and carried, *nem. con.*, Mr. J Carter proposed the third resolution —

"Taking into consideration that the improved system referred to will greatly conduce to the comfort and health of the public, diminish the losses to which the householder, shopkeeper, and foot passenger are now subjected, and the act that, if extended throughout the kingdom, will very probably give employment to 50,000 able-bodied poor, this meeting is of opinion that the commissioners of sewers be respectfully requested to adopt it in cleansing the streets, courts, and alleys throughout the city of London with the least possible delay."

Mr. Bates seconded this resolution, and

Mr. C. Cochrane, the president of the Street-cleansing Association having addressed the meeting, the resolution was carried unanimously.

Mr. Brewster moved a resolution, empowering the committee to lay before the Court of Sewers, at their meeting on Tuesday, the resolutions adopted, together with the memorial, signed by upwards of 7000 names.

This having also been seconded and carried, on the motion of Mr. R. L. Jones, seconded by Mr. Deputy Corney, thanks were awarded to the noble chairman for his conduct in presiding on the occasion.

Lord Robert Grosvenor having returned thanks, the meeting separated.

Without wishing to depreciate the value of such an institution in affording relief to the poor, it is nevertheless a duty not to be led into error. There are scavengers at present employed in all parts of England whom, we suppose, it is not intended to throw out of work; of course the number of these men must be deducted from the number whom it is stated will be benefited. We love philanthropy, but it must be based on fact.

A "GREASY DAY" ON THE LONDON BRIDGE STEPS.

first of these unequivocally associated uncleanliness with ungodliness, the second applauded the Association on its work over the winter of 1845/46, and the third directed the Association to lay its plans before the Court of Sewers of the City of London forthwith. Despite its apparent respect for the Association, the *Pictorial Times* concluded rather tartly – 'Without wishing to depreciate the value of such an institution in affording relief to the poor, it is nevertheless a duty not to be led into error. There are scavengers at present employed in all parts of England, whom, we suppose, it is not intended to throw out of work; of course the number of these men must be deducted from the number whom it is stated will be benefited. We love philanthropy, but it must be based on fact'. But more interesting than this verbal response are the two images, which dominate the page. Across the top of the page is an tidy line of orderlies brushing street detritus to the kerb. One man is looking out of the picture to the left, and another has paused to mop his brow, but the image primarily suggests organised, useful, even heroic, toil, carried out despite the slightly amused presence of a man and boy idly watching in the right foreground. Crucially the men are both in uniform and act in a uniform manner – the Association's scheme depended on the deployment of a massive labour force acting in concert under the direction of a centralised authority, and the image suggests the discipline that such a system was meant to impose. Counterposed against this image of disciplined activity is a representation, taken from below, of the stairs leading off London Bridge. At the top of the stairs an alarmed woman carrying a basket on her head and an apprehensive boy look down the steps on which increasingly violent accidents are taking place or about to take place – a man is sliding down the steps on his bottom, two men approaching the right angle turn in the staircase (one with a walking stick) look anxiously down to where a fishwife is hurtling downwards, her fish projected out of her basket as a flying shoal, and a man is inching his way on down clutching the stair rail. In the foreground, two further fallers, one with a basket, have collided in their headlong descent. The image is dramatically structured not just by the flying bodies twisted into various helpless or supplicatory poses but also by the complex shift of perspective suggested by the twist in the staircase. Writhing on down into darkness, the image suggests that this is the staircase to Hell, that uncleanliness is indeed next to ungodliness, and that a dirty, slippery city is a city going to Perdition. The image also recalls in its structure, however unconsciously, Rowlandson's famous etching of 'The Exhibition Stare-Case' which showed the twisting stair-case of the Royal Academy packed with



*opposite*
**5** *Pictorial Times* (9 May 1846), 296

a jumble of falling figures[70] – another image of a society heading towards damnation due to its moral failings, although Rowlandson's principal interest seems to have been as much in the lewd postures of the tumbling bodies as the moral conclusions to be drawn from the scene. Together, these two images present a powerful narrative of a newly orderly and efficient society, orchestrating a philanthropically assembled labour force to good purpose, sweeping away into the abyss the dirt and chaos of a previous order. Indeed, this full-page image is a stunning reminder of the power of the weekly illustrated press to forge grand social narratives out of minor news reports, however unrelated the text and images may seem to be.[71]

A further aspect of this image is worth consideration here. The line of street orderlies is structured to suggest the kind of concerted and co-operative physical activity of, say, a rowing crew, with the poses of the men and the angle of their brooms carefully aligned. There is also the suggestion here of a machine, and it was in the period from the 1830s on – the great moment of the march of intellect – that the possibility of a street-cleaning machine begins to appear within the press and popular literature. As early as 1834 *Bell's Gallery of Comicalities* pondered the possibility of 'Automaton Dusting' as part of the 'Progress of Mechanism'.[72] A wood-engraved vignette shows an image of a mechanical device, wearing a dustman's hat, filling a cart with refuse while a 'traditional' dustman watches. The traditional dustman, however, has been transformed by his new freedom from dirty activities into an exquisite with a plumed fantail, strapped sandals and a quizzing glass. Further satirical comment on the march of intellect follows:

> Destined to shine in future day!
> Descendent proud of Dusty Bob,
> Who danced with Sal of Africa.
>
> 'Tis pleasant, with prophetic glance,
> To peep into futurity;
> Of intellect to note the advance
> And mark what men of dust will be.
>
> 'A capital machine, egad!
> As e'er I cast my eyes upon;
> What think you of my wooden cad,
> My patent dust automaton?

'What fools our fathers were alack!
How limited in comprehension!
Who could have dreamt, three centuries back,
Of such a notable invention?'

The extensive situating of the dustman trade within the context of the march of intellect will be examined in detail later, but the point here is to stress the social will to take away the degrading and filthy aspects of the dustman's work through automation. While usually imagined through humour or satire, the humanitarian and reformist wish to automate the collection of waste and thus eliminate direct human contact with refuse is a recurrent theme of representations of the trade from the late 1830s on. *Punch* uses the idea for several cartoons, for example, including one where a dustman pushes a rigid soldier along the street so that the guard's bearskin hat can sweep away street refuse.[73] In practice, however, while street cleansing has been largely mechanised, the automation of dust collection has never really occurred, despite many attempts to introduce mechanisation.[74]

By the 1840s, then, the dust trade had undergone massive changes from the small-scale entrepreneurship and independence that had characterised its early practitioners. Municipal intervention, regulatory legislation, changing practices in domestic heating, and the combining of the traditional, rather specialised, role of dustmen with wider responsibility for street cleansing had made dustmen either quite large-scale entrepreneurs or else parish employees in the form of waged street orderlies working within a clear civic bureaucracy. Various schemes for even wider reformation of the trade were being discussed and tested.[75] It is at this late moment in the history of dustmen that their cultural presence becomes most visible – in the pages of urban sketch writers like G. A. Sala or R. H. Horne, campaigning journalists like James Greenwood, and, most prominent of all, in the social analyses of Henry Mayhew and in Dickens's late novel *Our Mutual Friend*. One central argument of this book is that the authority and detail of these Victorian versions of Dusty Bob have overwhelmed and repressed a more varied and culturally diverse narrative of his rise and fall, and that the most intense cultural 'moment' for the dustman is perhaps more properly located in the years between 1820 and 1840 rather than the years between 1840 and 1865.

2

# Picturesque and educative dustmen: the urban scene and its dirty denizens, 1790–1821

## Introduction

This chapter is concerned with the representation of dustmen in visual culture from the 1790s, when they begin to appear in various established and relatively widely disseminated graphic genres, up to 1821, the year in which the publication of Pierce Egan's phenomenally successful and widely imitated picaresque novel *Life in London* established the dustman, in his fictional and stage manifestation of 'Dusty Bob', as a ubiquitous and powerful representative of urban culture within popular consciousness. While the widespread preoccupation with the figure of the dustman is essentially a Regency and early Victorian phenomenon, the origins of the social obsession with waste and dust clearly emerge from the three decades considered in this chapter.

These early accounts of the dustman are considered within three differing representational traditions. The first comprises the many series of 'Cries of London', the alphabets and the children's primers which depicted dustmen prominently among visible London street trades, and which provided, however decoratively produced, a wealth of documentary information. The combination of the picturesque and didactic that characterised such images underpinned their attempt to familiarise children (and, to some extent, barely literate adults) with the commercial realities of early industrial London, and, perhaps more important, to allay their anxieties about the burly and aggressive figures they might meet on the pavements of London. These kinds of image, which clearly originated in this period, persisted well on into the Victorian period in a relatively unchanged form.

The second comprises the representation of dustmen within what might be called the 'urban picturesque' – that is in the costume books, watercolours and, in a less obviously decorative manner, single-plate caricatures of the early years of the nineteenth century, where the graphic codes of the rural picturesque were being adapted to accommodate a new curiosity about urban life and the inhabitants of the metropolis. A number of key images of the dustman – that produced by T. L. Busby for example – combined the urban picturesque with the didacticism and social curiosity of the traditional 'Cries'. In these images the dustman began to gain his visible distinctiveness, a distinctiveness constructed partly through clothes and accoutrements, but also the outcome of a range of gestures, postures and poses associated with the trade – most obviously the articulation of the dustman's famous cry of 'Dust Ho!'.

The third representational tradition discussed here is that derived from Pierce Egan's famous novel, and includes a number of both graphic and novelistic responses to *Life in London*. In these fictions the dustman became the subject of the indulgent gaze of young male adventurers in pursuit of low-life urban spectacle, presumably for the delight of Egan's predominantly genteel readers. The dustman was frequently shown in these images as an embodiment of the freedoms and rewards implicit in social liminality and willed transgression, and was thus constructed as a willed reproach to genteel respectability. Presented as a hedonist for whom the concept of manners did not exist, the dustman came to represent pleasures and satisfactions unavailable to the refined.

Drawing together the implications of these three modes of representation, this chapter also suggests the resolution, if not the assimilation, of these competing traditions of representational possibilities, into a stereotype – the construction of the dustman as a picturesque but potentially dangerous liminal figure, both attractive and troubling in his energy, cultural belligerence and transgressive potential. Yet, equally, the diversity of representational possibilities available also led to some of the ambiguities in the repeated use of such stereotypes, ambiguities which both fascinated and troubled later Victorian artists and commentators. It is this stereotype that provides one key focus for the prolonged meditation on the nature of street culture and its implicit meanings that is described later in this book. Important as they are in forming a prelude to the broader discussions of the politics of urban space, labour, dirt and leisure which follow, the early phases of the dustman's appearance in popular culture are themselves of considerable interest and, indeed, complexity.

## 'D' is for dust – dustmen for children

Dustmen make a regular appearance in the many series of 'Cries of London' produced in the early years of the nineteenth century. Dustmen can be found in at least ten collections of 'Cries' in the period between 1804 and 1823, and in several more from the mid-Victorian period.[1] They also appear in a wide range of literary sites which might be described as 'sub-cries of London'[2] – illustrated teaching alphabets aimed at children,[3] scraps destined for the carefully accumulated albums put together by young women, and various other ephemeral publications which, while lacking the aesthetic and cultural ambition of the 'Cries' genres, nonetheless drew purposefully on the visual representations of the streets.[4] Most commentators argue that the function of these images was 'reactionary in spirit' and concerned to teach 'orthodox pieties' of a 'moral religious and educational nature'.[5] Through a 'host of books … touching on trade' children 'were not discouraged from showing curiosity about the price of goods and how they were produced, and were taught to express gratitude for their daily fare'.[6] Many of these images are difficult to date, but surviving examples, despite their use of the forms, layouts and imagery of earlier images, seem to belong to the 1830s and 1840s – precisely that moment when dustmen are beginning to lose their traditional roles, customs and habits. Nonetheless, it is clear that most surviving images from this period draw on stereotypes and modes of representation established before 1830.

**6** 'Dustman' reprinted by Charles Hindley in *A History of the Cries of London, Ancient and Modern*

As compositions which decontextualised dustmen from the London streets and rendered their appearance by a linear outline (figs 6 and 7), it might seem that the simplicity of such images precludes any interpretation apart from a reiteration of the picturesque and documentary elements of the images, and a recognition that 'books of hawkers for youngsters divide into pedagogical and religious or moral'.[7] But it might be worth thinking a little more about their purposes and functions, which hover between the educative and the nostalgic/picturesque. One regionally produced image draws on retrograde typography, enclosing a tiny version of the dustman within an

*Dust, O !—Dust, O !—Bring it out to day,*
*Bring it out to-day, I sha'n't be here to-mor-row !*

DUST, O !—DUST, O !.

7 'Dustman' reprinted by Charles Hindley in *A History of the Cries of London, Ancient and Modern*

elaborate typographic border made up of curling tendrils and leaves – a singularly inappropriate setting for a dramatically posed urban dustman.[8] The picture is accompanied by a rhyme:

> Dust O! – Dust O!
> His noisy bell the dustman rings
> Her dust the housemaid gladly brings
> Ringing he goes from door to door
> Until his cart will take no more.

This Otley publication is evidently an educational one, a way of using a series of nostalgic urban images to introduce children to reading, a chore rendered all the more pleasant by the decorative nature of the page. The image, despite its bucolic border, depicts the dustman in an assertive pose, basket akimbo, against the background of his cart. His horse seems to be straining out of the left top corner of the image. The little verse, while stressing that the dustman is a welcome neighbourhood visitor, nonetheless also draws attention to his brimming cart, which is emphasised in the image by the prominent upright shovel driven into the waste in the cart. So, while a fundamentally educative picturesque re-drawing of the dustman as an urban presence, nonetheless this image does acknowledge the nature of his work and the belligerence of his street presence. Yet the anachronistic form of the image – a reference back in both typographic structure and literary manner to early chap books – and the jovial rhyme to some extent take the potential conflict out of the image and drain it of unpleasantness. It is interesting to speculate how the image might have been negotiated between teacher and taught in dame schools and cottages up and down the country.

Many other images in alphabet books provide a wealth of information about the dustman's trade activities within tiny, simply drawn images. One alphabet image showed a dustman front on issuing his famous cry of 'Dust Ho!', hand to mouth as megaphone, with his bell in his left hand and his basket and spade resting by his side.[9] In the background a colleague, viewed from behind, is standing on a ladder dumping waste from his basket into a high-sided cart. In a tiny space, all the key components of the dustman's activities – not to mention his cry and trade paraphernalia – are represented here. A similarly structured image forms part of a spectacular sheet of trades that combined the 'Cries of London' structure with the teaching of numeracy rather than the more usual alphabetical instruction. It is called *London Cries or Addition Made Easy*, and 'Dust O!' represented the number '4'.[10] Even the crudest little images – like the tiny block used by the Banbury printer Rusher in a variety of publications, which shows a dustman lugging an empty basket in front of his cart – have some documentary value.[11] The documentary and educative functions of such images provided the knowledge base, the 'norm' from which contemporary satirists built their more analytical and more emblematic versions of the dustman and his social meanings.

In *The Nursery Companion* Iona and Peter Opie reproduce an 1820s 'Cries' which shows a slightly caricatured dustman in the foreground (paired with a watercress seller) while in the background his colleague struggles up a ladder to throw the contents of his basket into the dustcart.[12] The Baltimore-published *Sam Syntax's Description of the Cries of London* pairs its dustmen with a watercress seller and again one of the paired dustmen does the shouting while his partner, sketchily drawn in the background, does the carting. In this instance, however, his shouting is regarded more as a nuisance than a quaint addition to the melange of street sounds:

Now out with your dust – for the Cart's at the door,
While forward goes Sam hoarsely bawling for more;
'Dust ho!' and 'Dust ho!' As he raises his voice
His bell stuns our ears with its dissonant noise.[13]

Images such as these made good use of multiple figures to describe the range of activities that comprised a dustman's function.

Even more explicit and detailed in its account of the trade is the dustman described in *City Scenes, or a Peep into London for Children*, an expensive and thorough Harvey and Darton publication of 1818.[14] Along with the scavenger, also illustrated as a hard-working and socially useful tradesman, the dustman was given a generous and welcoming response:

> A very useful set of men are these; they remove the dust and the dirt from the houses in the city. It is a very profitable business, for, by sifting and sorting what is taken away, every thing becomes useful. There are frequently found cinders for firing, ashes and breeze for brickmakers: bones and old rags, tin and old iron, are carefully separated from oyster-shells and stones, which have their several purposes.[15]

Complementing the engraving of the scavengers, who are shown shovelling waste into their cart, this image shows a dustman in the foreground calling out his trade and ringing his bell while his colleague empties his basket into the cart shown behind. The image is both naturalistic and vigorous. Here, the dustman, already heralded as a 'useful' member of society, was further familiarised and assimilated into children's consciousness by an accompanying verse:

My masters, I'm dirty, not can I be clean;
  My business it would ill become,
With my face and hands clean in the street to be seen
  While I carry my shovel and broom.[16]

So, despite his dirty appearance and association with both waste and physical effort, the dustman was carefully explained as an essentially benevolent figure – no bogeymen are welcome in this world of genteel childhood!

Other comparable images showed a similar blend of retrospective or nostalgic literary pleasure and educative functionalism. An undated woodcut set of 'Cries of London' was organised with some ingenuity as a 'Humorous Alphabet'.[17] At sixpence this little stitched chapbook would have been aimed largely at teachers, and was published by Mrs Hodgson, a successful dealer in scraps and down-market comic lithographs. This chapbook uses a self-consciously anachronistic format and manner. The images are organised four to a page, each with a brief verse underneath, and printed on one side of the paper only to stop the print bleeding through on to the next page. Again the publisher has sought to bring together several traditional genres here – the perennial 'cries of London' format was combined with both an educational primer and a sequence of diverting images. The images are not self-evidently comic, but they do suggest elements of caricature. Street traders are rendered in isolation against an empty background in as naturalistic a way as the small scale and clumsy technique allow, but with some comic exaggeration. The dustman, face on to the viewer, is holding his bell high in his right hand and using his left hand as an improvised megaphone. His fantail hat is hidden. Under his image the verse runs:

> DUST O! DUST O! Come maids, hear my Bell, be cleanly you must,
> I'm coming, you see, to take off your dust.

Once again, the dustman was presented as fulfilling a useful public service, and the potential unpleasantness of his trade was buried within the complex of traditional picturesque, educational and comic possibilities offered by the image.

The use of the image of the dustman amidst those many used to teach children their letters, to amuse the barely literate and to satisfy the nostalgic tendencies of those seeking to record and celebrate the street culture of a vanishing Regency world was clearly widespread. These textbook images tend to emphasise one or other of the possibilities depending on precise purpose. A magnificent late chromolithographed 'scrap', for example, celebrates the heroic presence of a fully kitted-out dustman with his horse and cart in a way that to some extent subjugates naturalism to decorative splendour.[18] Nonetheless, the image is packed with documentary detail and had a clear educative function. Another image from a late source, the 1847 *Little Mary's Primer* published by the prolific Joseph Cundall, showed a fully realised if tiny vignette of a dustman climbing a ladder to deposit the contents of his basket in a cart while his horse waited patiently. Ruari McClean notes that the book showed 'a more visual approach to book design for children' than many other instances, and had, indeed, become 'almost a strip' rather than a primer.[19]

Taken overall, these kinds of educative images, then, tended to serve as a means of domesticating and normalising the figure of the dustman. They familiarised the dustman for children as a street presence. While they were largely drawn in the picturesque mode, with its tendency to eliminate background and social context, nonetheless these prints did offer images of dustmen at work and showed in some detail their working tackle. They have, accordingly, considerable *documentary* value. In their informative functionality these kinds of images differ markedly from contemporary caricatures in which dustmen are seldom seen at work, and offer little contribution to social usefulness. The picturesque dustmen of these educational images tended to be colourful, noisy, jocular and familiar. They were generally acknowledged as people who undertake something of social value.

Alphabet books and series of 'Cries' certainly offered children a stereotype of the *useful* dustman, and thus frequently represented him as a life-affirming and picturesque figure, familiarised into the childish imagination through his famous cry. In invoking these attitudes towards dustmen, literature for children was at odds with the more fraught emblematic readings of contemporary caricaturists, described in detail in Chapter 4, who were on the whole more interested in the carnivalesque management of perceived threats to the social order than in the need to educate and inform young children. But it was close to both the self-consciously picturesque and cheerfully picaresque images of dustmen to be found in the costume books and illustrated fictions of the first two decades of the nineteenth century.

## Dustmen and the urban picturesque

As well as images specifically aimed at children with the intention of rendering street figures as useful, productive and unthreatening urban presences there were also graphic traditions for adults which sought to render street trades as both socially heroic and aesthetically pleasing. Such images might be properly called an early form of the 'urban picturesque', especially as such a term implies the extent to which these prints drew on the tropes, motifs and graphic codes of eighteenth-century rural depiction rendered in both watercolours and prints. This range of picturesque prints, most of them etchings, metal engravings or (after 1815) lithographs, are largely drawn from, or related to, established genres of print-making such as series of street cries, volumes of prints of regional or working costume, or prints of urban 'types'. Despite Shesgreen's analysis of the major changes taking place within the 'Cries' genre early in the nineteenth century, which 'aimed to replace … picturesque realism … and French pastoralism with a new antipastoralism founded on … caustic naturalism',[20] these images retain both the aesthetic aspirations and Romantic sympathy with the liminal and the outcast which had characterised earlier images within this tradition.

At one end of the scale, such prints overlapped in their formulation and purposes with the images drawn for children described above, especially in their use of formats derived from the 'Cries' or the Alphabet. For example, F. J. Mannskirsch's little 1797 aquatint of a dustman comes from a series which renders the 'Cries' idea as picturesque urban vignettes.[21] This tiny image, framed in an elaborate octagonal border to look like an oil painting, shows two dustmen at work, one loading a cart, while a housemaid stands watching at the door of a house. The street is quite fully realised, and there is a sense here of people quietly going about their business. This is a charming rather than an expository image and one that deliberately brings the idioms of the picturesque to bear on street labour.

At the other end of the scale, such prints occasionally substituted caricature and the grotesque for the picturesque, and expressed repulsion and repugnance rather than aesthetic pleasure in low-life urban subjects. There are, however, relatively few dustmen visible in caricature before 1821, and those that do appear have identities which correspond more with a range of street-cleaning activities than specifically with those belonging to the dustman.[22] There are a number of reasons for this absence. Most obviously, the trade was only slowly disentangling itself from the other groups of street cleaners. Although unlicensed scavengers were giving way to licensed dustmen in the period, and night-soil removal was becoming entirely the province of sweeps, some confusion over roles remained. The distinctive dustman 'uniform' – partly adopted, perhaps, to distinguish 'proper' dustmen from scavengers – was not fully established, and images from this period are not especially interested in such fine distinctions between trades.

But the issue is not just one of visual culture responding to empirically observed reality. The representation of dustmen formed part of a wider conceptual understanding of the urban poor, and eighteenth-century caricature was remorseless and savage in its account of this class. As Dorothy George noted in the Introduction to volume 7 of *BMC*, 'as before, social injustice is only by exceptionally subject of graphic satire',[23] and for caricaturists like Rowlandson, Woodward, Elmes, the

Cruikshanks (Isaac, Robert and George) and the other producers of the more 'social' images being issued or re-issued primarily by Thomas Tegg in the first two decades of the nineteenth century, the urban crowd remained essentially an undifferentiated and grotesque 'mob'. On those occasions when these caricaturists drew throngs of urban characters at fairs or other gatherings,[24] they were represented, to cite the description of *BMC* 11775, as 'a plebeian crowd, much caricatured'. In these scenes of undifferentiated grotesquery, one looks in vain for the distinguishing garb, equipment and posture of the dustman. Where workers in the dust trades were specifically rendered, they were represented through animalistic, brutalised physiognomy and bodies, and brought together ideas of contamination, contagion, dirt and lust, nowhere more savagely depicted than in Rowlandson's *Love and Dust*[25] from 1788, a masterpiece of animalistic revulsion.

Haunting in its joyous repulsiveness as *Love and Dust* remains, it is the self-consciously picturesque images by artists like Paul Sandby, W. H. Pyne and T. L. Busby which have come to dominate recent awareness of early dustmen and their activity.[26] Such images derived largely from an impulse to record and render urban street life in a pleasing decorative manner which combined the antiquarian project of recording 'vanishing' customary practices (like street cries) with an aesthetic which derived continuity and coherence from the representation of rural contentment. As Shesgreen suggests, a countervailing impulse towards naturalism and towards a sceptical reworking of the picturesque increasingly appeared in the work of Paul Sandby, J. T. Smith and T. L. Busby as the tradition moved on into the nineteenth century. But nonetheless, even in these images the rural picturesque and aesthetic self-consciousness remain standard reference points. Sheila O'Connell describes the visual structure and ideological implications of this tradition in the following terms:

> [By 1800] scholars and collectors regarded popular prints of all sorts as products of a lost innocence – conservative rather than radical. They were associated with an idyllic rural life rather than with urban streets ... Publications appeared of series of town and country 'types', their dress, customs and so on – W. H. Pyne *Microcosm*, 1806, T. L. Busby *Costume of the Lower Orders of London*, 1820. These emerged from the 'cries' of earlier periods that had been sanitized more directly by Francis Wheatley in his *Cries of London* of 1796, in which pretty girls in neat dresses sell their goods beside fine examples of civic architecture.[27]

It is this urban yearning for the rural and the picturesque – a process that decontextualised dustmen from the actualities of their filthy trade – that structured the relatively well-known images of London trades that emerged from the costume books of the early nineteenth century, most notably those produced by Pyne, Busby and Smith.

Dustmen appeared in a number of these key early nineteenth-century costume books, and these images have become extremely well known. Pyne's two famous images of dustmen, one depicting a dustman with a dog, from the *Microcosm* (1806) (Plate I and fig. 8) and

**8** W. H. Pyne, 'Dustman' from *Microcosm*

the other, drawn from *The Costume of Great Britain* (1808), showing a dustman looking back at the viewer over his left shoulder against the background of a street scene, have been frequently reproduced. In both these images, the dustmen are shown as dynamic figures frozen into poses which emphasise their vigour and vitality. Pyne's 1806 image has the dustman as one of four figures rendered in sepia to form a full page of the *Microcosm*.[28] The other figures on the same page, which is rightly entitled 'Miscellaneous', comprise a ferret seller, a bellows mender and a chair caner. Three of the figures are depicted in dramatic poses with sweeping arm gestures. Both the bellows mender and the dustman are shown calling out their trade, although the dustman, shown in frontal view both shouting and ringing his bell with his basket held on his right hip, is easily the most dramatic. A dog scavenges in the heap of dust at his feet – a bone is clearly delineated – in an emblematic reminder of the constituent elements of 'dust'. His fantail has somehow been transformed into a kind of shadow that envelopes his face, and he wears a waistcoat rather than the more usual top-coat – evidence, along with a Busby image from 1820, that the dustman 'uniform' took a while to become established. This image is a self-consciously aestheticised act of figure drawing, as much a model for amateur artists as an attempt at documentary realism. It remains, despite the dog, the bone and the dust, a resolutely picturesque image, interested in the aesthetic drama of the working figure rather than its social implications. The streets are here eliminated from the image, and the viewer is required to supply the urban context in which the figure functioned. It is unlikely that the owners of Pyne's folios would have wanted to re-instate the daily realities of filth, grime and waste which characterised the dust trade back into this image – it seems likely that they would have preferred to leave this manly and active figure as an essentially picturesque or even heroic one.

The 1808 image, ostensibly drawn to focus on the costume of the dustmen, nonetheless positions the dustman across a quite fully realised street scene, with the image receding towards first a cart with a second dustman shooting ashes from his basket and then further to a substantial, even palatial, town house beyond. Much in the style of the 'Cries' images, Pyne has tried to illustrate emblematically here the reach and nature of the street activities of dustmen. But the central dustman has been self-consciously posed both to make his characteristic dress entirely visible and to register his energy and virility as the figure twists to stare back at the viewer over this left shoulder. The back view taken of this central figure allows the fantail hat to be suggested in all of its mythologised extensiveness, and makes clear the classic sequence of loose white jacket, breeches, stockings and boots that characterise the dustman figure. The dustman is clean, and his clothes are in good order. Pyne's image seems to have served as the model for a decidedly similar view of a dustman looking over his shoulder and located against a street scene with a distant cart being loaded which appears in a volume called *Picturesque Representations of the Dress and Manners of the English* published in 1814.[29]

T. L. Busby's *Dustman*, drawn in profile, and one of few shown in trousers rather than breeches, is scarcely less well known.[30] Busby's dustman is a *working* dustman, half hidden by the vast basket he is carrying on his shoulder, and one of few dustmen depicted without breeches or a loose-fitting jacket – in this case, he wore a close-fitting dark jacket, clogs, and patched and holey trousers. Smiles, in discussing Busby in his study of costume books, focuses attention on the idea of the series and on the emergent relationship between developed letter-press and illustration as the costume-book genre established itself in the first decades of the nineteenth century, but singles out the unusualness of Busby's work in trying to humanise and individualise street characters, even to the point, Smiles suggests, of asking readers to offer aid to them when they met on the streets.[31] The detailed biographical evidence presented by Busby to explain his subjects has already been suggested in Chapter 1, which contains extensive quotation from the seemingly authoritative account of the dustman and his trade which accompanied the illustration. Busby's defence of the truthfulness, particularity and depth of his account of the people who inhabited the streets of London additionally suggests his humanitarian concern and compassion – as Smiles notes 'the poverty-stricken are shown to possess integrity and dignity which would sharply distinguish them from the undeserving poor'.[32]

**9** George Cruikshank, 'Dustman' from *London Characters*

Further indication of he ways in which the essentially celebratory 'Cries' tradition began to develop investigative as well as picturesque elements is provided by Cruikshank's *Dustman* (fig. 9), originally drawn as part of a series for the *Gentleman's Pocket Magazine* between 1827 and 1829, and then re-issued as *London Characters* in 1829.[33] As Vogler notes, 'Cruikshank's London characters closely resemble, but are not identical to, the many series of "street cries" popular during the late eighteenth and early nineteenth century'.[34] The differences depended on the much higher degree of naturalism that Cruikshank was bringing to his images in the late 1820s. Even the tiny vignettes (including several dustmen) he drew for such comic publications as John Wight's *Mornings at Bow Street* (1824), *More Mornings in Bow Street* (1827) and *Sunday in London* (1833) around this time show his responsiveness to Wight's literary marriage of Regency urban anecdote with a new documentary and investigative rigour.[35] It is no accident that Wight described his work as a 'Collection of Humorous and Comic Reports' in the sub-title to *More Mornings at Bow Street* because his work, amusing as it was meant to be, nonetheless sought the truthfulness of a police 'report' – his books comprised evidence as much as anecdote. In this *Dustman*, depicted with a slightly awkward tilt of the figure and a note of pleading pathos, Cruikshank did not shrink from an honest rendering of the character's presence – 'unshaven, unkempt, and knock-kneed' according to one commentator[36] – and yet he retained a sense of visual pleasure in the picturesque spectacle of the fully kitted dustman with his mighty bell, his characteristically flaring surcoat and famous fantail hat. This is an image drawn at exactly that moment when the urban picturesque, refusing the alternative exaggerations and complexities of caricature, begins to become centrally interested in reportage as a central mode for representing the city. Reportage is considered in detail in Chapter 6.

So far in this chapter the images considered have served didactic and decorative functions, often combining a documentary and an aesthetic impulse. These functions were largely expressed in images that isolated the street figures from their social context through the elimination of an explanatory background or visual context. Smiles describes such images as 'surface' representations of 'outward appearance', and suggests how in the first few decades of the nineteenth century these kinds of images give way to 'depth' representations where the working figure was individuated and increasingly presented with a carefully delineated social context for his or her activities.[37] Increased naturalism and attention to social context of this kind fed into the more imperative investigative and documentary tendencies of early Victorian literary modes, especially the social problem novel. But intersecting in the 1820s with these essentially naturalistic and aesthetic concerns were other emergent representational traditions – traditions which evolved the naturalistic and decorative aspects of the 'Cries' and urban 'characters' through exaggeration, the grotesque, the picaresque and the comic into versions of the dustmen as deviant or transgressive figures, distinguished by their a-social desires and appetites. It is here that the complex and enduring stereotype of Dusty Bob has its most fertile origin.

## Low life in the East – Pierce Egan and the transgressive dustman

Pierce Egan's illustrated novel *Life in London*, published in part-issue form in 1820–21, immediately became a cultural phenomenon. It gave instant rise to numerous theatrical adaptations and imitations, sponsored a range of imitative or downright derivative picaresque fictions, furthered the reputations of its illustrators (the brothers George and Robert Cruikshank), provoked a bitter row between Egan and George Cruikshank over its origins, and provided a prototype for the widespread marketing and 'merchandising' of cultural commodities. It was a book adored by Thackeray but one reviled by Dickens,[38] however influenced he may have been by it. It had an astonishing presence in early nineteenth-century consciousness. Much reprinted during the 1820s, *Life in London* has continued to enjoy a persistent afterlife.[39] It is a book that has still had less than its due in terms of scholarly interest, even though J. C. Reid's excellent *Bucks and Bruisers – Pierce Egan and Regency England*, which appeared in 1971, made a strong case for Egan's importance.[40] Subsequently, *Life in London* has often enough been pillaged for colourful illustration of early nineteenth-century pleasures,[41] but only recently served as a focus for detailed analysis or discussion.[42] Greg Dart argues persuasively that the popularity of *Life in London* was to create through its 'thick verbal texture … a polyglot vocabulary that was not tied down to any particular social milieu … In this way *Life in London* succeeded in capturing the age of "improvement" at its utopian moment, and the improvement it imagined was (in certain curious ways) highly inclusive and democratic in nature'.[43] The importance of Egan's use of slang as a democratising argot is clear.[44] Dart's further argument that, despite its ostensible focus on the misdeeds of young 'bloods' of unmistakeably genteel origins, *Life in London* is infused with a democratic vision in which class differences and hierarchies are acknowledged but accommodated, or even celebrated, is an important one for the cultural history of dustmen and serves as an important starting place for the argument which informs this book. Marriott, however, while he acknowledges that in the All Max in the East scene at least the book might be read as 'an assertion of the worth of an international proletarian culture' ultimately reads it as 'a celebration of middle-class Regency manhood in which the poor featured merely as a comic diversion'.[45] As such, he sees *Life in London* as a book which created conservative racial and social stereotypes that furthered the defusing of revolutionary tendencies among the politicised elements of urban society in the 1820s and 1830s.

The next chapter of this book argues that it is only *after* the publication of *Life in London*, and then in the theatre rather than in fiction, that the 'Dusty Bob' character, the central Regency device for the exploration of the dustman idea, begins to emerge clearly. At first glance, Dusty Bob's connection with the original text of Egan's novel is tenuous. Indeed, *Life in London* contains no character called 'Dusty Bob'. There *is* a coal-whipper called (significantly) Nasty Bob in it, who is a central character in the section of text and the subsequently famous illustration which describe an evening in an East End drinking dive, All Max in the East. While Nasty Bob pre-figures Dusty Bob in a number of significant ways, he is, as his name suggests, a different, less comic character who carried on a distinctly different trade which required different clothes. There *is* a dustman in *Life in London*, though you have to read the text carefully to realise this, as his role is not obvious. A section of the novel features a dustman called 'Chaffing Peter', who narrates a long story about Newgate in an extraordinarily elaborate rendition of street speech. Far from being a comic if transgressive pleasure-seeking representative of the proletariat like Dusty Bob, Chaffing Peter seems more an incidental comic diversion, a device through which the author can express an interest in the urban vernacular. Dustmen and related trade figures do, however, appear in the illustrations to *Life in London*, even if they do not function as important narrative presences. One, for example, appeared on the paper covers of the novel as published in original boards, drinking in a tavern over the caption 'Low' – and thus is seldom seen in bound or reprinted volumes.[46]

But two of the illustrations to *Life in London*, drawing on the visually similar figure of the coal-heaver or coal-whipper, do begin to assemble the repertoire of key motifs, tropes and concepts which would be rapidly attributed to Dusty Bob in his caricature and stage personae to construct him as a remarkably complex and useful social stereotype. The first depicts a visit paid by the pleasure seeking trio of Tom, Jerry and Logic (the novel's trio of picaresque explorers of urban entertainments) to a masquerade, a type of entertainment apostrophised by the author as a place where 'the searchers after *fun* may either *find* it or *create* it'.[47] The precise and extremely complex jokes involved in the event are not of concern here. More pertinent is the prominent figure of a coal-heaver, dressed identically to a dustman and located at the centre of the image in the midst of the revels. In this masquerade, one of the available adopted carnivalesque identities, alongside traditional figures like harlequin or a clown, is specifically that of a working man. To adopt such an identity for the genteel revellers is every bit as transgressive as adopting that of a nun – another of the central figures in the image. What is described here is the possibility of steeping out of the genteel and becoming, in however temporary, travestied and colourful a form, one of the 'low'. The picturesque dress of coal-heavers and dustmen, their unusually 'low' status due to the dirtiness of their job, and their apparent freedom from the constraint of any conception of manners, all made their identity one of particular appeal to a masquerader. Here, in a clear graphic form, is the model for many images of fantasised trangression from high to low, from refined to vulgar, from good manners to no manners which characterise the caricatures of dustmen produced between 1821 and 1850. The central structure of Egan's texts – the picaresque adventures of a group of young bloods willing to overstep experimentally the limits of good behaviour in a newly anxious urban setting – is being re-configured into graphic form.

*opposite*
**10** Henry Alken and William Heath, 'Tom and Bob among the Coster Mongers at a Donkey Cart Race'

Such re-configuration reaches its most refined form in the illustration to Tom, Jerry and Logic's most transgressive moment – their visit to an East End gin shop, All Max in the East.[48] In the dramatisations of *Life in London* this scene often serves as the play's finale, the ultimate destination of a journey outward from West to East, but also downwards from 'high' to 'low'. But in the novel, while a climactic moment of transgression, the scene appears about two-thirds of the way through. It is illustrated by one of Cruikshank's most famous images – Nasty Bob, at the incitement of the genteel visitors, dances a turn with African Sall, a black woman of doubtful profession and the owner of a small child and no husband. The caption describes Bob, Sall and their associates as 'the unsophisticated sons and daughters of nature', an allusion to their animality and energy as much as their ignorance. The issues raised by this scene, transferred from a coal-whipper to a dustman in almost every dramatisation of *Life in London*, are examined in the next chapter, but it is almost impossible to overestimate the impact of this scene, with its combination of interests in race, gender, class and language, on the history of early Victorian popular culture.

The other images considered here are all ones which, made during the first few years of the fashionable rage for *Life in London* and the picaresque exploration of London low-life which it engendered, exploited the stage transformation of nasty Bob the coal-whipper into Dusty Bob the transgressive dustman. Although these images draw on the theatrical versions of *Life in London* as well as on Egan's original text in formulating Dusty Bob as a popular cultural stereotype, and thus overlap with the playtexts and performances considered in the next chapter, they serve to maintain Dusty Bob's presence as a central motif in picaresque fiction. Thus the book that served as a sequel to *Life in London*, the 1821–22 *Real Life in London* (a book many believed to be by Egan), showed that its two illustrators, Henry Alken and William Heath, had readily understood the potency of the dustman as a characteristic element in the urban picaresque

as it had been defined by Egan's earlier work.[49] Dustmen are represented in the etchings for this book in several exemplary places. A Bob and Sal pairing (though Sal is white) appear in 'The King's Levee' in volume 1, where they carry on their courtship prominently in the left foreground of the image ignoring the ceremonial passage of the royal entourage behind. In volume 2 there are illustrations that include dustmen or coal-heavers in three characteristic locations – at the masquerade, as participants in a pony and cart race, and at an early morning street tea stall. All these images dwell on the association of the dustman with pleasure and transgression.

The masquerade shows genteel rakes adopting the permissive garb of the dustman or the coal-heaver to signal their freedom from normal rules of genteel good manners.[50] 'Tom and Bob among the Coster Mongers at a donkey cart race' shows a 'low' travesty of a horse race in which clumsy carts, incompetent horsemen and uncooperative donkeys compete. In one cart a fantailed driver has lost control of his donkey and fallen back into his cart while, in the distance, the upended breeches of another dustman charioteer are visible over the sides of a cart, his fall the result of the kicking exploits of his donkey (fig. 10). This is the first of many caricature images of dustmen as 'sportsmen' who act as either participants in or spectators of various more or less burlesque sporting contests. In a

TOM & BOB, taking a Stroll down Drury Lane at five in the Morning

third image Tom and Bob, as dedicated explorers of London's nightlife, are strolling home at five o clock in the morning after their night out through the already crowded activities of Drury Lane. A dustman, unceremoniously downing a dish of tea at a stall, is readily identifiable at the right of the image, an almost subconscious yoking together on the artist's part of transgressive pleasure-seeking and the working dustman (fig. 11). Again, this image forms a precedent for many other images, in both caricature and documentary mode, which represent dustmen at street stalls. *Real Life in London*, then, has a number of dustmen occupying characteristic spaces in the urban scene, suggesting how they have been rapidly and unselfconsciously ascribed to emblematic locations on the streets and in the taverns and clubs as result of the precedents offered by Egan's novel.

Further re-workings of Egan's text can be found in the graphic narratives, almost comic strips, which sought to translate the success of *Life in London* into a new form. William Heath's *A Midnight Go of Daffy's Elixir* elaborates many of the ideas suggested by Egan's description of All Max in the East (Plate III). In this instance, Bob and Sal have been relegated from a central role to the periphery of the image, where they drink, smoke (in Bob's case) and ignore the cries of Sal's squalling baby. This is an image of debauchery rather than one of pleasure. While Dusty Bob looks serene enough, he is too drunk to pour his drink into a glass, and the heart-shaped shovel leant against the wall at his side reminds the viewer that he has abandoned work for pleasure. African Sal is shown entirely unflatteringly – legs splayed apart she throws back her head to drain her glass of gin, barely able to hold on to the child that howls on her lap. This image is a critique of the ways in which the pursuit of pleasure leads to moral depravity, especially child neglect, and it stands in marked contrast to Egan's celebratory account of the animalistic vitality suggested by All Max in the East. One further point: for the first time here the dustman assumes the role of by-stander or spectator, located at the margin of the image, looking across the picture plane at the rich mixture of character and incident that the tavern interior provides.

*opposite*
11 Henry Alken and William Heath, 'Tom and Bob Taking a Stroll down Drury Lane at Five in the Morning'

*Doing a Little Low Life in the East* (Plate IV) is entirely dependent on Egan's account of All Max, although the various elements of the scene are slightly re-ordered. Dusty Bob, now clearly a dustman rather than a coal-whipper, occupies centre-stage with his dancing partner, but she is a buxom white woman rather that African Sal, who has been sent off to the left margin of the image where she begs a glass of gin from the genteel visitors. The one-legged fiddler performs without inducement, and there is none of vigorous interaction between the aristocratic low-life explorers and the proletarian denizens of the tavern which had structured Egan's vision in *Life in London* and formed the basis of the stage versions of the novel. While the scene has some elements of disorder in it – the reversed fantail of the dustman dancer, the public embrace of the couple on the right, the grotesque appearance of the man capering to the right of African Sal – it is a curiously static image, with the two genteel visitors towering disproportionately over the rest, and a number of quietly self-absorbed figures in the background. But the strangest feature of this image is the dustman in the right foreground, thrusting out of the main picture plane, but shown in back view staring into the image as if on the viewer's behalf. Here is the first of many dustmen whose main function seems to be that of a spectator surveying, on the viewer's behalf, the wonders of urban life.

Egan and his illustrators returned to dustmen again in later books that continued to exploit the idea of the genteel low-life adventurer. Robert Cruikshank's illustrations to Egan's *The Finish to the Adventures of Tom, Jerry and Logic* (1828), for example, included an emblematic dustman on its title page, as well as a dustman watching a play and a masquerader dressed up as a dustman – a direct reference back to the original *Life in London*. By 1828, of course, the stage fame of Dusty Bob had assured him of a constant presence in the popular cultural representation of metropolitan life, but it is in the illustrations to picaresque fictional texts of the 1820s, described above, that dustmen attracted to themselves the key meanings that were to be exhaustively repeated, analysed and developed by the caricaturists of the early Victorian period. These were largely emblematic and figurative meanings quite outside the didactic and documentary modes stressed in the costume books and 'Cries of London', which had relied on a combination of naturalism and the urban picturesque for their effect. These illustrations constructed a repertoire of complex interpretative possibilities which formed part of the stock in trade of an entire generation of comic artists, and are thus a necessary prelude to the chapters that follow.

First of all, in obvious contradistinction from the images in the 'Cries' and costume books, the representations of dustmen which emerge out of picaresque fiction located dustmen not at work on the streets but rather at leisure in taverns, gin shops and even, to some extent, on the streets in non-working roles such as tea-drinking. These are images that either deliberately made an association between the working activities and leisure pursuits of dustmen (they are depicted constantly in their distinctive working dress which formed a perpetual reminder of what they did) or else concentrated on the idea of what 'pleasure' might mean to the readers of the picaresque fictions of the 1820s. This shift of locale from the streets to taverns was not quite a shift from the public to the private or the domestic, but nonetheless it began to figure the significance of dustmen more in cultural than in economic terms. It was their significance as emblematic urban working men rather than the nature of their particular trade which proved a subject of fascinated interest. Alongside this hugely significant shift of focus was another – in these images dustmen were figured as much as spectators as participants, and they began to haunt the peripheries of images of urban delight as absorbed observers as well as occupying centre stage as pleasure seekers. As onlookers, dustmen, with their distinctive dress and willingness to be diverted, became irresistible to caricaturists seeking to fill out a busy urban scene. Dusty Bob and African Sal, sat watching the varied activities of the tavern from the sanctuary of a settle located at the margins of the image in *A Midnight Go of Daffy's Elixir*, or, even more graphically, the absorbed back view of the dustman spectator in *Doing a Little Low Life in the East*, form some of the recurrent motifs and frameworks out of which caricaturists built their images in the 1820s, 1830s and 1840s.

3

# Theatrical dustmen, 1820–60: not so Dusty Bob

## Dusty Bob reaches the stage and meets his match

Pierce Egan's famous novel, *Life in London* and its imitators did not, then, create the fame of Dusty Bob, despite making other central characters like Tom, Jerry, and Logic into popular cultural heroes. Indeed, the novel barely mentions Dusty Bob, and then as an obscure comic coal-heaver, who serves to swell a scene or two, rather than as a fully realised caricature of a dustman. What Egan does do in his novel, however, is to establish the picaresque tropes and imaginative possibilities that allowed the predominantly genteel readers to construct a vulgar yet inclusive, potentially dangerous but essentially genial, low-life 'other' which could be lived out, theatrically at least, in the 'cribs' and 'dives' of the 'East' with the 'unsophisticated sons and daughters of nature'[1] whose habitat this represented. Other writers and illustrators were quick to re-work Egan's mix of picaresque adventure, urban transgression and graphic satire. As already suggested, these yearnings for colourful and 'forbidden' low-life adventure shaped, too, the many stage versions of Egan's novel, and these theatrical and sub-theatrical versions of Dusty Bob and African Sal form the subject of this chapter.

It was the 'leaps from the page to the boards',[2] that is to say the dramatisations of *Life in London*, which made Dusty Bob famous. The stage versions of *Life in London* not only transformed a minor character in Pierce Egan's novel from a coal-whipper into a dancing dustman, but also created an enduring comic figure widely visible in popular culture for the next thirty or forty years.[3] This figure, Dusty Bob, became one of the key stereotypes through which urban anxiety would be formulated, examined and (perhaps) resolved in the early Victorian period. The staggering range, popularity, and diversity of these dramatisations has been described often enough, hardly surprisingly given that *Tom and Jerry* was one of the theatrical phenomena of the nineteenth century.[4] Under various titles – *Life in London, Tom, Jerry and Logic's Life in London, The Larks of Logic, Tom, and Jerry* as well as *Tom and Jerry* – Egan's original idea was dramatised in at least six different versions, to say nothing of minor variations and new productions of what became the standard text, W. T. Moncrieff's *Life in London, or Tom and Jerry*, which was originally performed at the Adelphi Theatre in November 1821. Moncrieff's version of Egan's novel was not the first stage adaptation, and had been preceded by at least two other productions of *Life in London*, one by William Barrymore at the Royal Amphitheatre in September 1821, and a second probably by Charles Dibdin at the Olympic in November 1821.[5] Over subsequent months in various productions Tom and Jerry were sent on visits to places as diverse as Paris (a George McFarren production at the Royal Coburg in December 1822)[6] and Brixton (The Surrey Theatre in 1823). In search of originality, difference and spectacle, productions featured such incidental delights as a Pony Race 'passing round and into the pit'.[7] A rare pamphlet in the Beinecke Library describes the horse race in some detail, and suggests that it must have been a very elaborate piece of staging involving six ponies, with one in black colours representing Dusty Bob. This version of the play is described as a 'New Pedestrian, Equestrian, Extravaganza and Operatic Burletta In Three Acts of Gaiety, Frisk, Lark and Patter'.[8] Dusty Bob was described as 'Clerk of the Course' for these revels. Other performances featured exhibition fights between leading pugilists of the period, which occupied the gaps between acts. In the May 1822 Royalty production of *Tom, Jerry, and Logic's Life in London*, Neat and Hickman obliged with what the playbill described as a 'set-to' and a 'real out and outer' which was 'repeated every evening'.[9] Another production featured the two most famous prize fighters of the time, Cribb and Spring.[10] Perhaps something of the spirit of all these productions can be gained from the Royalty's immodest but certainly entertaining description of its April/May version of *Tom, Jerry, and Logic's Life in London* – 'an entirely new Operat-ical, Melo Dramat-ical, Farcet-ical, Com-ical, Pantomim-ical, Gallimaufr-ical, Whims-ical, Tagrag-ical, Bobtail-ical, Costermonger-ical, and the real Corinthian-ical, elegantly elucidated, and most truly designated …'.[11] Or, to cite another not entirely restrained title page, 'an entirely new Classic, Comic, Operatic, Didactic, Moralistic, Aristophanic, Localic, Analytic, Terpsichoric, Panoramic, Camera-Obscura-ic, Extravaganza Burletta of Fun, Frolic, Fashion and Flash in Three Acts, called *Tom and Jerry*'.[12]

From all these various versions of the *Life in London* idea,

W. T. Moncrieff's *Tom and Jerry* became overwhelmingly the most famous and most popular. Hindley calls it 'by far the best of the whole *bunch*'.[13] Originally performed on the 26th November 1821, the play was closely associated with the Adelphi Theatre where it ran for over three hundred performances over two seasons, 93 consecutives nights forming the first season.[14] Moncrieff's account of the popularity of his own play, while probably neither modest nor truthful, does nonetheless point to the mythologised place *Tom and Jerry* occupies in theatrical history:

> This piece obtained a popularity, and excited a sensation, totally unprecedented in theatrical history; from the highest to the lowest, all classes were alike anxious to witness its representation. Dukes and dustmen were equally interested in its performances; and Peers might be seen mobbing it with apprentices to gain admission. Seats were sold for weeks before they were occupied. Every theatre in the United Kingdom, and even in the United States, enriched its coffers by performing it ... It established the fortunes of most of the actors engaged in its representation and gave birth to several newspapers ... In the *furore* of its popularity, persons have been known to travel post from the farthest part of the kingdom to see it; and five guineas have been offered in an evening for a single seat.[15]

While all such comments as this are hardly impartial, every commentator agrees on the unprecedented popularity of *Tom and Jerry*. However, none gives an entirely reliable or coherent sequence of versions, performances or performers. Charles Hindley's wonderful late Victorian miscellany *The True History of Tom and Jerry* assembles texts, anecdotes, reminscences, illustrations and various nuggets of more or less reliable information into a narrative which is almost post-modern in its fragmentation, diversity and self-consciousness. Reid's account of the play comes from his study of Pierce Egan, and is both heavily dependent on Hindley and coloured by its defence of Egan's originality and literary skills. Patten, too, in his massively detailed recent study of George Cruikshank, is concerned with issues about originality and authorship in a context where it may be better to regard the whole gathering of literary, visual and dramatic tropes amassed around the 'Life in London' idea as a repertoire of possibilities drawn on unrepentently and vigorously by a whole range of authors, illustrators and theatrical entrepreneurs.

Yet a number of things are obviously clear, and it may be sufficient here just to list those elements of the theatrical history of *Tom and Jerry* which bear directly on the construction of Dusty Bob as a comic stereotype. Firstly, the popularity of various productions of Moncrieff's play is beyond contest. Hindley states that in 1821 and 1822 ten productions of *Tom and Jerry* had occurred in London and surrounding districts alone. Reid and Patten give long lists of productions (fig. 12).



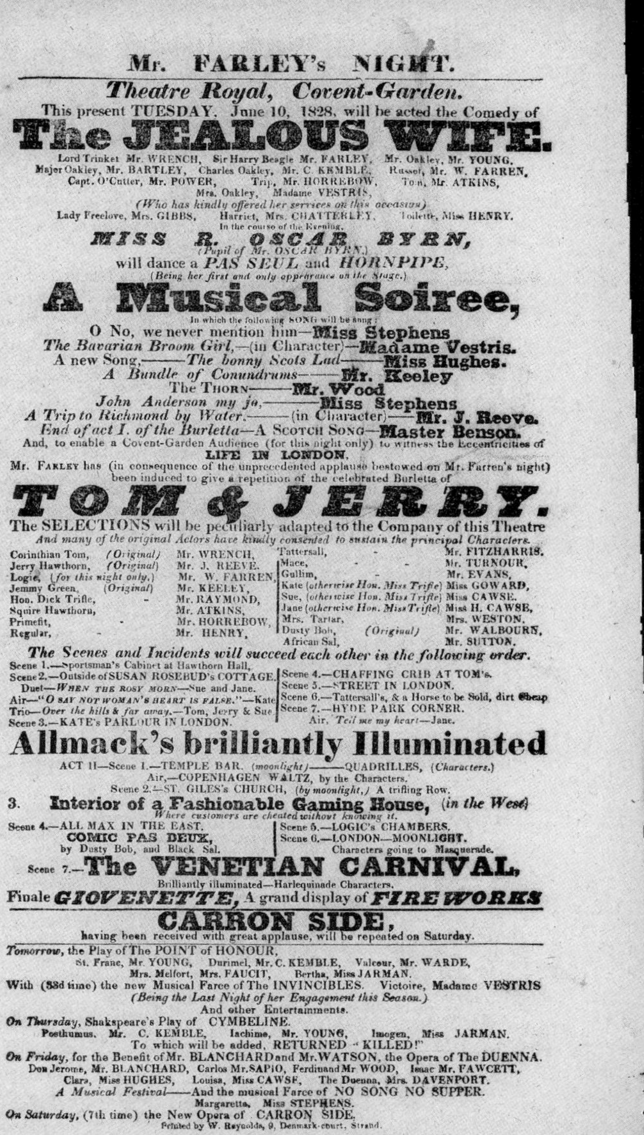

Mr. FARLEY's NIGHT.

*Theatre Royal, Covent-Garden.*

This present TUESDAY, June 10, 1828, will be acted the Comedy of

**The JEALOUS WIFE.**

Lord Trinket Mr. WRENCH, Sir Harry Beagle Mr. FARLEY, Mr. Oakley, Mr. YOUNG, Major Oakley, Mr. BARTLEY, Charles Oakley, Mr. C. KEMBLE, Russet, Mr. W. FARREN, Capt. O'Cutter, Mr. POWER, Trip, Mr. HORREBOW, Tom, Mr. ATKINS, Mrs. Oakley, Madame VESTRIS,

*(Who has kindly offered her services on this occasion)*

Lady Freelove, Mrs. GIBBS, Harriet, Mrs. CHATTERLEY, Toilette, Miss HENRY.

In the course of the Evening,

***MISS R. OSCAR BYRN,***

*(Pupil of Mr. OSCAR BYRN,)*

will dance a *PAS SEUL* and *HORNPIPE,*

*(Being her first and only appearance on the Stage.)*

**A Musical Soiree,**

In which the following SONG will be sung:

O No, we never mention him—**Miss Stephens**

*The Bavarian Broom Girl,*—(in Character)—**Madame Vestris.**

A new Song,——*The bonny Scots Lad*——**Miss Hughes.**

*A Bundle of Conundrums*——**Mr. Keeley**

The Thorn——**Mr. Wood**

*John Anderson my jo,*——**Miss Stephens**

*A Trip to Richmond by Water.*——(in Character)——**Mr. J. Reeve.**

*End of act I. of the Burletta*—A Scotch Song—**Master Benson.**

And, to enable a Covent-Garden Audience (for this night only) to witness the Eccentricities of

**LIFE IN LONDON,**

Mr. Farley has (in consequence of the unprecedented applause bestowed on Mr. Farren's night) been induced to give a repetition of the celebrated Burletta of

**TOM & JERRY.**

The SELECTIONS will be peculiarly adapted to the Company of this Theatre

*And many of the original Actors have kindly consented to sustain the principal Characters.*

| | | | |
|---|---|---|---|
| Corinthian Tom, *(Original)* | Mr. WRENCH, | Tattersall, - | Mr. FITZHARRIS. |
| Jerry Hawthorn, *(Original)* | Mr. J. REEVE. | Mace, - - | Mr. TURNOUR, |
| Logic, *(for this night only,)* | Mr. W. FARREN, | Gullim, - | Mr. EVANS, |
| Jemmy Green, *(Original)* | Mr. KEELEY, | Kate *(otherwise Hon. Miss Trifle)* | Miss GOWARD, |
| Hon. Dick Trifle, - | Mr. RAYMOND, | Sue, *(otherwise Hon. Miss Trifle)* | Miss CAWSE. |
| Squire Hawthorn, | Mr. ATKINS, | Jane *(otherwise Hon. Miss Trifle)* | Miss H. CAWSE, |
| Primefit, - | Mr. HORREBOW, | Mrs. Tartar, | Mrs. WESTON, |
| Regular, - | Mr. HENRY, | Dusty Bob, *(Original)* | Mr. WALBOURN, |
| | | African Sal, | Mr. SUTTON. |

***The Scenes and Incidents will succeed each other in the following order.***

Scene 1.—Sportsman's Cabinet at Hawthorn Hall,

Scene 2.—Outside of SUSAN ROSEBUD's COTTAGE.

Duet—*When the rosy morn*—Sue and Jane.

Air—"*O say not woman's heart is false.*"—Kate

Trio—*Over the hills & far away.*—Tom, Jerry & Sue.

Scene 3.—KATE's PARLOUR IN LONDON.

Scene 4.—CHAFFING CRIB AT TOM's.

Scene 5.—STREET IN LONDON.

Scene 6.—Tattersall's, & a Horse to be Sold, dirt Cheap

Scene 7.—HYDE PARK CORNER.

Air, *Tell me my heart*—Jane.

**Allmack's brilliantly Illuminated**

ACT II—Scene 1.—TEMPLE BAR. *(moonlight)*——QUADRILLES, *(Characters.)*

Air,—COPENHAGEN WALTZ, by the Characters.

Scene 2.—ST. GILES's CHURCH, *(by moonlight,)* A trifling Row.

3. **Interior of a Fashionable Gaming House,** *(in the West)*

*Where customers are cheated without knowing it.*

Scene 4.—ALL MAX IN THE EAST.

COMIC PAS DEUX,

by Dusty Bob, and Black Sal.

Scene 5.—LOGIC's CHAMBERS.

Scene 6.—LONDON—MOONLIGHT.

Characters going to Masquerade.

Scene 7.—**The VENETIAN CARNIVAL,**

Brilliantly illuminated—Harlequinade Characters.

Finale ***GIOVENETTE,*** A grand display of ***FIREWORKS***

**CARRON SIDE,**

having been received with great applause, will be repeated on Saturday.

*Tomorrow*, the Play of The POINT of HONOUR,

St. Franc, Mr. YOUNG, Durimel, Mr. C. KEMBLE, Valcour, Mr. WARDE, Mrs. Melfort, Mrs. FAUCIT, Bertha, Miss JARMAN.

With (33d time) the new Musical Farce of The INVINCIBLES. Victoire, Madame VESTRIS

*(Being the Last Night of her Engagement this Season.)*

And other Entertainments.

*On Thursday*, Shakspeare's Play of CYMBELINE.

Posthumus, Mr. C. KEMBLE, Iachimo, Mr. YOUNG, Imogen, Miss JARMAN.

To which will be added, RETURNED "KILLED!"

*On Friday*, for the Benefit of Mr. BLANCHARD and Mr. WATSON, the Opera of The DUENNA.

Don Jerome, Mr. BLANCHARD, Carlos Mr. SAPIO, Ferdinand Mr WOOD, Isaac Mr. FAWCETT, Clara, Miss HUGHES, Louisa, Miss CAWSE, The Duenna, Mrs. DAVENPORT.

*A Musical Festival*——And the musical Farce of NO SONG NO SUPPER.

Margaretta, Miss STEPHENS.

*On Saturday*, (7th time) the New Opera of CARRON SIDE.

Printed by W. Reynolds, 9, Denmark-court, Strand.

**12** Playbill for 'Mr Farley's Night' at the Theatre Royal, Covent Garden, 10 June 1828. The bill includes *Tom and Jerry*

The Moncrieff play, however, emerged as the 'standard' version of the Tom and Jerry idea, and it is this text that Hindley prints in the *True History*. The 'standardisation' of the text is important because not all the various plays had a part for Dusty Bob – Charles Dibdin's 1822 *Life in London, or, the Larks of Logic, Tom and Jerry* for instance, despite its claim to be 'founded on Pierce Egan's highly popular work', had no dustman

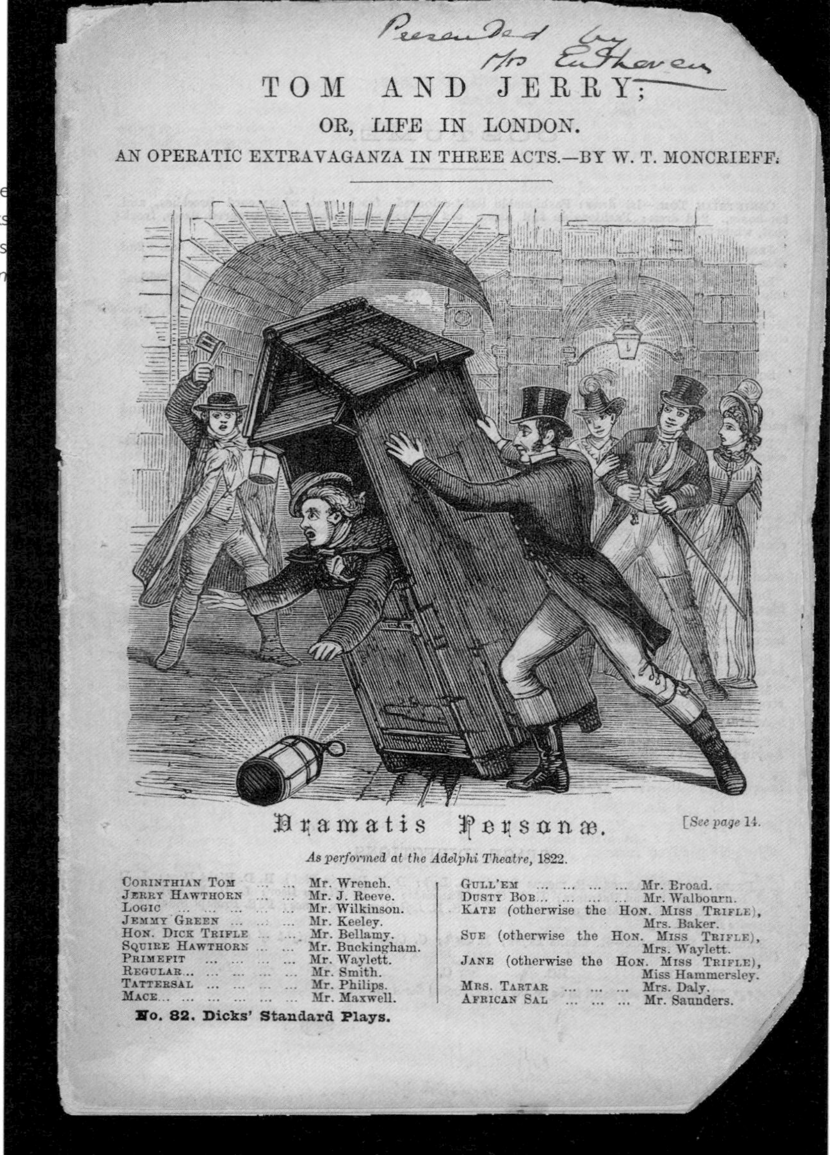

Presented by Mrs Enthoven

TOM AND JERRY;

OR, LIFE IN LONDON.

AN OPERATIC EXTRAVAGANZA IN THREE ACTS.—BY W. T. MONCRIEFF.

Dramatis Personæ. [See page 14.

*As performed at the Adelphi Theatre*, 1822.

| | | | |
|---|---|---|---|
| Corinthian Tom ... ... | Mr. Wrench. | Gull'em ... ... ... ... | Mr. Broad. |
| Jerry Hawthorn ... ... | Mr. J. Reeve. | Dusty Bob... ... ... ... | Mr. Walbourn. |
| Logic ... ... ... ... ... | Mr. Wilkinson. | Kate (otherwise the Hon. Miss Trifle), | Mrs. Baker. |
| Jemmy Green ... ... ... | Mr. Keeley. | Sue (otherwise the Hon. Miss Trifle), | Mrs. Waylett. |
| Hon. Dick Trifle ... ... | Mr. Bellamy. | Jane (otherwise the Hon. Miss Trifle), | Miss Hammersley. |
| Squire Hawthorn ... ... | Mr. Buckingham. | Mrs. Tartar ... ... ... | Mrs. Daly. |
| Primefit ... ... ... ... | Mr. Waylett. | African Sal ... ... ... | Mr. Saunders. |
| Regular... ... ... ... ... | Mr. Smith. | | |
| Tattersal ... ... ... ... | Mr. Philips. | | |
| Mace... ... ... ... ... ... | Mr. Maxwell. | | |

**No. 82. Dicks' Standard Plays.**

**13** Title page from the Dicks Standard Plays edition of *Tom and Jerry*

in it.[16] The popularity of Moncrieff's text was long lived, partly due no doubt to its continued availability first in Dicks's series of Standard Plays (fig. 13) and later in a French's acting edition.[17] Both series enjoyed wide popularity and were easily available in cheap formats right through the century. Productions of *Tom and Jerry* continued to be mounted in the 1840s, 1860s, and even 1870s.[18]

Another feature of the theatrical history of *Tom and Jerry* is the way in which particular roles in the play became associated with particular actors who seem to have moved on from production to production. A July/August 1822 Astley's production of *Tom and Jerry* makes proud mention on its playbill that Mr G. Raymond was playing Corinthian Tom for the fourth time.[19] Similar continuity is found across the variety of versions of the play, with much store set on retaining the original actor (that is the original Adelphi cast of the Moncrieff version) where possible.[20] This was particularly important in the case of Dusty Bob, as we shall see. There is at least one instance of a character from *Life in London* turning up in another play altogether. The Olympic Theatre's 1823 production of *Tothill Fields Tournament*, a quite dreadful-sounding burlesque tournament between the police and the Tothill proletarians, includes the character of 'Dusty Robert, Esq.' as one of the leaders of the Tothill Fields mob, a re-working of the Dusty Bob idea which even allowed Mr Linch to re-take the Dusty Bob role which he had already performed in a version of *Tom, Jerry, and Logic's Life in London* at the same theatre six months before.[21]

While the conclusion that the theatre-going public, which at this time certainly cut across social differences, could hardly have missed seeing a version of *Tom and Jerry*, needs to be treated with some caution, yet it seems likely that the repertoire of comic scenes from which all versions of the play derived and its central narrative assumption of the irruption of Tom, Jerry and Logic into a series of picaresque low-life adventures were widely known. But this more general popularity does not entirely explain the celebrity of Dusty Bob, especially as his character only appears in the Moncrieff versions of Egan's original text and a few other productions. Other scripts, like Dibdin's 1821 *Life in London*, invented alternative comic low-life characters in direct competition with Moncrieff.[22] The Olympic Theatre's *Life in London* ('More Lark! More Life in London!') of March 1822, for example, not only used a newly invented comic character (a ballad singer called Rag Tag) to replace Dusty Bob as a low-life grotesque, but also replaced Bob and Sal's dance with a 'favorite comic song' called 'Looby Lump's Life in London' sung by Mr Lancaster.[23] Some versions, as already suggested, had no 'low-life' elements at all. So Dusty Bob was not an obvious candidate for stage fame, and was often dispensed with in the cast list of versions of Egan's text. Even in Moncrieff's text he appears in only one scene, a scene which at first reading seems entirely ordinary.

The single scene in which Dusty Bob appears in Moncrieff's play, which occurs in Act 3 Scene iii of the printed text, and always towards the end of Act 3 in playbill descriptions of performances or towards the end of Act 2 in two-act versions, forms part of an act usually named 'Life in the East', which concludes a picaresque trio of increasingly burlesque activities (following 'Life in the Country' and 'Life in London'). Thus the movement of the play, in so far as there is one, is from rural to urban, from West End to East End, from high life to low life, from order into topsy-turveydom. As one version of Moncrieff's text, suggesting the pleasure of binaries, puts it 'Tom, Jerry and Logic have ever the best, Of the coves in the east, and the swells in the west'.[24] This movement is emblematically depicted in the play by a witty contrast between two London drinking haunts characterised in a classic example of Egan's word-play – 'Almack's in the West' and 'All Max in the East', the former a smart West End gambling club, and the latter a low-life tavern. This emblematic contrast between the binaries of high and low is underscored by extended wordplay. Almack's was a well-known and long-established club.[25] 'All Max' existed only figuratively, and its distance from respectability is marked by its name, 'max' being a vernacular slang word for gin widely used during the period.[26] The landlord of All Max is called Mace, again a slang usage, used as a verb meaning to cheat, impose or rob, or as a noun meaning a rogue.[27] As we shall see, much of the action of the scene depends on similar punning usage, puns which deconstruct, verbally at least, the distances of class, language, wealth and status which lie between Dusty Bob and the slumming aristocrats.

It is important to state initially that the scene draws very heavily on the relevant plate from Pierce Egan's novel *Life in London* discussed on pp. 51–2 in the previous chapter, with the obvious difference that Egan's coal-whipper has become a dustman. The scene opens with the entry of a crowd, which included the fiddler Rosin, Dusty Bob, African Sal, Sal's black baby Mahogany Mary, and various other low-life characters, into Mace's crib. They sing a 'glee' about the pleasures of gin, no doubt accompanied by much ceremonial 'swigging'. An extended dialogue between Bob and Mace ensues, with Bob ordering and paying for more drink ('heavy wet' or porter on this occasion, together with a twopenny 'burster', which required a complex mix of ingredients). The dialogue's comic focus is on Mace's suspicions about Bob's solvency and willingness to pay, and Bob's more generalised suspicion of landlords as a species. The dialogue is resolved by Sal's anxious hoverings round Bob's tankard, anxious because she is afraid her partner will not save her any drink. Mace calls for generosity to the fiddle player, which causes Bob to pawn his bell in anticipation of the evening's revelries. They are interrupted by first the noise and then the actual entry of Tom, Jerry and Logic, who treat Mace's customers as an inducement to collective pleasure. Mace calls on a willing Bob to perform a 'minnyvit' (though the following dance bears little resemblance to a minuet, let alone a 'pas de deux'). At Sal's behest, and referring to her by the derogatory racist name of 'Snow-ball', Logic prompts Rosin the fiddler with a drink of gin while at the same time smothering his face in snuff, and act of begriming which clearly echoes the racial mockery of Sal – it is important to remember that snuff is popularly called 'dust' in this period, and that 'dust' in this period also sometimes means 'money' as well as a fight.[28] Bob gallantly defends Sal from these racist insults – 'she's none the vurser, though she is a little blackish or so!' Sal, by way of reminding Bob of her many virtues, declares herself to be extremely popular with the Jack Tars, hinting that she is to be understood to be a prostitute. Tom soothes the ruffled sensibilities with a plea not to stand on ceremony, but rather to start the 'double shuffle'.

Given the centrality of the dance to both this scene and the argument of this book, it seems worthwhile quoting the full stage direction to this part of the scene:

> Comic Pas Deux –
> Dusty Bob and Black Sal.
>
> Accompanied by Rosin, on his cracked Cremona, and Jerry on a pair of Tongs to the air 'Jack's Alive'. In the course of the Pas Deux, when encored, Sal, by way of a variation, and in the fulness of her spirits, keeps twirling about; and the same time going round the Stage – Bob runs after her with his hat in hand, crying "Sarah, my Sarah, 'ant you well?" & c. The black Child, seeing this, and thinking there is something the matter with its mother, also squalls violently, stretching its arms towards her; at length, Sal, becoming tired of her vagaries, sets to Bob, who exclaims, "Oh! It's all right!" and the dance concludes.[29]

The dance represents the climax of the scene. Tom settles his bill, generously with a 'flimsy' or £1 note, and asks Mace to 'serve the change out in max for the covies'. Tom, Jerry and Logic leave, reluctantly leaving Rosin behind. Bob borrows more on his bell for considerable quantities of food and drink – 'must have the bell in the morning, you know, even if I spout the tops for it'. The assembled company then reels off – the reel referring both to a clumsy collective dance and their general drink-induced deportment.

This printed version of the scene accords closely to descriptions drawn from play-bills. The Royalty's 1822 *Tom, Jerry, and Logic's Life in London* describes the scene in very similar terms: 'Mr. Mace's crib – natives and foreigners – Barclay and Perkins – lots of heavy-trying upon tick – no go – false alarms – the agreeable surprise a shove in the mouth – Eastern beauties – all ripe for a reel – an elegant Pas de deux between African Sal and Dusty Bob – Queered in the upper story – nearly being stranded in Gravel Lane – and off in a rattler'.[30]

Clearly such bald descriptions do little to tell us why the scene became so famous. The position of the scene within the play's overall structure is obviously a significant factor in its continuing importance. The drive from country to city, from West to East, from genteel to 'natural' (Jerry remarks 'here we are among the unsophisticated sons and daughters of nature' on entering Mace's crib), from responsibility to pleasure, which propels the play clearly culminates in this glimpse of proletarian abandon. The scene in All Max in the East forms *Tom and Jerry's* necessary climax, the moment when the main protagonists' (and presumably the audience's) vision of good fellowship, 'naturalness', pleasure and community based on tolerance of difference (rather than denial of difference) is realised. So the scene is central to the 'meaning' of the play insofar as picaresque texts 'mean'. But the staggering popularity and longevity of the scene apart from its place in the overall structure of *Tom and Jerry* needs further thought.

Hindley ascribes the success of the scene largely to the brilliance of Bill Walbourn's performance as Dusty Bob. While a number of other actors clearly made some reputation in the part (most notably Fillingham and Linch) and each performed in several productions, Walbourn seems to have offered the definitive performance.[31] Hindley cites Egan's comments in *Life of an Actor* – 'as … giving him a title in the niche of fame beside John Kemble, Mrs. Siddons, and all the great actors'.[32] He continues:

> The personification of Dusty Bob, by the above actor, has been unanimously decided by the public to be one of the greatest triumphs of the histrionic art ever exhibited on any stage … a comic actor of

the greatest celebrity exclaimed 'Good heavens! Is it possible? Do my eyes deceive me? Most certainly it is a real *dustman* they have got upon the stage. I am very sorry the profession has descended so low as to be compelled to resort to the streets to procure a person of that description to sustain the character.' He left the body of the theatre in utter disgust – nor was it until introduced to Mr. Walbourn in person, behind the scenes, that he would believe it was an actor. *Further praise than this is superfluous.*[33]



It is interesting that Hindley here sees the naturalism of Walbourn's playing as his great strength, as this suggests that there is something intrinsically comic about dustmen regardless of what they are required to say and do on stage. But leaving aside the hyperboles of Hindley's celebratory manner, it still seems likely that the comic representation of this scene as drunken carnival is largely dependent on the nature of its performance rather than on any intrinsic brilliance in the dialogue or action. The playbills suggest that Tom and Jerry was characteristically performed as burlesque spectacle rather than sequential narrative – many performances conclude with fireworks, spectacular tableaux, or pony races round the pits. Theatrical performance generally in the 1820s was closer to what we might call circus, pantomime or spectacle than to 'plays'. We thus have to try to re-imagine what good actors might have made out of Moncrieff's apparently jejune script which led to Bob and Sal's 'Pas de Deux' being 'nightly honoured with roars of laughter and shouts of applause'.[34]

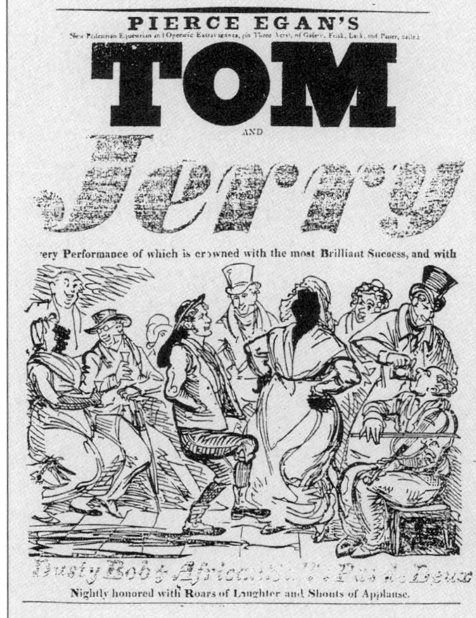


**14** A section of the original poster, drawn by George Cruikshank, advertising the Adelphi Theatre production of *Tom and Jerry* in November 1821

The above quotation, appropriately enough, comes from a copy of a Tom and Jerry play-bill which carries Cruikshank's publicity engraving, an engraving which was widely used in advertising peformances of the play, and which was distributed separately (fig. 14). Hindley suggests that the use of Cruikshank both as an advertising artist and as a scenery designer, and Cruikshank's choice of Sal and Bob's dance to represent the play's pleasures to a wide potential audience, was a major reason for the fame of the 'pas de deux'.[35] While

I think all these reasons offer a partial explanation of why Sal and Bob become famous, I think we need to turn to deeper issues concerning the series of social transgressions represented in Sal and Bob's scene in *Tom and Jerry* to understand its lengthy survival and significance in popular culture. These are issues to do with the complex dialogue between laughter, difference and fear which underpins all serious humour.

Act 3 Scene iii of *Tom and Jerry* depends on a number of complexly related issues – pleasure, drinking, money, class and race. It centres on acts of trangression which foreground pleasure at the expense of responsibility or respectability. Bob is coupled with a black woman, who has an illegitimate black child. Sal may also be a prostitute. She is also, evidently, in spite of Egan's and Hindley's insistence on the naturalism of the scene, a man dressed as a woman, and a white man at that playing a black woman. Bob pawns the symbol of his livelihood, his bell, for pleasure. He transgressively removes the symbol of his manhood, his hat, to pursue Sal in her giddy dance.[36] Tom, Jerry and Logic defy convention by being at Mace's crib at all. Everyone involved accepts the validity of an inclusive social moment of conviviality which suspends the 'normal' distinctions of wealth, class and social hierarchy without entirely denying them. In all these ways the scene might be described as transgressive.

Drinking is represented here at the same time as a form of appetite, a form of conviviality, and a form of consumption. The rituals of drink are elaborated and celebrated – the delighted cataloguing of picturesque slang names ('heavy wet', 'max' and 'burster'), the extended byplay between Bob and Mace over whether Bob's glass is full or not, Sal's anxious observation of the state of Bob's glass and pot, and the traditional exchanges between landlord and drinker over the ability to pay. The purpose of these rituals is that of sanctioning and formalising appetite. Drink is seen as a 'natural' appetite, a necessary part of self-expression. The scene opens with a song in celebration of gin, characteristic of those many convivial drinking songs to be found in every popular song-book of the period.[37] The first act of Logic on entering the crib is to give Sal's child, Mahogany Mary, a glass of gin, which he calls only half ironically 'a drop of mother's milk'. His aim seems to be both to show his own generosity and to make sure the child does not contribute vocally to the rest of the evening. Given the traditional argument that dustmen, by the nature of their calling, need to drink to wash the dust from their throats, and given their traditional association with drunkenness, it is no surprise to find this archetypical representation of the cultural milieu of dustmen to be centred on the heavy, ritualised consumption of alcohol, usually in the company of women. Yet alongside this defence of drink as a natural appetite, this scene also reminds us that drinking was a form of economic consumption.

The scene is as full of ritualised financial exchanges as it is of the ceremonial ordering of drink. Bob digs about in his pockets for the 'stumpy', muttering that 'My tanners are like young colts; I'm obliged to hunt 'em into a corner afore I can get hold on 'em'. The slang associated with money is again ostentatiously elaborated. As well as the elusive 'tanners', the scene boasts 'browns' (pennies), a 'flimsy' (a pound note), and 'duces' (twopence). The scene celebrates 'paying up', producing the 'stumpy' on the nail. The good-natured exchange between Bob and Mace – Mace withholds Bob's pot of porter until he has the money in his hand, and has evolved a special ritual gesture of exchange to make sure beer and money are simultaneously exchanged – over the need for ready money is underlined by the generosity by which Tom, Jerry and Logic leave a pound note to pay for a fourteen-shilling bill. Yet under this apparently good-natured and willing exchange of ready money more calculating elements are obvious. Mace's name reminds us that swindling is assumed to be the norm in the East, and the discussion on whether he has given Bob full measure underlines his pursuit of profit. The entry of the 'gemmen' from the West causes Mace to remark in an aside 'Regular trumps! I can charge vhat I like here'. The bill run up by the 'gemmen' reaches 14s. suspiciously quickly. The services of Rosin the fiddler require either cash rewards or payment in drink. But the most obvious financial issue here is Bob's willingness to pawn his bell – a necessary part of his trade equipment – to support his (and Sal's) evening of pleasure. Mace turns instantly, despite his denial of ever indulging in such transactions, into a pawnbroker. Although Bob is not without money in this scene, he can only gain more through selling his 'trade', by exploiting the financial potential of his own labour. Even as he relinquishes his bell, he remarks on his absolute need to redeem it from Mace the following morning 'even if I spout the tops [pawn my best clothes] for it'.

This scene then, far from denying the link between an instinctual appetite for drink and for pleasure and money, insists on their interconnectedness. Pleasure is depicted not as appetite alone but rather as part of a complex process of financial exchange. Even at his apparently most abandoned the economic status of the dustman is closely monitored. Pleasure, like everything else in the life of independent street tradespeople, is intimately connected with consumption.

Yet despite the startlingly financial terms that Moncrieff applies to discussions of pleasure here, the scene is informed by a vision of conviviality, of collective good times which cut across differences of class, race and gender. Hindley evokes, with characteristic overstatement, the sociability of the Coach and Horses, Nightingale Lane, East Smithfield (the inn he claims was the model for Mace's crib) during this period:

> The parties *paired off* to *fancy*; the eye was pleased in the choice, and nothing was thought about birth and distinction. *All was happiness!* – everybody free and easy, and freedom of expression allowed to the very echo. The group motley indeed; Lascars, blacks, jack tars, coalheavers, dustmen, women of colour, old and young, and a sprinkling of the remnants of once fine girls, and c. were all *jigging* together …[38]

It is interesting how the language Hindley uses here to describe racial characteristics echoes contemporary concerns about inclusiveness and difference – 'black' and 'women of colour' are terms we might use self-consciously today in order to acknowledge the potentially divisive nature of the language of racial depiction. As I've suggested, I don't think this scene is innocent of class distinctions, but nonetheless the vision of inclusiveness and harmony described by Hindley remains a crucial reference point for the discussion of the representation of dustmen as emblems of urban relationships. Clearly, the comic dramatisation of this scene would have needed to establish its tonal range. That range would have included absolute burlesque as well as good-hearted sociability. This scene clearly establishes many of the potential ways in which dustmen might be constructed within popular consciousness. We will see how that potential is realised more widely in caricature, song and fiction in the subsequent chapters.

The most startling element in this scene, however, is the relationship between Bob and Sal. In production this was presumably rendered as farce – a drunken proletarian figure of fun matched with a grotesque male impersonation of a black African prostitute and drunkard. Yet under that farcical possibility run some more complex issues. Sal is depicted in what ought to be an entirely hostile way. She has an illegitimate child. She may be a prostitute ('many de good vill and power me get from de Jack Tar'). She is certainly a little simple, and speaks in a way which is clearly derided for its stereotypical clumsiness. She is a hanger-on without economic resources of her own, and begs favours from Bob. She is a woman of ostentatious appetites for food and drink (shown in her ample figure) and few inhibitions. Yet the scene clearly defends her not just as an appropriate partner for Dusty Bob, but as an individual who, despite her 'difference' and vulnerability, deserves consideration and even celebration.

This defence is most obviously made in response to Logic's racist and familiar use of the term 'snow-ball' in talking to Sal. Ignoring all deference due to class differences, Bob immediately responds vigorously – 'Snow-ball, – come let's have none o'your sinnywations, Mister Barnacles, she's none the vurser, though she is a little blackish or so!'. Logic acknowledges the generosity of this response by treating everyone to Blue Rum. Sal rather piteously adds 'Massa Bob, you find me no such bad partner'.

'Blackness' and 'dustiness' are even more specifically addressed by the incident in which Logic, in asking Rosin to play his fiddle, rewards him not just with gin but also by smothering his face with snuff or 'dust'. The issue here is contamination, and the underlying assumption is one of contamination by association – Bob, who is 'dusty' and dirty, associates with Sal, who is black. They are rendered as appropriate partners because of their shared 'dirtiness', which constitutes the source of their social marginality, a marginality largely defined by fear of contamination. In his attempts to cover Rosin with 'dust', Logic seeks to reduce him to the status of those who are 'dirty', to contaminate him with the idea of dirtiness which lurks in this scene. This is a very direct expression of contemporary assumptions about race and colour, and a very deep-seated one. It is much to Moncrieff's credit that he does not leave the issue of race at this level of unexamined assumption, but seeks to find a more generous way of rendering Bob and Sal's shared 'dirtiness'.

Leaving aside the likely racist by-play which would have occurred in many productions of this scene, it is worth asking why *Tom and Jerry* figures Bob and Sal as an appropriate couple despite their evident weaknesses and failings, to say nothing of their cultural and racial differences. They are both spontaneous, driven by appetite and affection rather than manners or a sense of social deference. They are both marginal figures. They ignore difference and ceremony. They are free of all pretension and self-consciousness. They are ignorant of, or indifferent to, the constant mockery they have to endure. They have an energy, a sexual vigour, embodied in their dance, which makes them the antithesis to genteel restraint. In short, they collectively represent the antithetical 'other' to bourgeois restraint. Their role as a fantasised 'other' to gentility is discussed in the following accounts to their sustained presence in popular culture and in the discussion of caricature in Chapter 4.

All the transgressive possibilities of Bob and Sal are bound together by the delighted punning vernacular which dominates the dialogue of the scene.[39] Puns, as I've already suggested, link together the apparently diverse here. 'All Max' is a parodic 'Almacks' as well as 'All Gin'. Rosin is begrimed with snuff which is 'dust', and 'dust' in turn is a common vernacular term for money in the early nineteenth century. A 'dust-hole' is metonymically used to represent a nose even as it is metaphorically active to suggest a pit or orifice into which money is non-productively poured. 'Down with the dust' means both putting money on the table and drinking down the gin and ale which has to be paid for by 'dust'. The tavern keeper is called 'Mace', which is a common term for cheating. Bob, in a semi-comic way, accuses Mace of cheating. But even beyond these puns which structure the scene out of contradictory, but not necessarily incoherent meanings, there is a considerable amount of verbal inventiveness here, with the urban vernacular used to exploit social anxiety. If 'dust' is money, the money is 'dirty money', 'filthy lucre' (a truly nineteenth-century term) which structures social relationships through a cash nexus that thwarts instinctive generosity and inhibits pleasure. The linguistic energy of this apparently simple dramatic scene in fact takes us to the heart of a wide-ranging set of social anxieties, and it is 'dust' which provides the linguistic, ideological and metaphorical site for much nineteenth-century speculation on the nature of social structure and social order. Bob and Sal lead on to a more broadly pitched series of social debates, but the complexities they represent are seldom far from the minds of later caricaturists, writers and social analysts.

## Dusty Bob leaves the theatre for an unexpected journey through popular culture

As we have seen, the stage versions of Pierce Egan's *Life in London* constructed a continuing theatrical history for Dusty Bob through three decades, a history which also transformed him from a minor picaresque moment in Egan's original novel into a pervasive popular cultural stereotype. But one of the central arguments of this chapter is that popular theatrical characters, particularly when they became wider cultural stereotypes, cannot be contained entirely within the theatre, and began to pervade popular culture on a number of levels and across a range of genres. In the case of Dusty Bob this pervasiveness was partly the result of aggressive marketing – it was clearly in the interests of theatrical entrepreneurs like Moncrieff that their productions should be sustained within mass culture by a range of artefacts which were not only profitable in themselves but might also act to publicise their theatrical origins. But there was also an element of apparently unselfconscious, almost spontaneous, transmission involved, constructed out of a conjuncture between the fancies of popular taste, a particular moment in the history and development of the genres of mass culture, and commercial opportunism.

Outside the theatre, 'Dusty Bob' was sustained as a cultural presence over many years through a startling range of modes. The construction of 'Dusty Bob' within the traditionally genteel, but rapidly democratising, discourses of caricature between 1820 and 1840 forms the basis of the next chapter. In detaching Dusty Bob from his traditional roots in the drama in pursuit of broader socio-political meanings for proletarian figures, the caricaturists nonetheless frequently alluded to his theatrical origins. One particularly compelling example of this is a large single-plate etching of Peel as the national dustman, dressed in a very elaborate stage costume drawn from one of the many 'Dusty Bobs' who strode the London boards (Plate V). But quite aside from theatrical allusions within caricature, and leaving out the graphic flurry produced by Egan's novel which was considered in the previous chapter, there are a number of graphic images which bear specific relation to the theatrical life of Dusty Bob and which are considered here. These include images from the juvenile or toy theatre as well as prints which sought to represent performances of the play.

A second kind of Dusty Bob texts that are given impetus and shape by the theatre is formed by popular songs, and the next section of this chapter looks at a range of songs, glees and snatches derived from the theatre, especially the most famous song from Moncrieff's adaptation of *Life in London*, a song called 'The Literary Dustman', which came to enjoy a separate and sustained life within the song-books, broadsides and ballad sheets of popular musical culture. A more detailed look at dustmen in Victorian popular songs can be found in Chapter 5. But perhaps the most interesting of the ways in which *Life in London* was continuously reconstructed as a range of popular and largely independent texts and artefacts was the translations of the play's most popular comic moment – the burlesque pas de deux danced by the improbable but enduring popular pairing of African Sal and Dusty Bob – into something with an almost iconic cultural presence. The history of this famous dance and its exit from the stage into the mainstream of popular culture forms the last section of this chapter, although Bob and Sal's pas de deux will also reappear in later sections of this book.

Given the way the trade capitalised on topical events and theatrical celebrity, it is a pretty safe assumption that many graphic souvenirs of *Life in London* joined the song-books, broadsheet songs and Staffordshire figures which were produced to cash in on the play's phenomenal success. Just as Henry Heath and other caricaturists immediately re-worked Egan's text and the Cruikshank's original illustrations into independent (and expensive) narrative sequences of images, print dealers with any entrepreneurial ability must have seized the opportunity to broaden their market. I have only found fragmentary pieces of evidence for such opportunistic publications, but they are nonetheless broadly suggestive of the widespread commercial exploitation of the success of the play.

The first comprises a set of 'theatrical prints' published by W. West made up of small plain or coloured figures that could be cut out and stood up to form the substance of a toy-theatre 'performance'. The series was published in February 1822 under the title of 'West's Characters of Tom and Jerry, or Life in London', and costing 2d. plain, and plate 9 showed an 'All Max in the East' grouping which was clearly derived from Moncrieff's text. On the left Logic feeds gin to Mahogany Mary. Behind, Mace in a white apron carries a foaming tankard of beer. In the centre of the group Sal, rather finely dressed and less obviously obese than in most images, dances with Bob, with Tom and Jerry to the right, looking on and drinking.[40] Publication by West, the most prolific publisher of children's dramas, suggests that *Life in London* would have been an obvious candidate for re-publication in the form of the toy theatre, a form which, of course, required children either to read or invent a text to sustain their performances. In this way Tom and Jerry, to say nothing of Dusty Bob, entered the consciousness of many children unable for whatever reason to see stage performances of the play. The extent to which toy-theatre versions of *Life in London* had lodged in the popular consciousness can be guessed from a poem called 'The British Stage in Miniature' which is partially reprinted by Speaight from an 1829 publication called *The Parent's Poetical Present*:

> All people talk of London sights,
> For London's all the rage;
> But that which most a *youth* delights
> Is called 'THE BRITISH STAGE'.
>
> There's 'LIFE IN LONDON', Tom and Jerry,
> There's also 'LIFE IN PARIS'; ...[41]

That *Life in London* reached down into broad popular awareness can also be gauged from a series of prints published by J. L. Marks which offered a kind of comic-strip version of the play.[42] Speaight lists these as one of three toy-theatre versions of the play, but, while it is possible that these images were again intended as cut-out scenery for toy theatres, nonetheless they also comprise a graphic narrative that sought to be an equivalent for a production of the play.[43]

Less easy to categorise in terms of purpose and intended audience is a print published by the well-established caricature printer and dealer S. W. Fores in April 1822. Drawn by 'W.W.' and engraved by Gleadah, this single plate image shows 'All Max in the East, A Scene in Tom amd Jerry, or Life in London' and thus presents itself as a representation of an actual performance of the play (Plate II).[44] Yet it is clear that the image, while maintaining the central tableaux of Bob and Sal's dance, adds a range of tropes and ideas that are less obviously derived from the theatrical stagings of the play. Rosin is black, peg-legged and dressed in something approaching a sailor's uniform, Mahogany Meg is being fed gin by a villainous-looking nurse in the front right corner, a black man with a broom stands at the left in front of a crippled beggar on a board and a gin pouring ne'er-do-well, while Mace, in a white apron, stands with his arms folded at the right. In the background are deployed a range of predatory prostitutes and other sleazy denizens of the East. The visitors – Tom, Jerry and Logic – are scarcely distinguished at all from the general crowd. A timid, bespectacled figure behind an equivocal one in a cravat and straw hat at the centre of the image perhaps represent Tom and Jerry, and it seems likely that the ne'er-do-well pouring gin is Logic, but the differentiations of manners and class on which the theatrical scene depends are difficult to find here. Equally inscrutable is the representation of All Max itself, shown as an almost unfurnished and bare cellar reached by crude wooden stairs leading down from the street door. There is no attempt made to suggest warmth or conviviality. Bob's traditionally celebrated dancing style is reduced to awkward contortions and Sal fares little better. While it is possible to imagine that this image offers an accurate account of the stage set and dramatic content of a particular performance of the play, there is nothing in the print to link it to a precise theatrical context, and it may well be that it is intended to represent an unfocused gathering of *Life in London* tropes. Equally difficult to interpret is the intended audience for the print, which is extremely crudely drawn and, in the copy I have seen, primitively hand coloured. But engravings were still not cheap in the 1820s, and Fores mainly published for the traditionally genteel audience who bought single-plate caricatures. Would Fores's usual customers have wanted such a clumsy, poorly drawn image? And how would they have read it? Images of this kind, even if they were not commonplace, seem to me to suggest the ways in which anything associated with the theatrical success of *Tom and Jerry* enjoyed a ready market in the 1820s, and conspired to make the comic pas de deux of Dusty Bob and African Sal a famous event in the popular imagination.

## 'The Literary Dustman' reaches the charts

Several of the songs from stage versions of *Tom and Jerry*, as well as some which were written to cash in on the success of the play, had a wider life as independent cultural artefacts. Leslie Shepard's study of the ballad printer and seller John Pitts gives some indication of the extent of this response to commercial opportunity at the bottom end of the market.[45] Additionally, as already suggested, there were a number of up-market souvenirs of the play giving song-texts and sometimes music as well. These slight but energetic publications were often enhanced with a coloured illustration. But one song, 'The Literary Dustman', can be immediately connected with Moncrieff's versions of the play through its place in Moncrieff's 1834 *Songbook*, even though I have not found any descriptions of performances of *Tom and Jerry* in which the song is noticed.[46] Nor, given its references to the *Penny Magazine*, could the song have been written in this form before 1832. Nonetheless, the prominent placing of a framed picture of Dusty Bob and African Sal within the associated woodcut in the *Songbook* makes the debts to the stage obvious.[47] The song provides a detailed first-person description of one dustman's programme of self-education and social ambition, formulated tonally somewhere between bragging, pathos and vulgarity. It is among the most serious and generous acknowledgments of the social potential of dustmen despite the inevitable mockery of the way in which the literary dustman can ape the manners – but not the speech, refinement, or sensitivity – of the truly genteel. Nonetheless, the song also laughs at those genteel pretensions to culture which proceed from crass social ambition rather than true feeling. The ways in which this song links the figure of the 'literary dustman' to debates about the march of intellect form part of the substance of Chapter 4, and the social implications of the song are discussed in detail there. Here, the aim is the rather different one of illustrating, albeit sketchily, the extent to which this theatre song was relocated within a considerable range of different popular genres.

Firstly, 'The Literary Dustman' had a separate existence as a broadside song. In his study *Cambridge Street Literature*, Philip Ward describes the list of the printer Henry Talbot in the mid 1830s.[48] One sheet includes

'The Literary Dustman' alongside a patriotic song called 'The Soldier Who Died for his King'. This version, which appears to be exactly that printed in Moncrieff's *Songbook*, is accompanied by a totally inappropriate woodcut illustration of an old woman with a stick. Ward dryly notes that this illustration is also used, equally randomly, for another of Talbot's ballad sheets (he also notes a dancing negress among Talbot's blocks). Although it is hardly surprising to find a pirated version of a popular song on a provincial broadsheet at this time, it does point to the wide currency that Moncrieff's plays and their various popular cultural progeny had for many years in Regency and early Victorian Britain.

Another printing of the song, using an identical text, appeared in *The Quaver or Songster's Pocket Companion* (1854).[49] *The Quaver* was a characteristic cheap pocket miscellany of popular lyrics with the emphasis on patriotic, comic and drinking songs, and the presence of 'The Literary Dustman' in such an unselfconscious popular anthology confirms that the song enjoyed a long-lived independent life quite apart from its theatrical context. Even in 1854, several years after the journal had ceased publication, the references to the *Penny Magazine* are retained. Similar evidence of the interpenetration between theatrical songs and popular music comes from a couple of references in William Thomas Thomas's book *A Collection of Original Songs* (1856).[50] William Thomas Thomas was W. T. Moncrieff's real name, and the collection forms a reprint of many of his theatrical songs. Dustmen appear in several of the songs, including one ('A Round of Topers') in which an astonishing range of trades are depicted through phrases which (often punningly) link them linguistically to drink. Thus – 'The *Dustmen* gets *muddled*, till scarce he can stand'.[51] Another of Thomas's songs, 'A Batch of Ballads', ingeniously creates a new song entirely out of the titles of others. The fourth verse runs:

> 'I'm a jolly Pensioner'--
>     'Do you ever think of me, love?'
> 'Oh no, we never mention her'—
>     'Under the walnut tree, love!'
> 'We met'—'Deep in a forest dell,'
>     'Walker, the Twopenny Postman'
> 'Sweet Joe, from all he bears the belle'—
>     'The Literary Dustman!' ...[52]

A further song, 'Chapter of Slang', uses the pairing of Bob and Sal as characteristic low-life characters:

While Dusty Bob and Afric Sal don't stand upon gentility
But swear they're down, and leery coves with just the same facility:
And as your Toms and Jerrys on their sprees, larks, rambles pass this way
Old watchey swears that he's awake, and knows full well the time of day.[53]

Such re-workings of the *Life in London* tropes in songs reinforced Bob and Sal's interdependent history as well as their continuing role as representatives of the new urban proletariat.

While the evidence is fragmentary, it is sufficient to suggest the widespread survival of *The Literary Dustman* as a popular song beyond its immediate context in the theatre. Song-books drawing on theatrical performance were an important means both of marketing plays and of constructing literary commodities in their own right. Plays were also memorialised by reprints of popular texts together with small wood engravings 'drawn from performance'. In short, the popular theatre sustained a wide spectrum of cultural production initiated by performance, but subsequently disseminated in printed form of by graphic images, which in turn must have returned songs to oral transmission and performance. The figure of the dustman, sometimes figured specifically as Dusty Bob, with or without African Sal, but also more widely depicted as educated or drunken or comic, is certainly present in the theatrical song-books in a way which attests to his wide incorporation into the popular consciousness.

There is the further intriguing likelihood that Bob and Sal's presence in popular culture became associated with specific tunes named after them, tunes which were linked as much to dance as to song. The evidence for this comes from mid-Victorian play texts. In R. B. and W. Brough's 'Historical Extravaganza' *Alfred the Great: or, The Minstrel King* (1859), the burlesque text is constructed round airs and duets drawn from opera or other serious songs. At the end of the melodramatic first scene, one of the invading Danes, Haldane, sings, with the help of a chorus, a song to music drawn from Bellini's opera *I Puritani*. A footnote to the text, however, states firmly 'In non-operatic companies, this may be sung to the familiar melody of "Dusty Bob"'.[54] As well as confirming the transformation of Dusty Bob into a tune as well as a stage figure, a dance and a cultural icon, this offhand comment also situates Bob and Sal as low cultural alternatives to the 'respectable' theatre. The extravagant 'burlesque pantomime' by H. J. Byron, *George*

*De Barnwell* (1863), connects popular tunes called 'Black Sal' and 'Dusty Bob' even more closely with melodramatic representations of low-life London.[55] In a scene set in Ranelagh Gardens, and involving a plot both too complex and too ludicrous to be worth summarising, the two central characters, De Barnwell and Lady Milwood, become involved in a comically exaggerated dialogue, part declaimed and part sung, in which Lady Milwood incites De Barnwell to commit a murder on her behalf. The tune offered by the text for Lady Milwood's part in this dialogue is 'Black Sal', and on conclusion of their shady deal the two leave the stage dancing the jig 'Black Sal and Dusty Bob' as the stage fills with pleasure-seekers dancing an 'umbrella dance'. Again, then, Bob and Sal continue to be memorialised on the stage, over forty years after their first appearance in the London theatres, through the tunes which had become associated with the boisterous, low-life, but life-enhancing jigs and polkas which had been named after them. It is the geniality of this stage presence which is evident. Bob and Sal, metonymically present in the tunes which are named after them, commemorate or construct a version of popular pleasures which are free from vice, threat or viciousness, and recall to the harried Victorian urban consciousness an imagined theatrical (or even 'real') London of popular spectacle and low-life charm – London as a burlesque extravaganza of colour, good heartedness and clumsy energy rather than a city of darkness, sin, deprivation and urban danger.

## 'Double shuffle' – Dusty Bob and African Sal cut the rug, Regency style

As we have seen, one of the enduring, and enduringly popular moments in *Life in London* and *Tom and Jerry* dramatisations of Pierce Egan's original novel was the comic dance staged by Dusty Bob and African Sal. This dance is concerned with the ways in which lust, animality and instinct cross boundaries of class and race. It is not easy to interpret the interesting range of images which situate Bob and Sal together as sexual beings, and the bulk of the caricature images of Dusty Bob as a rather troubling amorous adventurer will be considered in the next chapter on caricature. But it is necessary here to think further about the cultural persistence of Bob and Sal's pas de deux on into early Victorian popular culture in graphic form. In these images, while Bob and Sal partially invoke an instinctual and animalistic potential for uncontrolled and unacknowledged Malthusian appetite, they are more usually represented in a genial, even an affectionate way as a celebration of, rather than a warning about, the power of human desire. Yet of course all these discussions are complicated by the doubts about identity (however comic) brought from their theatrical origins by these images – on the stage, African Sal is usually played by a white man. The images cannot, and do not appear to wish to, conceal these origins. Indeed, they contribute centrally to the construction of Bob and Sal as celebratory exemplars of proletarian lust – celebratory despite the fears about sexuality, class and race which they publicise. They belong more to the world of carnival, of a world turned comically upside down, than to a world of savagely wrought differences and conflicts.

Most representations of Bob and Sal together depict their clumsy yet affectionate dance. Viewed solely as representations of stage figures, these images of Bob and Sal offer some of the most genial and accommodating images of the Regency and early Victorian dustman. Yet these images are linked contextually to some of the more profound and disturbing elements within the graphic repertoire for delineating the urban proletariat. They also show a surprising level of persistence – even in the 1840s it is clear that allusions to Bob and Sal still carry much of the weight of their original appearances on the popular stages of the early 1820s.

Apart from the original Cruikshank plate in *Life in London*, the first and most important delineation of Bob and Sal dancing together was drawn by George Cruikshank, entirely appropriately given his involvement in designing scenery for the first Adelphi productions of *Tom and Jerry*, to say nothing of his disputed claims to the authorship of *Life in London*.[56] As we have seen, Cruikshank's original plate for the novel depicted a coal-whipper dancing with African Sal, but, apart from the crucial shift from coal-whipper to the similarly dressed dustman, his wood engraving for the Sadler's Wells poster shows an extremely close similarity to his original etching for Pierce Egan's novel despite the more traditionally vernacular medium and commercial purpose (fig. 14). The Sadler's Wells poster is important as it marks the moment when Bob and Sal's dance begins to exist as a separate act of popular cultural production. Although the image reproduced here was drawn for a play-bill, it was also circulated as a separate engraving. As Hindley notes, 'Mr. Walbourn as "Dusty Bob" was drawn and engraved by George Cruikshank, and sold with other character portraits, at the Adelphi Theatre'.[57] The publication of engravings 'drawn from performance', both to accompany cheap reprints of play texts and as separate prints, was well established by this date, but Hindley stresses the particularity of this image, with a named actor and a specific theatre. The association of Dusty Bob with

Walbourn and Moncrieff's definitive version of the play with its first home at the Adelphi was undoubtedly part of the process through which player, play and place became amalgamated into a single cultural artefact. But crucially here, Dusty Bob and African Sal, building on their stage fame, begin, by means of the independent distribution of Cruikshank's engraving, to be detached from their novelistic and theatrical origins, and become a discrete, even autonomous, popular cultural pairing.

As well as stressing the force of Cruikshank's engraving as a means of separating out Bob and Sal from their theatrical source, the image does offer an interesting gloss on the scene from *Tom and Jerry* which it depicts. There is sufficient detail to suggest that the engraving is meant to be naturalistic. In particular, the comic events shown at the right foreground, where Logic is suborning Rosin into playing his fiddle (and, Logic hopes, into accompanying him on further adventures) through drink, is a careful rendition of the precise action of the scene, or at least of printed versions of the scene. The figure of Bob, too (Sal rather less so) is drawn with a surprising degree of naturalism. Bob is not caricatured, but rather shown as, if anything, a heroic figure rather than a figure of fun. I think this is particularly important given the working of the caption below the image on the play-bill – 'Nightly honoured with roars of laughter and shouts of applause'. This chapter has been interested in the reasons why the All Max scene from *Tom and Jerry* was regarded as a comic masterpiece, and why it became famous in its own right. Was it because of its hilarity and geniality? Or was it because of the serious issues it raised in comic form? This engraving offers an ambiguous account of these issues – the scene is not depicted visually as an especially comic one, yet verbally there is an assertion here of its riotous effect. Even allowing for theatrical hyperbole, this version of Sal and Bob dancing offers little clear information to account for the persistence and significance of their pas de deux in subsequent popular-cultural image-making. In order to pursue the issue, the later use of the Bob and Sal pairing must be discussed.

One of the earliest joint representations of Bob and Sal I've been able to find belongs to a crowded c. 1823 Catnach broadsheet, versions of which are printed by both Gretton and James (fig. 15).[58] The lower sections of the broadsheet are given over to 'The Tears of London: or, the Death of Tom and Jerry' and the supposed 'Will' of 'Black Billy'. The woodcut of Tom and Jerry's funeral is the dominant image of the three strips which form the sheet's illustration, however, and there is an immediate insistence on the theatrical sources of the image through the depiction of a large sign for the Adelphi Theatre centrally sited behind the funeral cortege. The accompanying verses, while they lament the death of Tom and Jerry in a facetious mock-heroic manner, also stress the rakish, hell-raising popularity of the two stage characters, who are mourned by every louche street character except the 'charlies' or watchkeepers for their pranks, exploits and general debauchery. Dusty Bob, clutching a glass of gin, and African Sal, upending a large beer pot, bring up the rear of the procession, and are memorialised in a separate verse of their own:

> And Dusty Bob, and Afric' Sall,
> Are following of their masters dear
> At intervals Bob rings his bell
> And wets his grief with gin and beer.

15 Part of a Catnach broadside 'The Tears of London' showing the 'Death of Tom and Jerry'

The image may well have been drawn specifically to commemorate the ending of a long-running production of the play at the Adelphi (though it is hard to be precise about this) or just simply a 'final' attempt to cash in on the theatrical popularity of *Tom and Jerry*. The image and verse here situate Bob and Sal very firmly as street picturesques and as drinkers. Both are drawn in an entirely stereotypical way, Bob with prominent bell, hat and white coat, Sal with the voluminous skirts, white apron and mob cap through which she is invariably rendered. Her blackness, as well as her considerable bulk, is clearly delineated through an exaggeratedly Negroid profile and her bare, lifted arms. In this image, Bob and Sal are not so much a couple as separate images of the picturesque variety of street culture, linked more by their sociable fondness for drink and street theatre than by any apparent partnership or sexual liaison.

Other images of Bob and Sal, in addition to the ones from fictional imitations of *Life in London* examined in the previous chapter, represent their coupleness through their dance. A straightforward and anonymous engraving from the Victoria & Albert theatre museum, reprinted in Delia Napier's article on John Shelton, shows the classic formulation of Bob and Sal dancing. They are shown in profile, which was important in establishing the immediately recognisable silhouette versions of the couple which were subsequently alluded to by *Punch* as a form of graphic shorthand. Bob's dress and posture form a classic graphic dustman of this period – breeches, long socks, overshoes forming a thin lower profile set against a loose jacket, kerchief, and hat which place all the weight of the image in the upper half of the figure. Bob's attire suggests, characteristically, a somewhat dandyish dishevelment. Sal's profile is equally formulaic. The side view allows her Negroid features to be emphasised – receding brow, turned up nose, and thick lips. Her spreading long skirts are covered with a flowered, light-coloured apron, and both her skirts and apron have been hoisted up to show a considerable amount of her stockinged legs. Bob, a straw dangling from his lips, is ogling Sal, who returns his lecherous look directly if less enthusiastically. For all the rather stiff postures, the print emphasises the vigour, energy and sexual excitement of the couple. The spectator is invited to view their dance as something between comic parody of genteel pleasures and touching tribute to their improbable affection which crosses boundaries of colour and taboo, and allows sexuality – admittedly in comic form – to even the poorest and most degraded of the urban proletariat. To my mind, this is a celebratory image, in which the vigour of the popular theatre and of the animal energy of the poor outfaces contemporary assumptions about gentility, appropriateness, race and sexuality.

It is precisely this kind of celebratory image which allowed the dancing Bob and Sal to be turned into a celebrated popular cultural icon. The extent to which this image of the dancing couple was used within popular culture can only be guessed at from the few moments where recovery has been possible. One of these occurs rather touchingly in 1824, when a benefit at the Royalty Theatre on behalf of 'Master and Little Miss Linch' (the children of the owner) included 'the Little Pas de Deux of Dusty Bob and African Sal'.[59] Part of the poignancy of this moment comes from the fact that their father had taken the part of Dusty Bob in several earlier productions at his theatre, though it is hard to imagine what the effect of adding childishness to the many transgressive element already built into this pas de deux must have been. Further dancing Bob and Sals appeared on paired Staffordshire pottery figures produced by the firm of John Lloyd as late as the 1850s, although it is possible that only Sal survives in known copies.[60] Sal is shown dancing arms akimbo, and dressed in a sprigged muslin dress. She is instantly recognisable from the prints described above.

These admittedly fragmentary glimpses of Bob and Sal's dance suggest that the image nonetheless had embedded itself deeply enough within the repertoire of popular stereotypes of working-class energy, informality and animal vigour to be instantly recognisable across over twenty years of popular image-making (Plate XV). But the most remarkable evidence of the tenacity of the idea of Bob and Sal's transgressive proletarian caperings comes from that bastion of early Victorian middle-class respectability, *Punch*, although most of the relevant images come from the first few volumes published in the early 1840s when the magazine was still obsessed with the grotesque human body and with traditional jokes drawn from Regency bohemian boisterousness. Consider, for example, an image drawn from an early *Punch Almanac* (fig. 16).[61] The title strip for February 1842 is titled 'Valentine's

**16** 'February' from the *Punch Almanac* (1842)

Day – Cupid's Holiday', and shows a line of improbable lovers all being teased by the intervention of Cupid's sprites and cherubs. At either end of the strip are two quite naturalistically drawn versions of Dusty Bob and African Sal. At first glance it is not obvious that the two figures are connected, and in fact the viewer needs to have some awareness of the history of Bob and Sal to make sense of the image. On closer inspection, the narrative becomes clear. Bob and Sal are both depicted as lovelorn. Both are mooning over pictures of their beloved. Bob, in a posture of anguish, has one hand clutched to his heart. A mischievous naked cherub has thrust a pair of bellows up under his jacket to fan the flames of his lust. Sal, less obviously black than in many depictions, and certainly more ragged than usual, has been pierced by a large arrow from Cupid's bow. The overall image offers a relatively gentle satirical comment on the melodramatic agonies of proletarian desire, but it also invokes the long history of Bob and Sal as transgressive lovers. The assumption that the reader in 1842 will know this history confirms the depth to which the theatrical stereotype of Bob and Sal had penetrated popular consciousness.

A further dancing Bob and Sal pair, drawn as tiny silhouettes, appear on the title page of volume 4 (1843),[62] and an 1844 caricature confirms

17 'The Polka Pest', *Punch* VII (1844)

the persistence of Bob and Sal as a famous couple even twenty years after they first appeared on the stage (fig. 17).[63] This image accompanies a splenetic, but clearly fictional, letter from a reader deploring the social excesses of those who support and dance the polka, under the damning title of 'The Polka Pest'. The engraving shows a comically drawn Bob and Sal, ragged but enthusiastic, dancing their famous duet. Bob, who looks the worse for drink, carries his bell in his left hand. Sal, arms akimbo, is in her most unmistakably Negroid manifestation. The image is left unexplained by the accompanying article, except for the cryptic caption 'The supposed origin of the polka'. Again, the reader is left to construct the allusion and its implications for him- or herself out of what he or she knows of Bob and Sal. The implication is that Bob and Sal's dance was so famous that, according to popular mythology, it supplied the origin and prototype for the polka – a dance based on energetic contact between couples and thus controversial for many genteel and bourgeois Victorian families. Bob and Sal are in this way linked with the assault on Victorian respectability offered by dancing. The many images of the pair dancing, which posited the possibility of the ragged, racially mixed, overtly sexual pair of Bob and Sal in the drawing rooms of respectable England, make explicit the social threat represented by 'immoral' dances of foreign origins like the polka. Bob and Sal in this way come to represent the threats to, and anxieties of, bourgeois England. Even after their street presence has been rendered safe, and equally long after they came to fame as a theatrical pair, Sal and Bob still rise up to figure the dangers of miscegeny, overt sexuality and proletarian irruption to middle-class minds, dangers which will form much of the substance of the next chapter.

This chapter has looked at the theatrical presence of the dustman in the 1820s, a presence dependent on the establishment of a dramatic stereotype called Dusty Bob, whose role was inextricably linked to that of his stage partner African Sal. Dusty Bob was crucially a representative of the picaresque 'East' – a degraded and squalid embodiment of pleasure seeking low-life animalistic vitality. But as this mocking stereotype of vulgarity and ignorance gained popularity and was endlessly repeated across a range of popular cultural discourses, Dusty Bob became something more complex, and began to embody the pleasures and potential of transgressive carnival as well as continuing to provide evident threats to decency and gentility. It is this complex stereotype, as well as the picaresque and picturesque dustmen of the costume books, the novels of the 1820s by Pierce Egan and his imitators, the cries of London, and the children's alphabets (all examined in

Chapter 2), that provided the stock in trade of images and representational possibilities taken up by the caricaturists of the 1820s, 1830s and 1840s as a means of engaging with, and representing, rapid and disorientating social change. And it is in these comic images that the truly serious social resonances of the dustman are rendered cathartically present.

# 4

# Visual culture and the represented dustman, 1820–50: the public dustman

## Dustmen and visual culture, 1820–50

This chapter and the following one consider the apparent over-representation of dustmen compared to all other trades (except perhaps sweeps) within the visual culture of the period between 1820 and 1850. It was the wish to understand such over-representation that largely initiated this book. All the major comic artists of the period drew dustmen. George Cruikshank, Robert Cruikshank, Robert Seymour, William Heath, Henry Heath, John Leech, Charles Jameson Grant, Joe Lisle, John Phillips drew them recurrently. Henry Alken, Hablot Browne and Kenny Meadows drew them occasionally. Looking at obvious graphic sources alone, Seymour's much reprinted *Sketches*, essentially concerned with country pursuits ineptly and comically undertaken by townees, nonetheless has at least six plates that focus on the doings of dustmen – and dustmen appear centrally on the title page. Henry Heath's 1840 re-publication of much of his single-plate output from the previous two decades in his *Caricaturist's Sketchbook*, has over a dozen dustmen scattered through its pages, including two on its title page. There are nearly twenty images of or poems about dustmen in the *Comic Almanack* in its first ten volumes (1835–44). *Punch*, launched in 1841 right at the end of the dustman's glory years, depicted or lampooned dustmen on fifty occasions in its first ten years of publication. The short-lived fortnightly lithographed caricature magazine *Everybody's Album*, produced by C. J. Grant, has seven dustmen in its fourteen issues. The discourses constructed by a newly vibrant visual culture between 1820 and 1850, especially in relation to caricature and graphic satire, found dustmen to be an endlessly fascinating and complex subject.

These artists used every available form and mode in an increasingly diverse and complex market place.[1] While much diminished in its scope and acerbity, the single-plate etched or engraved caricature characteristic of Gillray and Rowlandson continued to have some presence on into the 1830s and 1840s, and these representations provide a number of the key images of dustmen discussed here. Many other images, however, derived from the widening repertoire of locales, modes and discourses opening up to comic image-makers in the early Victorian period. These developments in the modes and locale for caricature, essentially the product of the emergence of a mass market for prints even of a comic nature, necessitated considerable changes in the scale, size and organisation of the images produced (Plate XV). The increasing presence of wood engraving as a reprographic medium even in genteel or middle-brow publications resulted in the wide use of humorous vignettes in comic annuals, songbooks, broadsides and pamphlets. Wood engraving inevitably (given the use of end-grain blocks) caused both a reduction in the size of images produced and an increasing incorporation of images into texts, which in turn led to images being used for illustrative or narrative purposes. A further consequence of the increasing accommodation of images within linear texts was a tendency towards the thematic or narrative organisation of small groups of images. As David Kunzle has shown, one outcome of these developments was the emergence of the comic strip as a major genre, but many other kinds of comic image-making were affected.[2] The vignette-sized image, often organised into complex alignment with texts or other related images, began in the 1820s and 1830s to form the dominant way in which humorous social commentary was formulated. Lithography began to be widely used for comic and satirical images, usually in the single-plate format of eighteenth-century caricature. Such lithographs have been very little studied or appreciated for a number of reasons. The images were often crudely drawn and depict grotesque proletarian subjects, and thus were hardly decorative or likely to grace the drawing-room walls. Lithography, in Britain at least, has been generally studied as a means of reproducing fine art images rather than as a mass media for comedy, and thus incorporated into very particular art-historical narratives. Few collections of comic lithographs have been formed, as their 'low' urban subjects, poor draughtsmanship and ephemerality denied them status in the museum or gallery. Yet the three decades between 1820 and 1850 saw a massive flood of single-plate comic lithographic images, often produced in series by publishers like Tregear and Hodgson, and many of these images showed an interest in dustmen as urban subjects. By the mid 1820s, with the launch of the *Glasgow Looking Glass*, lithography was being used for magazines with pages built up out of an accumulation of small comic images a full fifteen years before *Punch*. Lithographic artists from this period were largely anonymous, and even those that are relatively visible, like Joe Lisle and Charles Jameson Grant, remain obscure. Nonetheless, the vigorous and inventive trade in lithographed caricatures provides many of the images of the dust trade studied here (Plates XII, XIII, XIV).

But, despite such new and animated diversity in the production of visual culture in this period, there is little evidence that the available audience for caricature, while massively expanded during this period, ever extended much beyond the relatively affluent and genteel classes of society. If the complex iconography and delight in the grotesque which characterised eighteenth-century caricature gave way to simpler, more jovial and better natured comic imagery during this period, there is no evidence that even the crudest of these new images, the lithographs published by Tregear, say, were aimed at or bought by the artisan classes, whose main access to caricature remained the print-shop window.

Accordingly these two chapters focus on representations of dustmen which emerge from, are produced by, and are consumed within an increasingly coherent and self-conscious social group which is identifiably becoming the 'middle class'. These are images which reflect growing fears and anxieties about the consequences of urban growth, especially ideas about proximity, contamination, intimidation, violence, drunkenness, and personal safety as aspects of street life. Such fears and anxieties are an aspect of the broader municipal and institutional interventions into the construction of urban space which are taking place during this period. But they are also images which are used to survey the middle classes themselves, with their aspirations, pretensions and manners subjected to the travestied reversals made available within the caricature-mode representation of their opposite. The dustman, at one level a not just a threatening reminder of the dangers and violence of urban life but also a representative of the 'waste' and detritus of an urban culture, also formed a yardstick 'other' through which the genteel or middle-brow aspirations of the emergent middle classes could be scrutinised. The dustman, despite his degraded profession and traditional vulgarity, might be understood as the travestied reversal of much that was increasingly becoming valued by the new urban middle classes – cleanliness, family life, quiet, 'culture', and the rituals of consumerism. The dustman's perceived 'otherness' made his espousal of the social habits and aspirations of his 'betters' available as a mode of self-understanding and, often, self-criticism among the sophisticated consumers of caricatures and other forms of visual culture.

Accordingly, the sections of this book which consider the representation of dustmen within visual culture between 1820 and 1850 are divided into two chapters. The first chapter deals with middle-class anxiety – those images of dustmen in their public presence on the streets as workers or, more usually, non-workers. The central argument here is that the many graphic representations of dustmen on the streets or at work that populate the discourses of emergent middle-class visual culture in this period can be most usefully understood a carnivalesque dispersal of fears and anxieties about the noise, dirt, waste, violence and class conflict becoming increasingly visible in Regency and early Victorian London. The represented dustman both publicises these anxieties and allows them to be discussed and, potentially, neutralised. The second chapter considers the representation of dustmen in their more private capacities – at home with their families, shopping, pursuing their new-found (and often ludicrously pretentious and inappropriate) cultural ambitions. These images serve as means of formulating middle-class self-awareness through the depiction of its opposite.

## What did dustmen look like?

What did dustmen actually look like?[3] The three standard histories of occupational costume,[4] which draw their evidence almost exclusively from picturesque and topographical illustration rather than from caricature, produce an account of the dustman's appearance in the early nineteenth century which is remarkably consistent. It can be easily summarised by brief references to written sources. Here is the stage direction for Dusty Bob's costume drawn from a popular and widely reprinted edition of W. T. Moncrieff's play *Tom and Jerry*: 'Dusty Bob: Dustman's fan-tailed hat, loose flannel jacket, velveteen red breeches, worsted stockings, short gaiters'.[5] These details are almost exactly replicated by an urban sketch published in *The Town* in 1838: 'The above sketch represents a familiar personage about town, especially to be met with in the morning portion of the day; his fantail hat, knock-knees, kicksey-casings, white gaiters and bell, are alike worthy of notice'.[6] Versions of this outfit will be found throughout the illustrations for this book. If there is a 'classic' or 'definitive' single image of a dustman in full rig, then I suppose it would be 'Paul Pry's' [Henry Heath's] well known *Dusty Bob – the Parish Dustman* in his 1829 series of engravings *Parish Characters* (Plate V).[7] This apparently naturalistic images shows the archetypal and completely accessorised dustman from his spreading fantail down to his boots, with classic loose-fitting jacket, plush breeches, striped stockings and gaiters in between. The combination of broom, shovel and bell represent the key tools of the trade, and imply the absent basket, and horse and cart. Even the short clay pipe is entirely characteristic. But some caution is necessary, as this image is concerned with documentary accuracy only in so far as it serves a satirical purpose – this image is in fact a mocking portrait of Robert Peel dressed not even as a 'real' dustman but rather as the famous stage figure of 'Dusty Bob'. While this caricature may offer a distilled essence of dustman, it is nonetheless a dustman seen through the refracting lens of both political satire and dramatic licence.

Nonetheless, the various written and graphic sources I have seen depict dustmen in the above terms with an extraordinary level of uniformity. Despite their fierce independence of status, dustmen appear to have dressed not so much uniformly but actually in a self-imposed uniform. Cunnington and Lucas assert that 'the clothes of early dustmen were probably undistinctive' but they go on to suggest that for the entire nineteenth century 'they seem to have followed a definite pattern'.[8] Although this view needs to be modified by the amply documented shift from independence into civic employees, and hence into uniforms, as 'street orderlies', in the middle of the century, the general point – that dustmen looked remarkably similar in the period between 1790 and 1840 – still holds. A similarity of dress established at the end of the eighteenth century was nurtured by a strong sense of trade identity and solidarity and given broad popular cultural reinforcement by the many stage appearances of Dusty Bob after 1821. There are a few 'undistinctive' dustmen within the graphic record, but they are unusual. Prior to 1790, dustmen, when they occur at all, are less easily recognised. Although the dustman in the background of Hogarth's *The Enraged Musician* (1741), for example, has the dustman tools of basket and bell, his dress is less than distinctive. Similarly, two dustmen in an undated, but probably 1790s, watercolour called 'Dust Hoa', while showing the classic tools of the trade, are dressed in slouch hats and smocks rather than fantails and fustian or flannel loose jackets.[9] A few other images, including the dustman from T. L. Busby's c. 1820 *Costume of the Lower Orders* and a stray dustman in one of Henry Alken's large plates, show dustmen in trousers rather than breeches and without fantails.[10] But these images offer a minority account. Overwhelmingly, the pattern of dustman dress is that identified by Cunnington and Lucas, which comprised a short but fully cut jacket, usually of a heavy material like fustian or flannel, and light in colour; an apron which protected the belly from dirt; breeches, usually brown or plush red velveteen; stockings often in light colours or even gaudy stripes; spats or gaiters and solid boots. Thus all the weight of the dress is in the top half (fantail hat to apron, head to waist) and the boots with these two masses of clothing connected by the thin line of knee breeches and stockings. Cunnington and Lucas suggest later variations – smocks for jackets after the middle of the century, and trousers beginning to replace breeches in many cases.[11] Certainly the first photographs of dustmen, from the 1870s, confirm such changes.[12] But by this time the role of dustman has been radically changed. Even so, as Cunnington and Lucas note, the basic features of dustmen dress, especially the hat and bell, remain, and these are relentlessly rehearsed in the many images of dustmen which throng the pages of this book. One image, a Henry Heath plate from his six-plate sequence *Nautical Dictionary* that comically re-defines 'Refit', even shows what dustmen wore underneath their ubiquitous fantails, jackets and breeches. In a moment of injudicious gallantry, a dustman offers a woman, bloodied but victorious in a street fight, his outer garments to cover her ripped clothes, thus revealing his ragged underpants to an assembled street crowd, while his companion, similarly moved by the woman's plight, is stripped down to his checked undershirt (fig. 18).[13]

**18** Henry Heath, 'Refit' from *Nautical Dictionary*

Such a widely and unanimously described working garb leads to the assumption that dustmen's clothes were essentially a dramatisation of necessity – the distinctive hat (frequently also worn by stevedores and coal-heavers) to protect the head from heavy loads, the gaiters to keep dust from seeping into the boots, the boots to protect the feet, and the apron to protect the midriff both from chafing and from dirt. Less obviously functional are the light-coloured jackets and the sometimes gaudy striped stockings. It is likely that the reason for the light-coloured jacket may, however, have been the outcome of necessity too. Fustian coats would have had to be left undyed in the natural fabric if they were to be frequently washed as the dyestuffs would have run and ruined the coat on washing. The breeches, too, sometimes seem to have been gaudy, although gaudiness may sometimes prove to be the outcome of the decorative impulses of colourists and printsellers rather than an accurate representation of what people wore. The first reference to a dustman in *Our Mutual Friend* refers to 'red velveteens'[14] and there are both literary and visual references to plush breeches, many of them red. These bright clothes might be explained functionally as an attempt to make dustmen ostentatiously visible (as they were audible) on the streets as they advertised for trade, although there is no doubt that any trade they might get would have quickly stained or discoloured the brighter parts of their dress.

**19** George Cruikshank, 'Lumber Troopers'

Many caricatures of dustmen exaggerate the size and density of the white or pale coat against the thinness of the be-breeched legs (fig. 19). If the coat was made of fustian, a common material for the coats of rural labourers, then its apparent stiffness and independence of shape would have been largely the product of the material used.[15] The extent to which dustmen became associated with their top-heavy coats can be gathered from an 1846 *Punch* cartoon, where a series of commodities advertised by sandwich boards become metonymically represented by the commodity itself in the place of sandwich-men. The 'Albert Coat' is thus advertised by a somewhat startled looking dustman almost overwhelmed by the voluminous white loose-fitting coat he wears.[16] The singularity, indeed uniqueness, of the dustman silhouette was a gift to caricaturists, especially those early Victorian artists who specialised in street scenes – the Heaths, Seymour, Leech, C. J. Grant and, in particular George Cruikshank.

One of the strangenesses of the dustman shape was that he was a figure even more distinctive from the rear than when viewed from the side or the front (fig. 19 and Plate IV). One consequence of this immediate visibility was that dustmen were frequently included in images of the street for a number of important reasons. First, their unique outline gave visual variety to street crowds. Second, dustmen were frequently drawn from the rear as spectators, as viewers of the urban scene sharing a slightly detached viewpoint with that of the viewer of the print. Third, the dustman shape was entirely suitable for rendering in a staggeringly simplified form, no more than a couple of lines in some cases.

A further issue concerning the nature of dustmen's dress concerns the relationship between their working clothes and their Sunday best. Even at home dustmen are seldom represented in anything other than their working clothes – indeed it is difficult to imagine how a dustman could have been depicted at all except through the differentiating medium of his unique style of dress. Many dustmen are shown as somewhat foppish dressers who exhibit some degree of self-consciousness and vanity in their clothes and appearance. Despite their engagement in a dirty, indeed filthy, trade, many dustmen appear to have taken considerable pride in their dress. Some are represented as something close to dandies, wearing their clothes with a masculine swagger not perhaps to be expected from such a lowly and contaminated trade. The dialogue between foppishness and assertiveness is an interesting one here. Dustmen were ridiculed both for their hot-tempered street aggression *and* for their feminised, rather effete dandyism. They could be satirised as both absurdly 'masculine' in their choice of clothes which dramatised their function as carriers, shovellers and lifters. But they could also be laughed at for their insistence on dandyish touches in their dress, touches that countered ideas of masculinity with the velvet textures and gaudy colours of feminine self-display. There is, accordingly, some element of ambiguity over gender roles in many caricatures of dustmen, although this may often have been merely a sly joke at the expense of their overstated male image. Either way, the pride dustmen are represented as showing in their dress adds further complexity to debates about how 'low' or degraded their trade actually was.

Certainly there are prints that specifically satirised this foppish element in dustman dress. One image from 1834 shows a dustman seated at his ease in a faux-Egyptian club chair reading a red leather-bound book (Plage XI).[17] At one side is a round library table on which sits a shaded lamp and a book. On the other side is a dramatic draped red curtain which deliberately echoes the red velveteen of the buttoned breeches. Under his fustian jacket and below his classic fantail, the dustman had added a white kerchief and a gold watch chain. Reading glasses are perched on his nose. In the upside-down world of caricature, the culturally ambitious dustman's clothes are easily gentrified into the lush textures and harmonised colours of the drawing room. While this image is a satirical one that quietly mocks the cultural aspirations of the proletariat, it is also acknowledges the possibility of the dustman as a civilised being, and transforms his street dress, with very little difficulty, into garb dignified enough to grace a cultured drawing room. Less admiring is an undated and anonymous *March of Interlect*[18] which implies, however ironically, that dustmen wore a 'Sunday best' version of their working clothes for social and fashionable purposes (fig. 20).

**20** Anon., 'March of Interlect'

Even on such formal occasions, however, the dustman clung on to his fantail hat. George Cruikshank, dressing up for a masquerade as a dustman, deliberately chose to bedeck himself in ragged clothes rather than the 'usual white flannel jacket and trousers of scarlet plush',[19] thus suggesting that a ragged dustman, at least on festive occasions, was an unusual sight. The conclusion to be drawn from this evidence must be that, as a consequence of their considerable economic status, fierce independence as a trade group, and masculine assertiveness as brawny, sexually charged working men, dustmen dressed assertively, carefully and with a sense of style which alludes to their increasingly significant social status. The apparent ambiguities here between dirt and stylishness, between aggression and vanity, between 'male' assertiveness and 'female' decorousness must be seen as part of the wider social and ideological ambiguities described throughout this book.

Of course it is the hats which provide the most obvious graphic emblem of dustman-ness, distinguishing dustmen easily and instantaneously from among the urban throng (Plates II, IV, VI, VII, VIII and IX all show characteristic fantails). To take one or two obvious examples: a strip panorama of a street gathering drawn by Charles Keene for the *Illustrated London News* as part of a full page of small images shows a dustman unmistakably present in the centre of a crowd characterised by every conceivable variety of hat and bonnet (fig. 21).[20] A vastly crowded Cruikshank image of a theatre audience nonetheless picked out the distinctive headgear of the dustman, turned away from the play and focusing on the pleasures of the audience at the top right-hand corner of the image.[21] Another Cruikshank plate, *Tobacco Leaves No 1*, has a strip of characteristic smokers across the top of the image, and again the dustman is immediately recognisable on account of his fantail (fig. 22).[22]

**21** Kenny Meadows, 'Metropolitan Election Sketches'

The fantail was a close-fitting leather cap with a long, flowing, leather patchwork 'tail' which covered the neck. It was used by coal-heavers, draymen and other heavy carriers as well as dustmen.[23] Christabel

**22** George Cruikshank, 'Tobacco Leaves No. 1'

Williams Mitchell's *Dressed for the Job* gives a useful diagram showing how the hat was put together from irregularly shaped pieces of leather.[24] Long use and dirt, however, seems to have welded these hats into a distinctively shaped and highly personal badge of their owner's trade. It is very rare to find a representation of a dustman, even in depictions of domestic interiors or shops, that does not show the fantail hat. The hats, like the full dustman body-shape silhouette, formed a unique shape that obsessed caricaturists in particular. They became stylised in graphic image making into a kind of shorthand which represented, often in dramatically simplified form, the whole complex of social meanings implicit in the street presence of dustmen.

There were, however, some complications over how best to depict fantail hats within the repertoire of caricature tropes. Basically, there were *stiff* fantails and *floppy* fantails. Stiff fantails, which often appear as a kind of huge inverted dinner plate jutting out fiercely in every direction and having little relation to the diminutive human head on which they have been jammed, were popular with the more genial caricaturists and urban satirists like Cruikshank and the *Punch* artists as well as with the more naturalistic versions of dustmen to be found in the urban sketches of the 1840s and 1850s. Such stiff and extensive fantails have a heroicising effect, providing dustmen not just with a trade identity but also with a wider emblem of physical strength and social utility. In the caricature and documentary record, the fantails tend to become less flap-shaped and more like fat cigars later in the century. But less generous, more disillusioned artists like C. J. Grant, who worked in a determinedly grotesque mode, rendered the fantail as a tight-fitting and often rather alarming skull-cap to which a floppy neck-piece had been crudely attached – a version of the fantail which may allude back to its origins as a protective piece of sacking roughly tacked on a skull cap (Plate XII). Dustmen are very seldom shown with their fantails removed from their heads, and then only in very particular circumstances all of which are associated with women, drink and disarray. On a few other festive occasions the fantails are, grotesquely, worn in reverse (Plate IV).

Dustmen are seldom shown cap in hand, except when 'unmanned' by female company or royalty, and even more rarely as hatless, even in environments like shops and drawing rooms where genteel manners would insist on the removal of hats.



Fantail hats, it is clear, while primarily a necessary form of personal protection, were crucial to a dustman's sense of autonomy and identity. As well as asserting a trade allegiance, dustmen's fantails also declared a certain kind of masculinity associated with hard and dirty manual trades. They are both comically picturesque and emblematically complex. At one level the dustman's hat, so lovingly invoked by *My Fair Lady* and Lonnie Donegan, is an endearingly eccentric symbol of a visible street trade and of urban spectacle. It is a shape that is both individualistic and representative, and it becomes almost an abstracted symbol of the carrying trades within the vocabulary of Victorian graphic culture. But it is also a hat not to have any truck with – a defiant, aggressive hat, never doffed in deference or politeness, a reminder of the physical aggression and proximity of a potentially contaminating proletariat. Such a complex of meanings deserves further detailed consideration in the following pages as part of the wider debate on the social meanings of dustmen.

## Dustmen at work

There are so few images of dustmen actually working among the range of caricatures produced between 1820 and 1850 that it might seem a risky project to say anything at all about the issue of labour except to make the central point that it wasn't the working life of dustmen that fascinated caricaturists. After 1850, there are an increasing number of images of cinder sifters, dust yards and the economic exploitation of waste, many of which are discussed in Chapter 7. One way of reading this absence of labouring dustmen from caricature, especially given the enormous range of images of dustmen *not* working which makes up the bulk of this chapter, is to ascribe it to popular stereotypes and urban mythology. Genteel society believed, however wrongly, that dustmen were bone idle, easily distracted from their work, and unwilling to work. As such they fulfilled hostile middle-class stereotypes of the urban workforce. Another more theorised way of reading this absence of pictorial interest in the actuality of dustman labour would be to argue that what is occurring is a widespread act of repression. Unlike Regency culture – which was willing to accept and acknowledge dirt, waste and ordure as a visible and necessary element of social experience – it might be argued that increasingly genteel, even prudish early Victorian bourgeois values (let alone the changing market for satirical images) pushed images of dustmen actually working into the collective subconscious, and instead began to concentrate on their presence as an economic phenomenon rather than a psycho-social one. However, enough images of working dustmen exist to make some useful commentary before moving on to consider the vastly more complex issue of *non-working* caricature dustmen.

Despite the temptation to make a clear distinction between work and leisure, it is not entirely useful to frame any description of caricature dustmen in terms of any such simple binary opposition. If there were almost no depictions of dustmen actually at work in caricature of this period, nonetheless the distinctive nature of dustman work both as an economic reality and as a metaphorical projection of social relationships was almost always implicit in their representation largely through the presence of their shovels, brooms, carts and bells, let alone their fantail hats and spats, in almost every image from this period. Also, it is hard to decide exactly what constituted 'work' for a dustman as various street activities were read by contemporaries more in terms of their social impact than as a form of labour. Shouting and ringing bells for custom, for example, was frequently shown in caricatures, but it was usually represented as a form of street nuisance, as noise pollution rather than a symptom of necessary work. Similarly, it was the often messy consequences for passers-by of shovelling up dust into (or not into) carts that formed the focus of comic images rather than the nature of the labour involved in clearing the streets.

Where dustman work is represented it is usually suggested by the massive presence of the dustman's cart, towering up high enough to require the dustmen to scale a ladder to throw in his load. Easily the most vigorous and evocative image I have seen of dustmen at work is an undated watercolour by Rowlandson called *Dust Hoa*.[25] Rowlandson's ink and wash image depicts two dustmen as ragged plebeian grotesques who are showing almost manic energy in pursuit of their calling. It offers a remarkably full and vigorous repertoire of dustman activities and accoutrements. Against a sketched-in background of a genteel London street (complete with two separate characters craning out of windows to engage with the street spectacle passing below), one dustman, having struggled up the ladder, shoots his basket of dust on to an already laden cart. The cart, with its massive metal-shod wheels and stout boarded sides, is being drawn by a solid if somewhat bent-backed horse, dynamically rendered by Rowlandson from a three-quarters rear perspective. Dramatically, indeed sensationally, counterpointed against the receding perspective of the scene, is the central figure in the image, a coarse-featured dustman swinging a bell in an upward arc in his right hand while dangling a presumably empty basket from his left by way of a counter-balance to stop him swinging himself right off his feet. The watercolour suggests that Rowlandson was both repulsed and yet fascinated by what he sees. The energy and sheer physical ebullience of the dustmen is offset against the patient horse and the genteel neighbourhood. It is almost as if the filthy cart and its crew bars off access to the wealthy and privileged world beyond. This image is clearly something more than a caricature – for all its stylisation and use of eighteenth-century conventions for representing the labouring poor, the brilliant drawing here suggests something more profoundly naturalistic and complex than ridicule. Certainly, the image provides more sense of the actual effort and strain of dustman labour than any other image reproduced in this book.

Elsewhere, even caricature images of what must have been extremely heavy manual labour tended not to be dominated by notions of hard work. Instead, the images are comically subverted by ideas of mishap, clumsiness or misadventure drawn from the repertoire of eighteenth-century caricature, where dustmen and similar dirty tradespeople were generally brushed aside as social grotesques, entirely brutalised by their trade, and related to genteel society only by their nuisance value (fig. 23).

"Raising the *wind*," not always "down with the *dust*."


**23** Robert Seymour, 'Raising the *Wind*'

A small *Punch* image of 1841 demonstrates this continuity with previous tradition.[26] A dustman, having got his full basket halfway up the ladder to his cart, overbalances backwards so that his load of dust tumbles over a stout passer-by, knocking off his hat as well as destroying his amour propre. Such images serve to draw attention away from the physical demands of street labour towards ideas of the inevitable contamination of the genteel world by its daily contact with street culture.

One or two images managed to offer some more extended, less farcical comment on dustmen's work. The most fascinating of these, Henry Heath's *No Genius* (Plate VI) is naturalistic and comprehensive enough to represent the perceived nature of dustman activity. The two foreground figures use the two basic tools of waste gathering, broom and shovel, and they stand by low heaps of dust that they have brought together. Behind them is positioned a high-sided cart, with massive iron bound and studded wheels, presumably to gain grip on slippery dirt-strewn streets. The cart is piled high with dust. While the image does not show the dust being transferred from road to cart by means of basket and ladder, enough other images existed for this process to be implicit. The distant figure of the sweeping apprentice, who seems to be reacting in surprise to some comment from the watching bystander, is wielding his broom with considerable intensity. This caricature thus offers a rare and full account of what dustmen actually did when they collected dust. Such images did contrive to establish the working practices of dustmen, ranging from crying out their presence through the accumulation of dust by sweeping, the transferring of the dust into carts, and, to some extent, the sifting and disposal of the accumulated waste. Some of Heath's *Scenes in London* show various work activities undertaken by dustmen including shovelling dust into baskets (No. 12) and a distant view of sifters on top of a prodigious urban dust heap (No. 29). Another urban dustheap and its workforce forms the strangely beautiful setting for a moment of dustman self-admiration delineated in the subtle pastels of lithography (Plate XIV). But seldom do these earlier images of dustheaps resonate with the socio-economic meanings so important to later Victorian commentators.

## The dustman as spectator

Previous chapters have noted the remarkable extent to which dustmen are represented in caricature primarily as enthralled spectators of the urban scene rather than as active participants within it as labourers or workmen. While the main explanations for such a denial of the working life of dustmen may lie within social and economic history, or even in the popular prejudices exploited by caricaturists in pursuit of ready sales, others derive more particularly from art history, and in particular from the way in which images of the urban streets were constructed during the first half of the nineteenth century. Dustmen may figure in these images for a number of artistic reasons: their distinctive clothes and silhouette lend variety to a potentially undifferentiated urban crowd; the comic potential of their disruptive social presence was widely recognised and exploited by caricaturists; and, most significantly, their backs are were distinctive as their fronts, thus permitting, perhaps even encouraging, the representation of the urban streets from a point directly behind the viewpoint of a foregrounded and visually distinct spectator. The dustman's gaze becomes the viewpoint, if not the medium, through which the viewer experiences the London scene. In the caricatures, the nature of this gaze has to be acknowledged, if only partially shared, by the viewer. It is a gaze which is fascinated, knowing, amused, detached, and disenchanted all at once. Seldom surprised by the urban spectacle, dustmen nevertheless maintained their capacity for wonder, their enthusiasm for the kinds of visual pleasures, events and diversions inherited from Regency street life. Essentially observers, unwilling or unable to construct narratives out of their visual pleasures, dustmen nonetheless led, and still lead, the viewer of comic images into the urban scene by presenting it as an endlessly varied and fascinating visual spectacle, and thus, by implication, a source of both pleasurable and thought-provoking interest. It is, thus, little wonder that dustmen appear so frequently in caricature formulations of London street culture.

But, as if to emphasise that the viewer can only partially identify him or herself with the dustman spectator, dustmen have a curiously peripheral role within the caricatures, lurking on boundaries and margins, as often half turned away from the viewer as viewed directly from the back. The caricaturists of the 1830s and 1840s clearly learnt these visual tropes from the illustrators of *Life in London* and its imitators, as a quick glance back to the illustrations to Chapters 2 and 3 will make clear. In these on the whole celebratory images from the 1820s of fictional and theatrical scenes dustmen were viewed as socially transgressive urban adventurers in the pursuit of sensual gratification, thus permitting the vicarious participation of the genteel viewer in low-life pleasure. Such dustmen might be represented either as spectators or as revellers, positioned on the periphery of pleasure as both amused and thoughtful spectators as well as joining in the general merriment. Both spectating and partying dustmen sometimes appeared in the same image (Plate IV).

Caricature images drawn in the 1830s and 1840s continued to depict dustmen both as peripheral spectators of the urban scene and as instinctual hedonists, and thus maintained a dialogue between indulgence and apartness, revelry and contemplation. Their amused and perhaps evaluative eye was caught by a broad range of social activity – ranging from political demonstrations through the gamut of street events to a staggering variety of street entertainments, both deliberate and inadvertent, – all of which depended on crowds and gatherings. The relationship between the watching and often partially isolated figure of the dustman and street gatherings formed much of the substance of these images, which raises issues about the relationship between contiguity and contact, separateness and community, and class division within the early Victorian crowd. It is this awkward and sometimes violent dialogue between uncleanness and isolation, watching and belonging, noise, nuisance and gathering that focuses this chapter and shapes its account of the street culture of the 1830s and 1840s.

*opposite*
**24** Robert Seymour, title page to *Sketches by Seymour*

Apart from their general delineation as thoughtful (or is it incomprehending?) spectators, what was it precisely that dustmen watched? They were certainly shown as fascinated spectators of any form of deliberately organised diversion or entertainment, especially when it was free. They appear at the many fairs which delineated the vernacular year at regular intervals, usually depicted from behind as part of an involved audience for sideshows, freak-shows and circus performances. A few examples from well-known sources will give something of the flavour of the recurrent motif of the roughly assembled stage or dais with its row of fascinated fantails. An early Laurie and Whittle broadsheet of Bartholomew Fair from 1811, comprising both an etching and a text, and depicting a mad bull charging through the Fair, has a lascivious dustman handling an ample woman up steps into a gaudy sideshow at the right-hand edge of the image.[27] Bartholomew Fair in the early nineteenth century, according to the Fair's historian, boasted Richardson's Theatre as its 'Chief Dramatic Booth' among the peep-shows, giants, tumblers and wild-beast shows. With its 'platform lined with green baize, festooned with crimson curtains, and lighted with fifteen hundred lamps' Richardson's platform also boasted 'moneytakers sat in Gothic seats' and 'a band of ten beefeaters' and 'a parade of his dramatic force'.[28] Given all this spectacle, it is hardly surprising that dustmen found Richardson's platform as compelling as any show that might have gone on inside. The irresistible attraction of such places is suggested by the Richardson scrapbook in the Theatre Museum,[29] compiled early in the twentieth century, which contains a number of views of his stall. In several of these dustmen eye up the available entertainment with a characteristic combination of insouciance, scepticism and delight. A little wood engraving by J. Walmsley of 'Bartholomew Fair As It Was'[30] with a dustman staring at a sideshow is echoed by another anonymous small image of a dustman watching a circus called 'Village Fair'. Another image, drawn from a series of toy theatre sheets called *Webb's Scenes in Harlequin – Red Riding Hood* shows another dustman looking at a circus.

If these images are relatively obscure, the same cannot be said of the title page of Seymour's much reprinted *Sketches*. In a book full of images of dustmen, many of them represented in archetypal activities, the title page shows two fantailed dustmen exchanging expectant looks as a rubicund showman drums up punters for his show (fig. 24).[31] The *Sketches* thus adopts the idea of the street 'show', with its variety, geniality and vivacity, as a metaphor for its own literary and graphic practices, suggesting that whatever might attract dustmen in person is equally likely to attract vicarious spectators out for the pleasures offered by its pages. Equally well known was James Grant's *Sketches in London* (1838), an important and popular work in developing both the observational codes and the literary modes of urban reportage. Grant's discussion of 'Penny Theatres' is accompanied by a splendidly vivacious Phiz illustration called *A Scene before the Curtain*.[32] On the stage of 'The Royal Victoria Theatre' scenes of mayhem, murder and desperate over-acting are taking place, largely to the indifference of a benchful of plebeian urban types who chatter and fidget their way through the performance. The exception is a dustman at the right margin whose prominent fantail is perched at a jaunty angle which furthers the totally enraptured involvement of its owner in the melodrama being acted

out on the stage. Other equally rapt dustmen can be found lurking at the corners of several of Cruikshank's depictions of theatre audiences, including the large 1836 etching *Pit, Boxes & Gallery* which shows, looking out from the stage, three tiers of spectators.[33] The highest, roughest and noisiest of these three tiers, though by no means the least interested in the performance, is the gallery, which is inhabited by a demanding and rowdy cross-section of the lower classes, a sweep's boy and a sailor among them. At the far right of the gallery is a dustman, pipe in hand. He is turned away from the stage, and clearly regards the performance going on among the audience as far more interesting than anything that might be happening on the stage. In every respect this figure represents an archetypal caricature dustman. Located at the right-hand edge of the image, both of and yet outside the crowd of 'low' urban types on display, adopting a posture that implies contemplative fascination but which simultaneously withholds the interpretative significance of the his gaze, this representation of the dustman reoccurs throughout the caricatures of the 1830s and 1840s even when watching events as different as radical political gatherings, frost fairs, Punch and Judy, or hangings.

Circuses, sideshows, penny theatres, performances and fairs, then, form one locus classicus for spectating dustmen. Even when dustmen do not have the stage of a sideshow to lean over or yearn towards, they find themselves a secure place to watch the assembled pleasures. One particular kind of street theatre, the Punch and Judy show, is worth examining in rather more detail both because of the frequency with which dustmen appear among its clientele and because of the potential common ground between the violent and transgressive Mr Punch and his assembled dustmen admirers. The high booths in which Punch and Judy shows were performed provided the sites for one of the crowd-gathering London street spectacles which were represented over and over again in the literature and graphic imagery of the first half of the nineteenth century. As George Speaight puts it in *Punch and Judy – A History*, 'there can be little doubt that the first showmen who took to the streets found there in the great metropolis the vast unhurried audience that will still gather and stare at any new thing'.[34] His book gives many illustrations of street crowds focused round the Punch and Judy booth, ranging from watercolours by Rowlandson to vignette wood engravings by the Cruikshanks. As Speaight further comments, 'In the last quarter of the eighteenth century Punch first established himself in the London streets, and during the first quarter of the nineteenth century he increasingly made his home there'.[35]

Given their propensity to be diverted by any passing street distraction, it is hardly a shock to find dustmen represented among these crowds. A tiny William Heath image published in the *Glasgow Looking Glass* in 1825 showed a small crowd gathered round a puppet booth. The crowd, characteristically, contained children, a cavalry officer, and a dustman.[36] Speaight gives an image of a crowd watching a street Punch and Judy show taken from a toy sheet published by I. Green and estimated by Speaight to have been published around 1810.[37] The image offers a classic formulation of a picturesque London crowd at this time. The members of the crowd form a busy frieze across the lower half of the image. While some of the crowd are depicted from the rear as they concentrate on the show, others are half- or three-quarters turned towards the engraver's viewpoint. A number of sub-narratives are formulated in the foreground – a child steals from a stall while its owner is diverted by the puppet show, – while many of the crowd are individuated by dress (a rustic and a sweep's boy for example) or by tools of their trade. An attentive dog shares the general absorption in the performance. At the centre of the composition, viewed directly from the rear, is the unmistakable back view of a dustman, characterised and differentiated fully by his distinctive dress even at this early date. Again typically, the dustman is both part of the crowd and distinctly separate – his fantail hat, dark in colour, forms the precise focal point of the image as it thrusts above and punctuates the line of the crowd.[38]

Ever present at organised commercial street entertainments like Punch and Judy shows and fairs, dustmen were equally associated in caricaturists' minds with the accidental and contingent 'shows' provided by everyday street culture. Perpetually poised in their street lives between work and leisure, it is no surprise that dustmen were seen to be ever ready to leave their duties to respond to the siren call of any passing free spectacle. If the caricatures are to be believed it took very little indeed to divert the interest of a dustman away from work. Violence attracted them particularly and is discussed in detail in a later section of this chapter. Other forms of street disaster seemed to form one particular source of pleasure for dustmen spectators, who were, of course, often a cause of them. One dustman in the *Comic Almanack* looked on quizzically as bailiffs distrained a household for rent arrears.[39] An unmoved dustman in conversation with a one-legged crossing sweeper formed one of a crowd watching a sabbatarian Puritan hanging a cat for illicit mouse-hunting on a Sunday in one of the large-scale and caustic woodcuts that formed C. J. Grant's lengthy series *The Political Drama*.[40] A tiny image from another of Grant's caricatures, this time a multi-panelled lithograph which satirised the almanac format, showed a dustman dancing in pleasure as a judge was hanged over a fire, though whether he is dancing to keep warm or as a political gesture is not entirely clear.[41] Other dustmen could be found watching a different kind of street disaster, street musicians (Plate VII). A dustman in one of Seymour's *Sketches* pauses to watch a group of musicians perform upon a harp, a cello, a flute and a fiddle (fig. 25).[42] The dustman is joined in

**25** Robert Seymour, 'Low Musical Connisseurs'

his leisurely appreciation of the music by a man in a bonnet delivering hot food, who opines 'Well now if that ant so moveing [sic] I could stop all day', thus suggesting the continued delight shown by caricaturists in the leisured idleness of street tradespeople as well as exposing their execrable taste. Equally characteristic is the image's title – 'Low Musical Connisseurs' [sic] – which raises the central interpretative issue faced in reading images of leisurely spectating dustmen. Was their gaze one derived from a knowing and knowledgeable aesthetic of street culture available only to connoisseurs or merely from the combined pleasures of idleness and vacuous gawping? A similar question is posed by the smoking dustman seated among a street gathering listening to an exposition of Paine's political philosophy which forms the frontispiece to W. T. Moncrieff's comic poem *The March of Intellect*.[43] Is the dustman Robert Cruikshank depicted here, deeply attentive but obviously at ease, a mocking or an admiring presence? Given that the representational mode of these images is satirical, if not quite caricature, it is hard to say, although in Seymour's image the musicians are drawn naturalistically (if sketchily) and so, too, is Robert Cruikshank's dustman. Seymour's dustman, however, offers a profile with a receding chin and forehead that verges on the grotesque. Even the graphic language of these images, then, negotiates between naturalism and caricature, drawing on both comic tropes and close observation.

But the particular enthusiasm of caricature dustmen spectators was for races, contests and sporting events where accidents, reversals and indignities could be viewed and savoured literally at leisure. The prototype of this image was drawn from picaresque precedent, namely *Tom and Bob among the Costermongers at a Donkey Cart Race*, a plate from *Real Life in London*, an image that shows the two genteel spectators looking on at a low-life version of Royal Ascot that has been transferred to Tothills Fields or a similar location (fig. 14). Among the four carts depicted, one has been upended by its complaining donkey in the distance. Of the three still racing, the two higher-sided carts are driven by dustmen, one of whom remains largely in control of his donkey, while the other has fallen into his cart in a heap. In this image, dustmen are shown mockingly as competitors – mockingly because their horses and donkeys were nearly always in poor condition which rendered them incapable of any kind of rapid movement. But the event – a semi-parodic low-life equivalent of the rakish entertainments of men about town – was exactly the kind of spectacle that attracted the dustman caricature gaze, and there are several caricatures that elaborated these ideas. The most spectacular of these is *Buttercups and Daisies – a Sketch from Low Life*, a broad but narrow panorama print that focused on a race between dustcarts, in this instance drawn by lumbering though still potentially fractious horses.[44] While one dustcart makes relatively speedy progress towards the finishing line, another has been upended, throwing its driver violently out of the cart backwards. The rest of the picture plane is occupied by a colourful and varied assortment of street characters – a one-legged veteran, two fighting women, a cripple on a dog-drawn sledge and a midget among many others. These low-life freaks and grotesques, all drawn with cheerful insouciance, march across the picture plane in a grimly determined way oblivious to or refusing to acknowledge the spectacle offered by the cart race. However, in the centre of the image stand two unmistakeable dustmen spectators cheering on their fellows. One offers a classically constructed dustman back view, while the other cuts a caper and waves his fantail hat. Here, then, the dustmen are specifically rendered in their central role as both spectators of and participants in the urban theatre.

A similar ambiguity between watching and doing informs a boisterous etching by Henry Heath of a game of street football that in fact resembles a riot more than a sporting event.[45] Among the varied pedestrians involved either in or by the game, a dustman, carried away by the general excitement, stamps on the neck of a fallen pedestrian in his mad pursuit of the ball. A number of crude little images offering a jaundiced view of simple proletarian pleasures – including a sack race, the pursuit of a slippery pig, and a donkey race with the jockeys facing their mounts' tails – appeared in William Heath's early lithographic caricature periodical the *Northern Looking Glass* under the headings of 'British Field Sports' and 'Sporting Scenes'. Dustmen appear in these as both spectators and participants, and one image – the sack race – has the classic combination of both an animated dustman in profile and a back view of a colleague among the lookers-on.[46] While never shown betting, caricature dustmen clearly loved sporting events of a rough and ready kind and those contests which involved reversals, accidents and those kinds of comic upheaval which were particularly damaging to human dignity. They are shown both as hapless if enthusiastic entrants in such events and as perennially enthusiastic spectators of them. In caricature at least no unlikely contest, race or game was complete without the presence of the perpetually fascinated dustmen.

One other important arena for the spectating dustman remains to be discussed – that of street politics. Nothing in the primary and secondary sources suggests that dustmen were in any way politically engaged or active. Indeed, commentators from Busby and Wight to Mayhew and Sala tend to suggest the opposite – that dustmen were too preoccupied with drinking, eating, smoking, courting and pleasure-seeking to know anything much about the world beyond their immediate patch. Their presence in the graphic representation of the march of intellect might be read more as a metaphor for social anxiety than a realistic account of dustman cultural ambition. Certainly, they were never represented as in any way part of any radical protest, though they sometimes appear as representatives of various discontented or grumpy trades.[47] Thus the frequent graphic association of dustmen with street politics may be nothing more than an extension of their fascination with any kind of urban spectacle, especially free shows. But there is something particularly compelling about the street presence of dustmen in caricature accounts of the street theatre of politics which singles them out as observers, if not as commentators. The composition of many such images gives extremely pronounced, perhaps undue, visual and compositional stress to the presence of dustmen among the noisy crowds that assembled to see their leaders and political representatives as they conducted their public duties. William Heath's *Leaving the House of Lords*, for example, which shows Wellington galloping through a hostile crowd in Palace Yard, has an especially prominent enraged dustman gesturing furiously as the most emphatically positioned and fully realised member of the crowd that fills the left half of the image.[48] It is not clear whether the dustman has any understanding of the reasons for Wellington's unpopularity or whether he is merely echoing the general sentiment of the crowd. Another of McClean's publications, a lithograph from *McClean's Monthly Sheet* called *A Meeting of the Trades' Union*, shows a Painite orator in the centre of the image standing on a kneeling henchman's back as a podium surrounded by bemused or indifferent passers-by.[49] But the tonal structure of the image actually gives most prominence to a wonderfully relaxed dustman, legs crossed and leaning back on his broom, and viewed from behind. Again, the dustman's expression gives no clues as to his political understanding. More remarkable still is another lithograph *General Assembly* held in the Library of Congress collection, which shows with considerable distaste an extraordinary group of disaffected and radicalised urban representatives including several black men, a soldier and a ranting orator standing on a bench to harangue his audience.[50] There is a dustman among this throng, but the entire composition is dominated by the presence at the right-hand front corner of the print of a dustman spectator seen from behind almost in silhouette and sprawled over a Windsor chair pulling on his long clay pipe in order to contemplate the assembled company at his leisure. As if to emphasise his distinctiveness and evaluative presence in this scene, a seated man has turned round to bring his startled gaze to bear on the dustman, thus emphasising the separateness and lack of obvious fraternity represented by his gaze. Dustmen, while showing no obvious powers of comprehending the significance of political events, frequently appeared in comic graphic representations of political life as a means of devaluing or satirising the whole procedure. The fear of the mob has metamorphosed by the time of the first Reform Bill into an anxiety about any extension of the franchise which might, in its logical conclusion, allow even such vulgar ignoramuses as dustmen access to political influence. Here, as in much else, dustmen were used to figure the dangerous extremes to which progressive or reformist social policies might lead. The patent absurdity of imagining a dustman as politically literate underlies these images, an absurdity that was as much a nervous tic as it was a comic reaction.

It is tempting, but dangerous, to think of the many dustmen shown by caricaturists on the streets of Regency and early Victorian London as something approaching that centrefold of Modernist iconography, the *flâneur*. Dustmen do have a curious and emphatic graphic presence as spectators on the streets depicted in early nineteenth-century comic art, and without doubt their gaze is curiously detached and different from that of the other figures that fill these images. Often the on-looking dustman is placed within the image in such a way as to offer the audience for prints an angle of vision, and an attitude, from which to survey the urban scene. The 'attitude' or stance of the dustmen was of considerable importance, as their posture and facial expression were frequently constructed as amused but knowing, pleasurably diverted but seldom surprised. Thus dustmen were shown to have evolved a form of pavement connoisseurship which offered the contemporary consumer of prints a vicarious point of view which permitted prurient glimpses of urban life without actually having to brave the nuisances, dangers and dirtiness of London streets. However, it is not clear whether the middle-class or genteel consumer of prints was meant to identify him or herself wholeheartedly with this dustman point of view. Because of their trade, as has already been shown, dustmen did occupy a curiously privileged space on the streets – dirty enough to create a space between themselves and fearful passers-by, fractious enough to keep fellow pedestrians at a clear distance, lazy or privileged enough by their particular trade to be able to stop and stare at will, dustmen might well have offered the timorously genteel but curious print-buyer an interesting and well-defended site for vicarious spectatorship. But the attraction of any invitation to share the dustman viewpoint and its licence was severely mitigated by the sustained *vacancy* and *incomprehension* of the dustman gaze. Spectating dustmen are easily amused, but seldom illuminated, by what they see. In this respect they are as far away from the self-consciousness and willed openness to experience that characterises the *flâneur* as it is possible to be. There is nothing aesthetic about their gaze – it is, in fact, a gawp rather than a gaze. Yet the emptiness of dustman spectatorship does not entirely negate its significance, and the watching that dustmen did characterised a new insistence on close observation and urban investigation that, in the mutated form of Boz, Mayhew and the

**Plate 1** W.H. Pyne, *Dustman*

**Plate II**
W.W., engraved J. Gleadah
*Almack's in the East, a Scene in Tom and Jerry or Life in London*

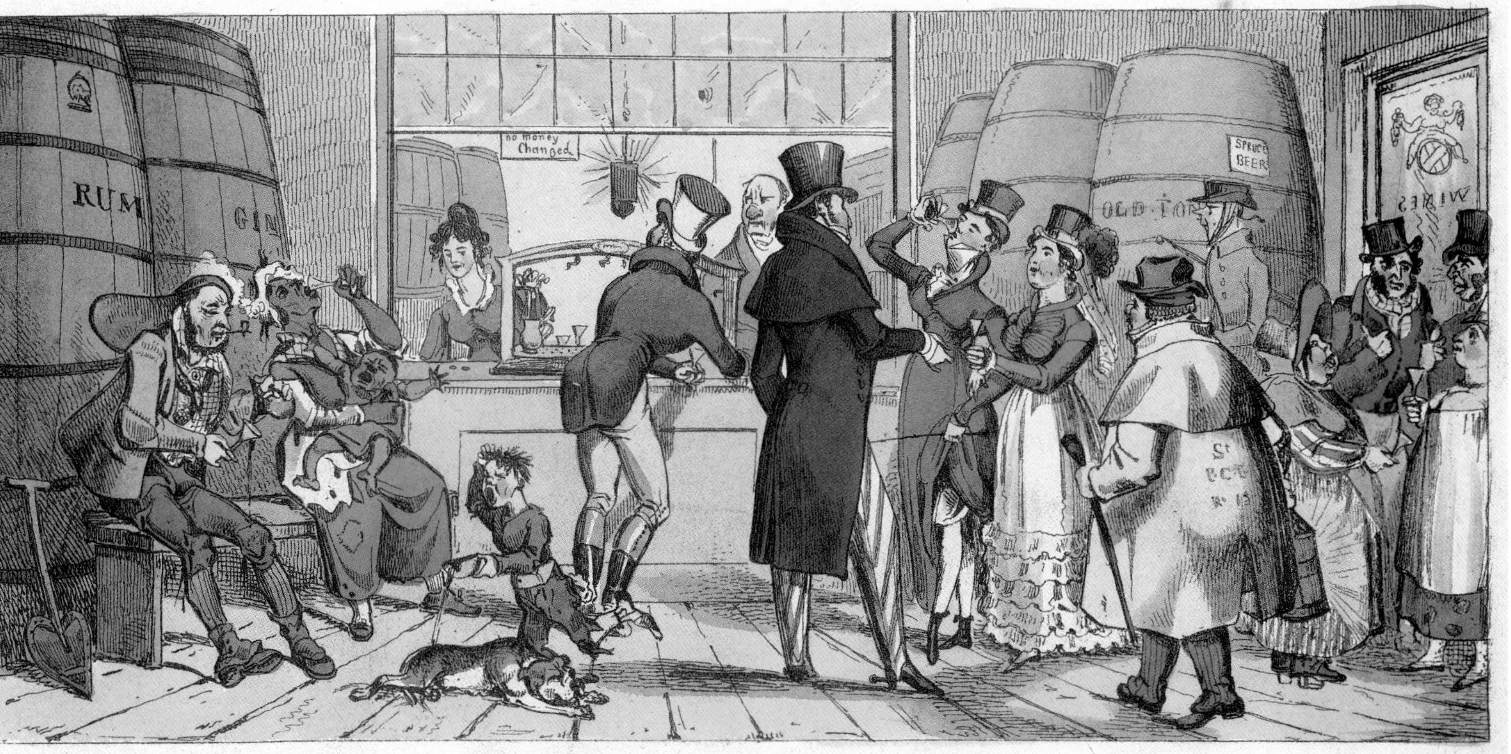


**Plate III** William Heath, *A Midnight Go of Daffy's Elixir*

**Plate IV** William Heath, *Doing a Little Low Life in the East*

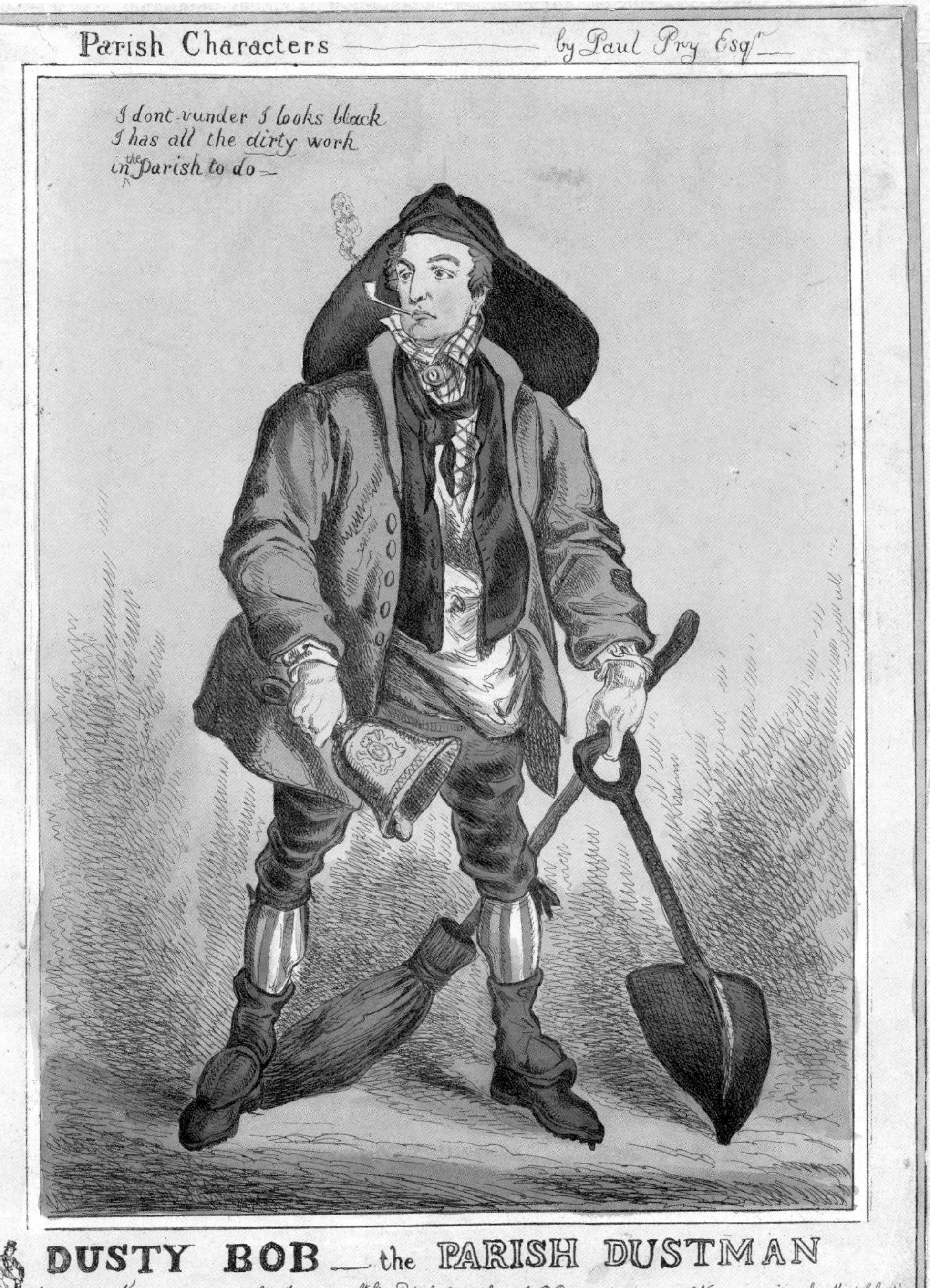

Parish Characters — by Paul Pry Esqr
I dont vunder I looks black
I has all the dirty work
in the Parish to do —
DUSTY BOB — the PARISH DUSTMAN
Pub June 1st 1829 by S Gans 15 Southampton St Strand (Sole Publisher of P Prys Caricatures — (None are original without S Gans' name)


**Plate V** 'Paul Pry' [Henry Heath], *Dusty Bob – The Parish Dustman*

**Plate VI**
'Paul Pry' [Henry Heath], *No Genius*

**Plate VII** George Cruikshank, *Les Savoyards*

**Plate VIII** J.L. Marks, *London Nuisances – The Dustman*

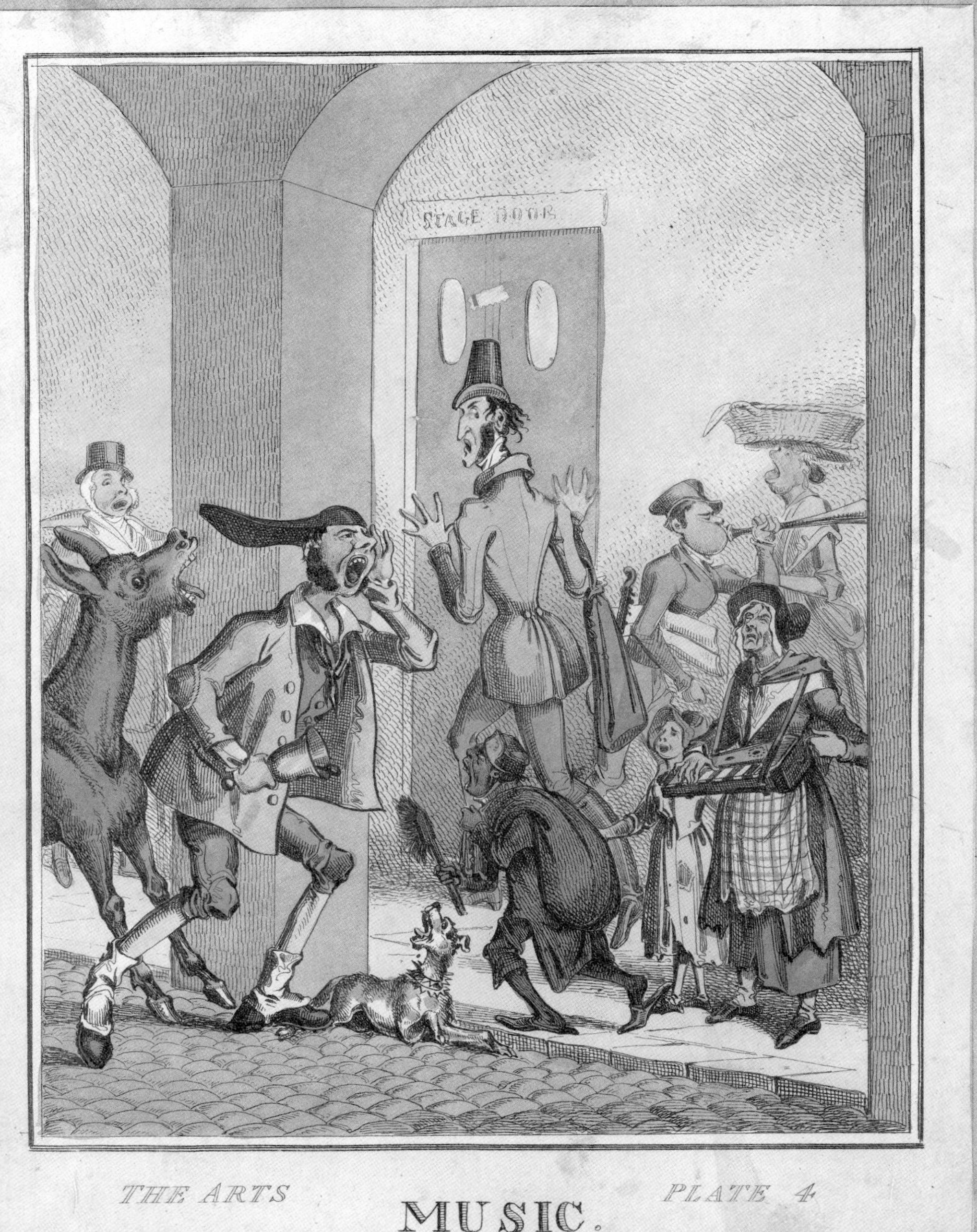

STAGE DOOR
THE ARTS
PLATE 4
MUSIC.
Published by G Humphrey 74 New Bond Street & 24 St James's Street
March 25 1823
WH fecit


**Plate IX** William Heath, *The Arts – Music*

**Plate X**
[Henry Heath],
*Fears*

**Plate XI** Henry Heath, *Intellectual Character – One of the Club at his Studies*

A CHALLENCE A LA MODE!

You Blackguard how dare you run against eny person like this 'ere, I shall demand Satisfaction, y'r Card feller, here's mine — Vell vell my good man dont go for to shove it in my face. I arnt my Pocket book vith me, but jest mention the place of meeting? — At the back o'the Bone bilers, — Y'r Veapons? Vy Shovels — I generally prefer Pistols, but I arnt perticKler, name y'r Time? — This 'ere evening presidedly at harf arter 8. Wery vell I'm y'r Tulip.

**Plate XII** C. J. Grant, *A Challenge a la Mode*

**Plate XIII**
Anon., *The Laughing Stock No. 11 – How vulgar!*

FLOWERS OF LOVELINESS.

NARCISSUS.

TREGEAR & LEWIS, 96, CHEAPSIDE.

W. Lake. Litho. 170 Fleet Street.

**Plate XIV** Anon., *Flowers of Loveliness – Narcissus*

**Plate XV** A page of small coloured engraved scraps with African Sal and Dusty Bob on the right of the second row

**Plate XVI** Henry Heath, *The March of Intellect*

Riverside Visitor, gave bourgeois London the information and awareness that drove progressive Victorian socio-political reform.

## Violent and noisy dustmen

In one of the many parodies of Hogarthian 'progresses' that filled the pages of early nineteenth-century comic journals, Robert Seymour, a specialist in sporting topics, re-drew the career of a successful prize fighter for *Bell's Life in London* in a series of nine wood-engraved vignettes with accompanying verses (fig. 26).[51] 'The Pugilist's Progress' traced the progress of a lowly born 'thriving lusty sprout' through childhood, school, street and public bar violence into the only licensed arena for his talents – the prize ring – and on into honourable retirement as an acknowledged 'gentleman' of the ring turned bar owner. 'There may the Fancy Lads repair, / A friendly bowl to drain' the verse comment in valediction of a 'manly' and 'honest' boxer who has earned repose and respect. However genteel his later career may have been, the pugilist's mettle was developed and most severely tested on the streets where 'milling' or brawling was widely understood as an aspect of the pavement collisions and traditional animosities that lived in the hinterland between Regency London 'nuisances' and early Victorian anxieties about the urban 'crowd'. In step the fourth of his 'progress', the pugilist encountered not one but three famous brawlers outside a pub. They were, of course, dustmen, and, as the author noted, 'Few worthies, I believe, can bang / The men of Dust and Coal'. But the budding pugilist was up to the task – 'Two Coveys are already down – / And 'tother soon must follow' – even if his method was somewhat unsophisticated. 'Your sturdy frame and courage high / Require a little science' before 'my hero tough' emerged into fame and fortune in the ring despite his

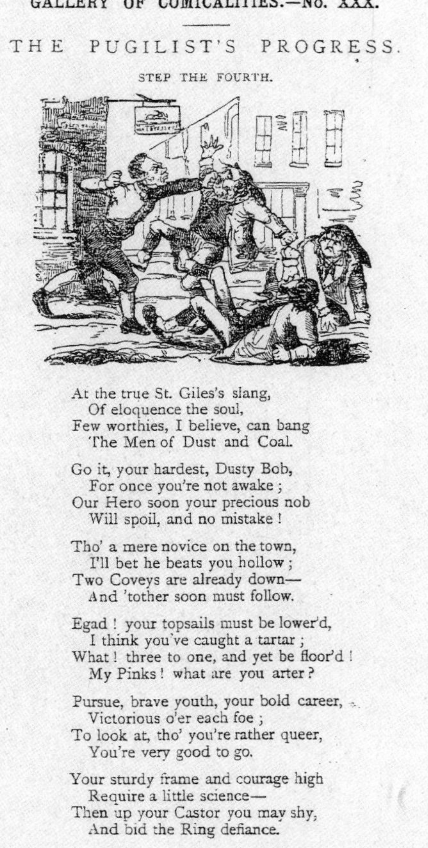
GALLERY OF COMICALITIES.—No. XXX.

THE PUGILIST'S PROGRESS.

STEP THE FOURTH.

At the true St. Giles's slang,
Of eloquence the soul,
Few worthies, I believe, can bang
The Men of Dust and Coal.

Go it, your hardest, Dusty Bob,
For once you're not awake ;
Our Hero soon your precious nob
Will spoil, and no mistake !

Tho' a mere novice on the town,
I'll bet he beats you hollow ;
Two Coveys are already down—
And 'tother soon must follow.

Egad ! your topsails must be lower'd,
I think you've caught a tartar ;
What ! three to one, and yet be floor'd !
My Pinks ! what are you arter ?

Pursue, brave youth, your bold career,
Victorious o'er each foe ;
To look at, tho' you're rather queer,
You're very good to go.

Your sturdy frame and courage high
Require a little science—
Then up your Castor you may shy,
And bid the Ring defiance.

32

**26** Robert Seymour, 'The Pugilist's Progress – Step the Fourth'

poverty-stricken 'yokel' background. While Seymour here may only be paraphrasing the Romantic veneration of the prize-fighter as manly (or indeed 'gentlemanly') typified by writers like Hazlitt and Pierce Egan, nonetheless he was forced to acknowledge that the streets offered a full education in violence, and that few teachers were more adept than dustmen.

Within caricature and the literature of urban exploration, dustmen were legendary for their violence and willingness to be drawn into brawls, scuffles, 'mills' and street fights. When they weren't actually fighting they could be found proximate to fights – indeed, brawls were one of the street events they are most often found watching. Mention has already been made of one of Henry Heath's *Caricaturist's Scrap Book* images which shows two dustmen admiringly offering their outer clothes to a woman after they have watched her brawling on the street (fig. 18).[52] One of John Leech's illustrations to *The Comic Latin Grammar*, for example, shows a dustman gawping at a street fight between a genteel young passer-by who has rubbed up against another dustman, who has stripped off his hat and jacket to square up against his slender and fashionably dressed opponent (fig. 27).[53] Here the dustman appears as both spectator and protagonist in a scene that evokes a combination of caricature tropes of aggression – class difference, over-stated masculinity, a comic punctiliousness about 'manners' among the working classes, and the dangers of street collision. A sardonic commentary on the scene is provided by the caption, ostensibly constructed to illustrate a point of grammar, but more apposite as a mocking account of the genteel 'art' of fisticuffs – 'The faithful study of the fistic art / From mawkish softness guards a Briton's art'. A more complex gathering still of accumulated caricature meanings is assembled by *Rouge et Noir*, discussed later, in which ideas about race are added to issues to do with collision, contamination and spectatorship.

Caricature dustmen persistently brought the threat of violence into any street situation where they were to be found. Perhaps this is unsurprising – dustmen were understood to be a rough, uneducated bunch who undertook a socially demeaning job which required little of them except physical strength. They may have had every right to feel aggrieved with their lot and hostile to their 'betters' who treated them with disdain and contempt. But there are particular reasons why dustmen were so consistently associated with violence, some of which were to do with the singular nature of their work. Characteristically, it was the burden of symbolic and metaphorical meanings that dustmen bore which rendered them so often as aggressors and antagonists in the caricatures from the first decades of the nineteenth century. By its very nature, the work of a dustman fostered aggression. As previous sections of the book have suggested, dustmen had to defend their 'round' from the depredations of 'flying dustmen' – illicit dustmen with fast horses and a contempt for regulation who were eager to pounce on and run off with dustheaps left for the legitimate dustmen. The vulnerability of

**27** [John Leech] illustration to [Percival Leigh], *The Comic Latin Grammar*

their work to the incursions of chancers, cheats and opportunists was particularly visible in their sustained anxiety about Christmas boxes, an anxiety explored in detail below. The need to make their presence visible and audible among the competing clamour of the streets in order to ensure that their due of dust and ashes was laid out for them must also have encouraged an aggression in their legendary bellowing of 'Dust ho!' and frantic bell-ringing. The physical demands of the job meant that dustmen, however frequently rendered as physical grotesques with knock-knees, repulsive faces and strange body shapes by the caricaturists, had something of the masculine swagger still associated with, for examples, labourers in the building trade. The difficult act of getting about the crowded streets with their clumsy carts amidst the ebb and flow of pedestrian and horse-drawn activity also led to conflict – dust-carts are frequently shown blocking off streets, often with their drivers leaning over their tail-boards to observe some eye-catching street event.[54] Containing their dust in such ways as to avoid soiling or besmirching passers-by can never have been easy for dustmen, and resulted in many an altercation with genteel passers-by.

But it is the weight of symbolic meanings which go furthest in explaining why dustmen are so thoroughly associated with violence and aggression. At one level, as debased labourers, they were perceived within the tropes of eighteenth century caricatures of 'low' urban workers as animalistic 'naturals', and thus victims of their uncivilised impulses and appetites. They are represented cheerfully and good-naturedly as such in a tiny image from the *Comic Almanack* where, on a blustery March day when the wind has made dust containment difficult, three dustmen have got into a fight with two gentlemanly passers-by whose fashionable garb has been soiled. The image is presented above the punning title of 'The Bell Savage' thus bringing together ideas of animality and savagery with notions of class, noise and dust – a potent and expressive combination of elements.[55] Such physical conflicts between men of differing classes also touch on important issues about the nature of proper or legitimate masculinity. In this instance, the gentlemen, with their raised canes, occupy dominant fighting postures, in one case slashing at a fallen dustman from above, in the other forcing the broom- and bell-wielding dustman on to the back foot to avoid a blow to the chin. The third dustman slyly takes advantage of superiority of numbers by emptying his basket of waste over one of the gentlemen. Dressed after the manners of early policemen and represented in postures which are startlingly reminiscent of prints of Peterloo, the two gentlemen come out of this image rather badly – by pressing home their class superiority on defenceless proletarians going about their business in difficult conditions, the image sides strongly with the dustmen in this instance. The viewer can't help sharing the delight of the third dustman as he gleefully showers a genteel combatant with his filthy basket-load of dust. But nonetheless the dustmen here are represented as clowns, yokels or, most powerfully, as 'naturals', so that their violence can be associated with their instinctual animality.

But more often violence was the result of street contact that involved perceptions of class difference and the ownership of public space. It wasn't even necessary to collide with a dustman to invoke his ire. In one caricature instance, for example, sneezing near a dustman was enough to provoke hostility.[56] But physical contact, with all the implications of contamination and despoliation implicit in street collisions, was the usual precursor of violence. Again, *The Comic Latin Grammar* could find an appropriate classical tag for such an event – a hybrid figure in a toga but sporting a fantail hat, a bell, and a clay pipe runs into a similarly ambiguous coachman under the heading 'Cave cui incurras, inepte: Mind who you run against, stupid'.[57] In another caricature, under the revealing title of *Fears*, a dustman again confronts a coachman – more or less his equal in terms of a reputation for thuggery and aggression (Plate X),[58] – while, in the most violent image I have found a hideous dustman is rolling on the ground, locked into a desperate conflict with an equally repulsive woman (fig. 28).[59] Only C. J. Grant of the caricaturists of the 1830s and 1840s could have chosen such uncontrolled and taboo violence as a subject for a comic image. It was inevitable that such a shocking violation of middle-class manners should be attributed to a dustman Running into a dustman was, in caricatures at least, an extremely risky undertaking, as another of Grant's vigorous grotesques makes clear (Plate XII). In this characteristically scathing image a dustman has collided with a sweep's boy, and, in a sustained parody of genteel

**28** Lithograph 'She Stoops to Conquer' from unknown source, possibly by C. J. Grant

etiquette, the two men, despite their savage appearance, work out the mechanics of satisfaction through setting up a duel. Once again, ideas of contact, contamination and violence – to say nothing of notions of race and 'aboriginal' instinct – are brought together in a moment of everyday street culture.

One image more than any other brought together the symbolic aggregation of meanings which attended the public violence of dustmen. *Rouge et Noir* was one of several plates published under the general title of *Hoyle's Games* – a joking reference to the standard book which explained the rules of card games.[60] The caricatures thus derived from a travesty of the efforts of *Hoyle's Games* to establish the rules and etiquette through which a civilised society should operate – accordingly they depict social transgressions. *Rouge et Noir* depicts a classic moment of street transgression – a splendidly dressed soldier in buckskin breeches and a red coat has bumped into a sweep's boy, and the two have taken the matter to fisticuffs. Thus collision and contamination lead to their inevitable outcome – violence. The fight is being scrutinised by a dustman, perched as usual on the right-hand margin of the image turned side on to the picture plane, with something of the discrimination of the connoisseur. The fight is watched by an urban gathering organised across the back of the image as a frieze and comprising a classic caricature cross-section of pavement figures – a jaunty female tradeswoman with a flat basket on her head, a coachman whip in hand, a hat-seller with his wares perched on his head, an attenuated fop of extraordinary height and a guardsman practically overwhelmed by his rampant bearskin. The contrast between the fashionably dressed and the uniformed on the one hand and the dirty and unkempt street tradespeople on the other brings issues not just to do with class but also, given the punning title of the image, to do with racial difference into consideration. Here, in one tiny image are found an extraordinary range of middle-class urban anxieties – fear of the violence of the urban mob, fear of bodily contact with its attendant likelihood of contamination at both a literal and a metaphorical level, fear of the breakdown of the rules and etiquette through which genteel conduct was managed, and, not least, fear of the racial implications held by the idea of the 'noir', here personified by a sweep's boy. Ideas about gender are even displayed here, with the feminised and foppish soldiers and the genteel by-stander contrasted with the aggressive masculinity of the sweep's boy, the dustman and the coachman, all them under the amused scrutiny of the pretty woman street trader who watches them all from the centre of the image like the arbiter of a medieval tournament. This caricature, then, summarises the anxieties about class conflict, urban space, masculine violence and the contaminating touch which preoccupied caricature accounts of the urban scene in the 1820s and 1830s. The threats offered by the association of dustmen with street violence, even when, as here, the dustman did nothing more than watch, were deeply inscribed into increasing middle-class anxiety about how to manage an increasingly complex and divided urban society.

The complexity of this middle-class anxiety and sense of threat can be best illustrated by the one moment when dustmen were brought into direct contact with the householders that, at a distance, employed them – the claiming of Christmas bonuses. Two images by George Cruikshank provide the key evidence here. In the first image, a small, densely crowded, and heavily annotated etching from a multi-image plate called 'Christmas Time' which was published on the seemingly incongruous date of 1 May 1827,[61] a genteel householder or housekeeper is being besieged at her front door by a mass of tradespeople demanding their Christmas box (fig. 29). She reels back in alarm from the importunate

**29** George Cruikshank, 'Christmas Time'

parish beadle, the street foot patrol, the turncock, and the postman. Further back the waits performers have 'taken the liberty of waiting upon you'. On the periphery, and less articulately, smaller petitioners, including a sweep's boy, try to attract her attention. But in the centre of the image, occupying a space of their own between the clamorous petitioners and the approaching waits musicians and players, two dustmen, one angular

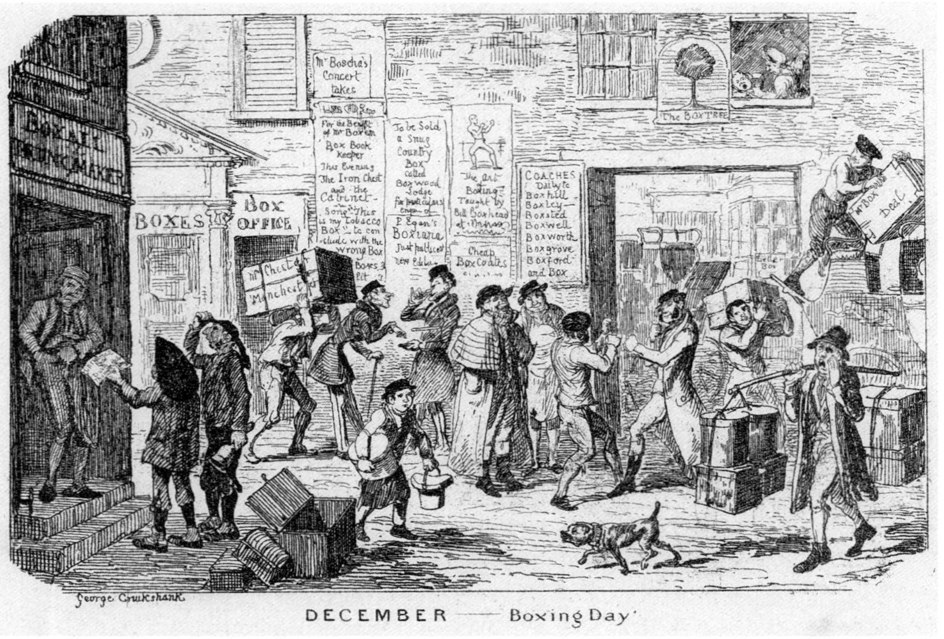


**30** George Cruikshank, 'Boxing Day'

and bent-kneed, the other thick-set and squat, contest their respective claims on a Christmas box. The sturdier dustman, bell tucked aggressively into his armpit, exclaims 'Vy you an't the riggular Dustman! Vat do you vant here? if you vants a X-mas Box, I'll give you vun, my Tulip.' His less well-endowed colleague replies 'I'm as good a dustman as you any day in the veek'. As we shall see, Cruikshank has picked exactly here on what seems to have been a major issue among dustmen, that their devotion to their particular geographical area of activities could be usurped by unauthorised imposters. So the two dustmen are literally contesting their territory here.

The second image, located as the final 'December' plate in the *Comic Almanack* for 1836 (fig. 30),[62] forms a larger, but still densely packed, etching full of verbal and visual jokes on the idea of 'Boxing' Day. A less contentious, more genial image than 'Christmas Time', 'December' is built out of a series of puns, jokes and double meanings implicit in the words 'box' and 'boxing'. For example, a poster advertising coach trips lists only places with 'box' in their names. A sign over a door announces the presence of a box office. A pub sign directs us to The Box Tree pub, where a small child is having its ears boxed by its infuriated mother. Two men are sparring (boxing) in the centre of the image. A wooden crate is being sent to a Mr Box in Deal. A large box or chest is being carried to Mr Chester in Manchester. And so on, through a genial riot of visual and verbal puns. At the left of the image, in the shadow of a high façade, two dustmen, one of them holding out a handbill or envelope inscribed 'Christmas Box Dusty Bob', the other touching (but significantly not doffing) his hat, seek their Boxing Day reward from a less than delighted employee of Boxall, Trunkmaker. Again the two dustmen are represented as a physically contrasting pair, one tall and attenuated, the second smaller and more powerfully built. The dustmen bring to their task a respectful if determined manner, and the trunk-maker gives off the air of one caught out in a necessary but hardly agreeable or willingly undertaken task.

These images might be read off merely as yet another manifestation of the variety of street presences occupied by dustmen if it wasn't for a considerable amount of supporting evidence, both documentary and humorous in nature, which attests to both the commercial and emotional intensity which surrounded the collection of Christmas bonuses. One lithographed caricature – a strip of six vociferously disgruntled trades-people comprising a lamplighter, a dustman, a scavenger, a beadle, a turncock and a 'charley' (nightwatchman) – cut from a larger plate called 'Symtoms [sic] of a Bad Boxing Day' offers a further glimpse of the pent-up aggression that surrounded Christmas tipping.[63] The *Comic Almanack*, in its first year of publication, had already interested itself in the fraught etiquette of Boxing Day, publishing a comic poem in December 1835 that outlined the trials of householders in warding off the persistent reminders of tradespeople to 'remember them at Christmas'.[64] The poem concludes:

> The Bellman, Dustman, Chimney-sweep,
> Bring up the rear in smart array.
> And all get drunk, and strip to fight,
> To prove it is a *Boxing Day*.

There are several handbills in the Guildhall Library, dating from the late 1820s and early 1830s, which explain the extent to which the dustmen's Christmas box was subject to territorial dispute, fraud and deception. Here is a typical example:

> To the inhabitants of the Parish of St. Lukes/To prevent imposition and fraud/ We the constant Dustmen of this Parish make humble application to you for A CHRISTMAS BOX, Which you are usually so kind as to give; and to prevent imposition on you, and Fraud on us, which was attempted by a set of idle, Disorderly Fellows who frequented the Parish last year, by defrauding the poor Dustmen of your little bounty; and to prevent Fraud, you will please not to give any person who cannot produce a Young Man with TEN FINGERS and TWO THUMBS.[65]

This plea from Shoreditch is preserved alongside others from Cornhill, Walbrook and Southwark,[66] though the others are forced to use less spectacular means of identifying the true dustmen than by the number of their digits. Most, in fact, seem to have used badges or medals, sometimes especially struck to represent dustmen (one had a basket and ladder, obvious tools of the dustman's trade, engraved on the recto), but more often commemorating other events or anniversaries. (It is, of course, interesting that the dustmen would not have been known to the householders and their servants by sight.) The handbills were also quick to point out and defend the distinctive status of dustmen – 'No connection with the Scavengers' a Southwark bill of 1828 insists.[67]

It is precisely these issues – the persistent impersonation of dustmen for fraudulent purposes during the Christmas season, the peculiarities of the ways in which dustmen identified themselves as 'authentic' or 'regular' representatives of the parish, and the determination of dustmen to distinguish themselves from 'lower' trades like scavenging – which re-surfaced in three articles in *Punch* which, despite being written over twenty years later, suggest that little had changed. The first comprised a pastiche play-text called 'The Christmas Boxes', which was one of a series of satirical 'Dramas for Every-Day Life'. The play-text dramatised the plight of an impoverished barrister ('Briefless') facing the annual householder's nightmare of a succession of tradespeople demanding their Christmas boxes. As the stage direction has it – 'Dustmen, Porters, Newsboys, Watchmen, Beadles, &c. &c. appear at the door, and continue increasing in numbers'. The dustman, described by Briefless as 'a character not easily sifted', takes a leading role in pleading for his bonus.[68] The second *Punch* piece appeared in 1853[69] and confirmed the magazine's interest in the urban sparring that took place between anxious but determined householders and their unseen but all too apparent tradesmen. A third *Punch* article in volume 28 (1855)[70] was similar enough to suggest some judicious reworking of the earlier article was going on, although the second piece actually recounts a meeting with the dustman in order to test the credibility of the 'token' of authenticity. The two *Punch* articles stressed both in content and tone the enormous cultural and social distance between the writers and the dustmen they described. Far from being concerned with the aggression and fractiousness of the Christmas box system, these two articles instead focussed on the dustman as belonging to a different, rather quaint, England, where impossibly fine distinctions between lowly trades were met with incomprehension and, indeed, condescension. By the mid-Victorian period, there was no longer the sense to be found in Cruikshank's images, of collective participation by all classes in a street carnival which might prove dangerous but which was also rumbustuous, entertaining and invigorating. Instead the *Punch* articles viewed the world of the dustman as distant, antique and comic in its bizarre practices, distinctions and parochial concerns. Mid-Victorian respectability sharpened social distinctions as well as social anxieties.

What, then, is to be made of these brief but significant glimpses, drawn from documentary evidence as well as graphic satire, of dustmen competing for their Christmas bonuses? As usual when such significant details are seized upon by Cruikshank, they reveal a number of different but overlapping emblematic social anxieties. The first is that, because the giving of Christmas boxes required the front door importuning of householders (or at least their upper servants), Boxing Day represented an unusually direct moment of contact between the respectable middle and professional classes and dustmen. A relationship usually mediated through the 'invisible' removing of rubbish is made manifest in a rare moment of personal confrontation in which the middle-class householder is forced to acknowledge their dependence on, if not always entirely their gratitude towards, the lowly trade practised by dustmen. A second anxiety was a response to the undoubted aggression with which tradespeople seemed to claim their seasonal due, aggression which undoubtedly confirmed the persistent genteel anxieties about the potential for social disorder represented by street trades. There is clear element of physical threat represented in the Christmas entreaties represented by Cruikshank, which added to a more general sense of middle-class apprehension about burly working men keen to assert their rights and dignities.

Such sense of threat must have been considerably augmented by the distribution of the handbills described above which made clear the levels of self-defence, aggression and conflict which existed on a daily basis within the dustman's necessary and legitimate defence of his own trade. It can have been of no comfort to genteel sensibilities to learn of the trade disputes and even criminal activities which were part of the everyday experience of dustmen. That dustman needed to be physically aggressive not just to do their job but also to protect their interests against the threats of unfair trade can only have increased the general middle-class sense of dustmen as members of a violent, fractious or even sub-criminal fellowship. Bringing these secular fears and anxieties to Christmas, increasingly a time of family celebration and Christian good-will, must have further alienated dustmen from genteel sympathy. The greed, aggression and sharp practices surrounding Christmas boxes offered something more than another subject for the caricaturist – they also represented the more general fears of disorder, working-class threat, and social division which were troubling an increasingly self-conscious urban middle class.

Noisiness was central to the dustman's trade, and previous chapters have made clear the extent to which the famous cry of 'Dust ho! had penetrated into popular urban mythology as an emblem of street culture. The meanings attached to the noise that dustmen made, as we have seen, ranged from nostalgia for remembered childhood pleasure to fury at the central role dustmen took in the construction of urban hubbub and the consequent annihilation of middle-class longings for silence or, at least, a reasonably quiet environment. Some reference has already been made to the legislative attack on street noise in the 1840s, and the privileged status that dustmen were accorded in such legislation – a recognition that the disposal of waste was a higher metropolitan priority than, say, the activities of sweeps or street sellers of comestibles, and certainly not to be compared to the perpetual nuisance of organ grinders or street musicians like the Savoyard band shown in Plate VII. Yet, for all the formal recognition of the legitimacy and, indeed, the social necessity, of noisy dustmen they were nonetheless constantly depicted by the caricaturists through their proximity to less defensible kinds of noise as guilty parties in the creation of the collective hubbub of early nineteenth-century London. Characteristically, in caricatures at least, the din dustmen made was largely figured as an aspect both of their more generally threatening street presence and of the more widespread problem of urban noise. A classic formulation of the idea of noise as threat can be found in Plate VIII, where the bell-toting, shouting dustman violates not just street peacefulness but also the ears of a genteel female passer-by. The title of this print – *London Nuisances – The Dustman* – deliberately invoked that long sequence of graphic 'Nuisances' which provided one of the key structures through which caricaturists figured the urban scene. But the noisiness of the dustman is here clearly linked to his invasion of the personal space of passers-by, and even to a form of sexual threat expressed by the superimposition of the dustman on the female figure behind.

While there is some justice, however, in considering dustman noise primarily as a form of threat, aggression or violence, several significant caricature images were more interested in ideas of class. These depictions of street noise concentrated on the ways in which public din offered a travestied version of the primarily genteel preoccupation with music-making, especially the parlour recitals of young women and the practice rituals of professional musicians and music teachers, who required the quiet of their living rooms to maintain their profession. As always in such caricature images the satire cut both ways. Street people and the proletariat were mocked for their lack of finer musical ability – all they could create was the immensely discordant cacophony that characterised the pavements of early nineteenth-century London. But (almost) equally the middle classes were also satirised for their increasingly prissy defence of harmony and quietude as central, and hence necessary, values. The comic potential of this equation between middle-class professional aspiration and the unrepentant noise generated by the common people was recognised by many early printmakers, and certainly by Hogarth in his 1741 print of *The Enraged Musician*. A dandified violinist, trying to practise in his ground-floor music room, stands at the window covering up his ears while below on the street is assembled a vigorous cross-section of street 'music' which includes a child with a rattle, another child with a drum, various street ballad singers and tradespeople bawling out their wares, and an exotic performer on a primitive-looking clarinet or oboe. There is even a dustman to the rear of the print making his own characteristic contribution to the decibel count. The ambiguous standpoint of the print suggest the complexity of the urban understanding involved here – at one level a professional is kept from his work by an unselfconsciously vulgar crowd whose din re-iterates the importance of his defence of music, but at another level the print celebrates the variety and energy of pavement culture. Everyday street life is comprised here of confused hubbub and competing shouts for attention, yet it is not entirely dismissed. While a travesty of refined cultural ambition, nonetheless the culture of the pavement offers a visual (if not aural) spectacle potentially as valuable as genteel music-making.

The complexities of perspective exploited by Hogarth can be found in simplified form in later caricatures. Plate IX, an 1823 etching by William Heath in a four-plate series called 'The Arts', offers a vigorous reworking of Hogarth's print.[71] A wasp-waisted musician, his fiddle sticking visibly out of a bag, fights his way through to the stage door of a theatre through an improbable – but not impossible – assemblage of accumulated noisiness. To the traditional human sources of street din, ranging from street musicians to a post-boy, a milk maid, a sweep and (inevitably) a dustman, are added the animal contribution of a barking dog and braying ass. A more refined and delicate reformulation of similar ideas can be found in one of George Cruikshank's small but crowded full-page etchings for the *Comic Almanack* (fig. 31).[72] In another image

**31** George Cruikshank, 'St Cecilia's Day'

that both celebrates and derides urban din, Cruikshank memorialises St Cecilia's day with a panorama of street noise. Every available suspect has been rounded up into Cruikshank's crowd – from a bagpiper in full Scottish costume to a family of itinerant singers, to a military band and a child with a banjo. A dustman, left hand to mouth and bell in his right hand, thus adopting the pose so often used in the 'Cries of

London' and children's books of the previous decades, occupies the centre of the image framed by the structure of a Punch and Judy booth. Like Heath, Cruikshank has even managed to introduce a barking dog and braying ass into his image. Undoubtedly this image is primarily satirical of both the quality and extent of urban noise, which in this instance is produced by a ragged and even grotesque assemblage of talentless and socially liminal people. Caricaturists were quick to ridicule the ludicrous 'connoisseurship' which led by-standers to admire street musicians, as shown in the sketch by Seymour, mentioned earlier, *Low Musical Connisseurs*, depicting a grizzled dustman and a pie-man pausing on the street to listen to a band.[73] The pie-man comments 'Well if that ant so moveing [sic] I could stop all day' (fig. 25). They were equally derisive about the quality of street music itself, and often hostile to the itinerants, often of foreign origin, who performed it. Yet in many images, street noise was understood as an important contributory factor of the urban spectacle, and there was positive recognition of the contribution made by the dustman's cry and bell to a longing for urban variety and tradition even when the din he created was a major source of irritation or even threat. It is in these ambiguities between celebration and anxiety that middle-class understanding of the city is most succinctly revealed.

5

# Visual culture and the represented dustman, 1820–50: domestic dustmen and cultural challenge

## Courtship and the amorous dustman

The topic of courtship links together ideas about dustmen contained within the graphic record which concern the interconnectedness between ideas of social threat, dirt and 'lowness' on the one hand, and concepts of gender, sexuality and manliness on the other. The aggressively male sexuality of dustmen, while always implicit in their physical appearance and sometimes confrontational street presence as a workforce, to say nothing of their general tendency towards social aggression, was nonetheless considered important enough to require widespread and specific response within caricature and comic image-making. Furthermore, images of dustman courtship persistently foreground the inter-relatedness between the public working life of the dustman and his domestic and leisure activities. But in practice it is hard to keep the private life of dustmen entirely separate from perceptions of their wider street presence.

There is no doubt that the representation of amorous dustmen in the first half of the nineteenth century is at the same time more complex, more forgiving, and more troubled than the robust dismissiveness found in the ur-text for this debate – Rowlandson's brilliant 1788 engraving of cinder sifters called *Love and Dust*. Indeed, if you were looking for a means of charting the change in social attitudes and representational methods between the 1780s and the 1830s, depictions of vulgar sexuality would provide a good starting place. *Love and Dust* is an image which establishes a deep and unsettling connection between dirt and sexuality. It also suggests the appalled objectivity of the eighteenth-century caricaturist's gaze – a willingness to make repressed anxieties grotesquely physical and aesthetically compelling. Its underlying social message was a profoundly assured and untroubled dismissiveness of proletarian culture, of creatures so irrational, so depraved and contaminated by the way they live that they have sunk into irrational animality, and are driven solely by their baser instincts. For Rowlandson, and presumably his audience, such a denial of human attributes was nonetheless essentially a comic spectacle, a restatement, through the representation of the inverted other, of the value of the rational, the polite and the genteel. This key combination of attributes – poverty, animality, lust, the grotesque and social marginality – was largely either rejected or significantly modified by later caricaturists, but it remained as a powerful memory for the later caricaturists considered here.

The reasons for the increased complexity of later (1820 to 1850) images of lustful dustmen partly derive from the social and cultural issues already described. Like modern-day builders' labourers, Regency and early Victorian dustmen had a highly visible street presence. They also had the time to stop and stare and to engage passers-by in conversation. When this was combined with their social aggressiveness, their penchant for diversion, their lack of shyness, and the physicality of their job (which clearly did, if the caricature record is to be believed, make them extremely self-conscious about their bodies, both in terms of the need for strength and in terms of the need to avoid contaminating physical contact with others), then it was hardly surprising that dustmen were endowed with a reputation for predatory male public conduct. While such a reputation in itself may have been more likely to provoke disgust or laughter than lust among those women picked out for attention, it is also important to remember that dustmen were beginning to be regarded as people of some economic status by the 1830s. Despite the degraded nature of their work, by the early Victorian period dustmen might just have been, in material terms at least, something of a catch for a domestic servant or a labouring woman. Historical sources also stress that dustmen, like sweeps, maintained their franchise and trade as a family concern, and that the business was inherited on down through the family. A vignette from Henry Heath's *Caricaturist's Scrapbook*, however mocking its intention, shows a complacent dustman protectively guarded by one housemaid from a discomfited colleague above the caption 'PRIZE – a vessel captured from the enemy' (fig. 32).[1] Perhaps the prospect of a dustman suitor was not as much of a laughing matter as eighteenth-century caricaturists had believed, especially for precariously situated urban women with little choice of trades, let alone careers.

And if the financial status of dustmen was more ambiguous than it might seem at first glance, so perhaps was their physical appearance.

Prize – a Vessel taken from the Enemy.

**32** Henry Heath, 'PRIZE' *The Nautical Dictionary No. 4*

The discussion of the dress and appearance of dustmen in Chapter 4 should have dispelled the idea that dustmen were simply and unequivocally repulsive. Despite their refusal to dress as anything other than a dustman, even on ceremonial occasions, their clothes expressed a certain dandyesque turn, a self-consciousness and pride in their appearance which seems at odds with the necessities of their trade. Dustmen were endlessly mocked by the caricaturists for their physical appearance, be it because of their pitifully thin angularity and awkwardness of posture, their almost parodic brawny maleness, their distinctive, and often bizarre, silhouette, or their self-evident filthiness. Even when compared to other trades, or even beggars, dustmen were perceived as uniquely unattractive (fig. 33). But, as we have seen, these characteristics did not prevent many artists – within picturesque, documentary and caricature traditions alike – rendering at least some dustmen with dignity or even heroic masculinity.

The visual record emphasises a number of these complexities, and again it is probably most useful to assume that artists are drawing upon a repertoire of tropes, figures and ideas which express a wide range of sometimes contradictory perceptions of the urban labour force, especially when manifested in its most degraded and yet, paradoxically, most successful form of the dustman. Within caricature it is possible to identify a number of overlapping, perhaps even interconnecting, representational patterns. The first of these read amorous dustmen as essentially childish, regressing from their rugged street assertiveness into something approaching helplessness and pathos when confronted by a woman. They were essentially 'unmanned' by the shift from the streets to the parlour, and are reduced to feeble-minded, ludicrous acts of deference, self-abnegation and diffidence by their need for a woman to think well of them – a need that is seldom met. Several dustmen appear on their knees making their suit to amused housemaids and domestic servants. Sometimes the dustman's object of desire responds not just with laughter but with mockery – 'Lor Mister Snub. I'm a feard as how you wants to deceive me like! Why you ain't ever afeard o' me Miss sure?' is one response to a proposal made to an ample housemaid by a dustman with his Dutch courage still visible in his hand (Plate

**33** J. Phillips, *Four Friends*

X).[2] Another amorous dustman, ensconced on a tavern bench and surrounded by a group of female 'admirers', has so far lost his sense of male identity that he has taken off his hat (fig. 34).[3] The caption, one of series of ironic dictionary definitions, runs – 'Monopolize, v. to engross the whole of a commodity to one's self' – thus making clear that a dustman was a prosperous enough potential mate to attract the interest of available females, even if their primary motive may have the immediate rewards of the prostitute. Another dustman brought to his knees in front of a woman forms one of a range of tiny images in

**34**
'Monopolise' from an unidentified lexographical series

the lithographed caricature title page *Frontispiece to the Musical Books*, accompanied by the complex punning caption of 'Overture to Esther'.[4] In these instances, the failure to reconcile the male world of street, dust and masculinity with the domestic world of parlour, family and the feminine makes dustmen open to the contempt of caricaturists, who are quick to exploit the discrepancies between public and private which haunt many dustman courtships. If never reduced to the animalistic grotesque of *Love and Dust*, nonetheless many a Regency dustman, in caricature at least, is rendered both foolish and laughable through his amorous proclivities.

Yet, interestingly, many of these images of foolish love are overlaid by a curious sense of courtesy and manners in which diffidence might be read as a perverted form of gentility. In one image by Henry Heath, two dustmen offer their clothes to a brawny woman whose dress has been shredded in a street fight (fig. 18).[5] Even given the comic relocation of notions of gentility to street brawling here, there is something artless and charming about the dustmen's offer of their filthy work clothes to help such an obvious reprobate. Even more touching is a later *Punch* image which, implicitly evoking the often tender pairing of Dusty Bob and African Sal, shows two spooning lovers, a dustman and a cinder-sifter, swooning over coarsely drawn but affectionately meant Valentines at either side of an elaborate almanac image of St Valentine's day activities (fig. 16).[6] The dustman's affection is being fanned by somewhat coarsely directed puffs from a cupid's bellows, while his cinder-sifting partner, who has thrown down her sieve, has been pierced through by the arrow of love. Some of these caricatures seem to have drawn on the idea of inappropriate but often moving tenderness which can be found elsewhere in Victorian culture – I am thinking here of, for example, Dickens's Sir Leicester Dedlock in *Bleak House*, whose anachronistic chivalry is depicted as both utterly inappropriate for contemporary society and yet somehow heroic in its regard for a world which has been lost. Several images of amorous dustmen are shot through with a similar, if more comic, vision, of burly working men clinging to notions of chivalry, decorum and good manners within a brutalised world of street violence, refuse, licence, and predatory capitalistic entrepreneurship. These ambiguities between the brutal and the courtly have already been suggested by the complex relationship of Dusty Bob and African Sal, which was figured both as an animalistic transgressive manifestation of lust, fuelled by drink and sleazy sociability, and framed within discourses of racist abuse *and* as the product of a curious, even transgressive, tenderness in which 'true love' might overcome barriers of race, wealth and difference. Yet none of the Bob and Sal images can figure the protagonists in a domestic context – they remain in a transitory world of taverns and public spaces, forever excluded from the domestic by the taboo nature of their declared partnership, just as many of the later dustmen are mocked and excluded by the housemaids and indoor servants who form the object of their desire.

Some images of the dustman, however, did manage to figure him as a domestic creature, though admittedly a sometimes rather ludicrous one. Many of these images will be discussed in relation to ideas of popular progress, and these are fundamentally concerned with the projected assimilation of the plebeian into the genteel as part of a hegemonic middle-class enterprise. Startled by a 'world turned upside down' in which dustmen go to lectures, read avidly, organise ballet lessons for their daughters, and superintend their sons' piano lesson, these images, especially those drawn by the relatively genial Robert Seymour, nonetheless do manage to predicate a domestic 'other' for the street monster who haunts so many caricatures of this period. Similarly, images like *The March of Interlect* (fig. 20) suggest that, however difficult it might be to separate out working and family life, it was still possible to imagine a domestic, and domesticated, dustman. Indeed, one interesting aspect of dustman's dress, already discussed in a previous section, was the way in which his leisure clothes, even his 'Sunday best' was merely a dramatisation of his work garb. Thus, without losing his male trade identity, it was possible for a dustman to connect work with family and leisure. The dandified dustman could also be the domestic dustman. It is important to maintain this sense of dustmen as having a life beyond the streets. While the overwhelming number of caricatures and images position the dustman crucially on the streets and in the taverns of metropolitan experience, the possibility of the domestic is never entirely denied. If dustman courtship is primarily the efflorescence of street aggression, a public overflow of swaggering maleness, more threatening than tender, nonetheless the potential for tenderness is not absolutely withheld.

Against this range of images of amorous dustmen rendered through ideas of absurdity, tenderness and childishness there exist many images of their courtship rendered as an act of aggression, even violation, in which any courtliness or kindness of behaviour is undercut by naked self-interest or animalistic desire. In these images dustmen are the stuff of nightmares rather than fantasies of domestic or emotional fulfillment. They are dirty, threatening and grotesque, a throwback to concepts of the irredeemable eighteenth-century urban poor. One especially powerful version that refers directly back to eighteenth-century precedents comes from a single-plate caricature structured as a frieze of three couples and ironically called 'The Tender Passion' (fig. 35).[7] The central of the three couples depicted comprises a vigorously angular dustman holding out a fuming short pipe demonstratively in his right hand and with his left arm possessively round his partner's neck, and a full-breasted, ample and certainly not unwilling young servant. The dustman declares that 'it [the tender passion] plagues the poor as well as the rich', an idea certainly confirmed by the spooning dandified soldier and overdressed woman passionately courting over a cast-aside guitar on the left of the image. The aim of the print is of course to offer a vision of 'the tender passion' as nothing more than lust.

Lust certainly seems to have driven the dustmen figured in other single-plate caricatures drawn both in the traditional engraved manner and the new medium of lithography. In particular, they are often paired with, or impinge on, women with their aggressively virile street presence. The dustman portrayed by J. L. Marks in his *London Nuisances* series,

**35** 'Paul Pry' [William Heath] 'The Tender Passion'

in what is centrally an image concerned with street noise, nonetheless contaminates not just the ears but the entire decorous space of a fashionably dressed young woman (Plate VIII). In other images the relationships of dustmen with women are directly associated with violence. They fight not just *over* women; sometimes they fight *with* women, not always successfully if one particularly nasty image drawn by C. J. Grant is to be believed (fig. 28). Using these kinds of images, dustmen, even in their more personal relationships, conform to ideas of animality, aggression, violence and threat among the urban underclasses which we have seen elsewhere within the genteel discourses of caricature image-making. But the most profound threat to be rendered in terms of images of sexuality finds its outlet in a couple of startling images of contamination in which a young, clean, virginal bride is visually associated with a dustman characterised by everything that troubled early Victorians about their urban culture. The first of these is a lithographed plate, probably by J. L. Marks, in which a characteristically burly dustman, pipe in mouth and incongruously holding an umbrella, escorts his pretty young partner dressed in virginal white along the street. He meets a dustman colleague, who expresses surprise at his 'coming out' with such an incongruous beauty.[8] In a wonderfully comic reply the enamoured dustman makes it clear that he is fed up of being represented by caricaturists as comic and vulgar, and that he is off to Marks's shop to get a caricaturist to make a proper and admiring image of the lovers. While the self-referential joke is an interesting one that gives comic shape to the meeting, nonetheless this image remains a rather shocking representation of the innocent, the coy and the virginal at the mercy of the besmirched, smelly and deeply undesirable dustman. The central premise of this image is reformulated in a similar if even more anxious form in *Punch*, where another dustman, the worse for drink, shows off his trophy bride in a moment of public triumph.[9] The dustman is old, dirty, smelly and physically grotesque, and thus every parent's nightmare bridegroom, despite his traditionally rumoured wealth.

These two striking images are fundamentally images of violation and contamination, and they summarise the deepest anxieties expressed in relation to dustmen. Going way beyond long-standing tropes of mismatched couples, these images construct middle-class anxiety with an intensity that not even their comedy can conceal. They are extremely revealing expositions of the fears of a fluid, newly urban culture in which the 'hitherto mute and irrational' (to use Carlyle's term for the urban poor) were beginning to reveal their social ambitions and purposes.

But even these images of the threat of uncontrolled lust to social decorum and hierarchy, let alone to notions of female vulnerability, are decorous compared to a small image that appears in the first issue of the *Northern Looking Glass* in 1826.[10] This image represents the concluding moments of a caricature discourse drawn from eighteenth-century precedents in which society could be depicted through the use of grotesque stereotypes as utterly lustful, animalistic, untouched by decency or reason and in spell to a gender politics driven solely by male desire. The tiny image is called *The Last Woman* and shows a negress in the centre of the image under assault from lust-fuelled hordes of grotesquely dressed and physically repulsive representatives of various ranks and orders of society – a bishop, a cavalry officer, a gout-ridden squire, and on through the repertoire of caricature types. Almost inevitably, a crazed-looking dustman sporting a stiffly threatening fantail occupies the left-hand margin of the image. Such unconstrained acknowledgement of degraded human instinct becomes increasingly less obvious in the caricature of the early Victorian period, where the carnivalesque replaces the grotesque as the dominant mode, and where the appalled contemplation of basic human instinct is replaced by a middle-class reformist desire to manage, reform and assimilate the potentially damaging effects of proletarian animality. Such a process of managing social anxiety by recourse to the carnivalesque seems to me apparent in the range of images of dustman courtship assembled here – not just in those that relatively openly acknowledge the sexual threat of dustmen to vulnerable women often from a different class, but also in those images that seek to represent dustmen as to some extent still capable of honourable or genteel conduct. The issue at stake was whether even dustmen – archetypally a degraded, dirty, ignorant, aggressive and oppressively male sector of society – could be incorporated into world of manners and conduct defined as acceptable or manageable by middle-class ideas of social order. The range of differing and sometimes contradictory representational possibilities suggested by caricature images of courtship suggest how contested and fraught these kinds of debates within the middle classes had become, and how central the cathartic potential offered by the carnivalesque was to bourgeois sanity.

## Smoking

For dustmen, smoking was a necessary accompaniment to lounging, and even a cursory glance at the many images of lounging dustmen in this chapter and the next shows how often their spectating involved peaceful or wondering performances on a clay pipe. They smoke at even the most inappropriate moments – while courting, for example (fig. 35) – and were inextricably represented by their pipes, which became emblematic of their 'lowness', dirtiness and smelliness as well as their propensity for standing and staring. Metonymically, pipes represent the kind of complex of associations that is evident in all the graphic accounts of dustman paraphernalia, a complexity that regards dustmen as people as ease with themselves as well as a nuisance to others. Some of the most naturalistic and affectionate images of dustmen depended on their ability to lapse easily from work into a contemplative and relaxed leisure proximate to their street labour, and smoking metaphorically represents the importance of such a close and socially significant relationship between labour and lounging. The marvellously refined wood engraving from the *London Saturday Journal* discussed in more detail in Chapter 7 epitomises these graphic connections between smoking, leisure and the street presence of dustmen (fig. 47).

But if one substantial caricature narrative about smoking dustmen is constructed as part of a wider consideration of their role as spectators and street loungers, a second belongs more precisely to the interest of comic images in this period in ideas about class, and especially in the complex ways in which the imitation of genteel manners and enthusiasms by the lower orders lent themselves to satire. Such satire, of course cuts two ways – the exposure of the fads, fashions and foibles of the rich in all their ludicrousness is every bit as amenable to mockery as the pretence of the vulgar to the airs and graces of the wealthy. The depicted contrasts between genteel and vulgar smokers that involved dustmen suggest the variety of ways in which early Victorian caricature was beginning to manage the cross-class encounters that enabled artists and their audiences to think through the social implications of an increasingly hierarchic society in which class mobility nonetheless was beginning to become an important factor. Such images were built up as either as friezes of contrasting characters, as pavement encounters, or as street panoramas of crowds of pedestrians drawn from all levels of society. The classic frieze formulation is suggested by one element of a packed multi-image etching by George Cruikshank called *Tobacco Leaves* (fig. 22).[11] This vivid etching offers a comic overview of the inconsiderate habits of smokers – a dandified gentleman offering his 'distressed' sister a Havana cigar as solace, a caddish young blade blowing smoke over two passing and primly genteel girls, a fashionable lover punctuating his proposal to his beloved (herself smoking a cheroot) with lengthy pulls on a pipe while declaring that he loved her 'dearer than my pipe', and so on. But across the top of the image is a frieze of seven smokers ranging from the vulgar, the raffish and the downright low to the passably genteel, all gathered under the banner headline 'Men & "Gents" (who are really respectable) may now be seen Smoking in the Streets – even with bla'guard short clay pipes – a practice which was formerly only indulged in by Common Thieves,

Outcasts, Sweeps and Dustmen! "Put that in your pipe & smoke it."' Both a sweep's boy and a dustman figure among the smokers, with a contented, even beatific, rough-looking dustman placed, as usual, on the right-hand margin of the image. Cruikshank's point is a telling one – in the widespread decline of formal manners, the general run of society found itself adopting the everyday habits of those previously dismissed as low, vulgar and beyond the reach of any concepts of manners or socially acceptable behaviour. In the world-turned-upside-down of the new urban culture, manners may as easily be derived from below as from above, with the urban proletariat proving as influential as the gentry. The conflict between pleasure and gentility is frequently acted out in images of this kind in the comic art of the early Victorian period, many of which feature exactly the kind of dustman Cruikshank sketched so vividly in *Tobacco Leaves*.

The street encounters and panoramic street views which depicted smokers were centrally structured by two ideas – the general contamination of the atmosphere (to say nothing of good manners) caused by smoking, and the ludicrous ways in which fads and fashions infected the social structure, drawing not just the rich but all levels of society into absurd excesses of behaviour. Smoking thus provided an important example of the models of social structure increasingly adopted by caricature in the 1820s and the 1830s – while the separate social classes attempted to maintain their own individual and separate space, they were increasingly drawn together both by their spatial contiguity, especially on the streets, and by their growing mutual awareness of each other's habits and manners. *Puff, Puff, It Is An Age of Puffing*, a large single-plate caricature from 1827, at the height of the so called 'cigar mania', is an excellent example of this graphic model of social relationships.[12] The image shows a range of traditional caricature pedestrians promenading across the picture plane, – ludicrously overdressed women barely capable of carrying their massive hats and layered flounces; fashionable men with nipped-in waists and flared trousers; a genteel lawyer with briefs under his arm, skin-tight buckskin breeches and shoes as delicate as dancing pumps; a tradesman's boy; and, at the right-hand margin, a burly dustman with mutton-chop whiskers, the only character in the image to look directly at the artist or viewer. But as these people pursue their separate paths across the pavement that forms the picture plane, they are also drawn into the collective fug caused by the ostentatious clouds of smoke produced by the pipes and cigars that all the men are smoking – much to the discomfort of the women who are holding handkerchiefs to their streaming eyes. Here the habits of the fashionable rich, however exaggerated and excessive, are imitated (or even parodied) by the vulgar, thus causing a general social discomfort and pollution.

Similar images with similar sub-texts can be found elsewhere, in all the various modes of caricature image-making. An 1834 lithograph called *The Cigar Mania* forms the characteristically febrile centre-piece of an issue of C. J. Grant's caricature magazine *Everybody's Album* (fig. 36).[13]

**36**
C. J. Grant, 'The Cigar Mania' *Everybody's Album* No. 12

Here the variety of urban figures caught up in the enthusiasm for smoking on the streets reaches almost manic proportions – tradesmen's boys, coachmen, a town crier, a dandy, a dog's meat man, a crippled beggar are all united in their consumption of tobacco. They are represented through several of the tropes already seen in *Puff, Puff.* Women endure smoke blown into their faces, the quality of the cigars is debated (a sweep's boy holding a cigar on a pin inquires of a passer-by 'Is yourn Hawannah?'), and people request a light from each other. As usual, the dustman in this scene is found on the right-hand margin, dashing into the urban scene half-hidden by the image's margin, and, in his haste, stabbing his cigar into the eyes of a well-dressed, even dandified, passing Jew. His cigar is held in a holder, a touch of gentrification that renders his aggression even more spectacularly than his posture. In this image, Grant's unique eye for the grotesque and his preference for lithography and the low are nonetheless shaped by a conventional caricature ordering of the streets – separate comic groups or individuals are brought together into contiguity and contact caused by their common interest in fashionable or faddish excess.

Even the tiny banner wood engravings used by George Cruikshank in the *Comic Almanack* show similar structural patterns. An *Almanack* page from November 1840 devoted to 'London Smoke', for example, has a crudely drawn frieze of figures as its headpiece. Two well-dressed gentlemen emerge arm-in-arm from a cigar divan at its centre, a sweep's boy buys a smoke from a street cigar-seller puffing away on one of his stock, and even a ragged woman street trader on the right with a smoking bucket in her hand is drawing on a short clay pipe. At the left of the image a dustman, pipe in mouth, has stopped to buy a glass of gin from a seated woman, herself smoking vigorously. The accompanying poem equates the peculiar meteorological characteristics of a polluted London November with the contribution made to its misery by the accumulated smoke generated by the pipes and cigars of its inhabitants. The poem concludes:

> Smoke will have sway; a very dingy yoke
> It keeps us under, and 'tis time we broke it;
> Alas, we can't, and e'en our merry joke,
> Reader, we find, is nothing till you smoke it.
>
> Smoke and November, then, go hand in hand,
> Till time dismiss them thro' his 'chaos' gates;
> Time is a man of taste, he clears the land,
> And just like smoke itself – *he vapour hates.*

Smoking is here, as in the other caricatures discussed above, understood as a form of pollution contributed to by all levels of society, and a pollution that imagistically figured other forms of contagion and contamination to do with class, contiguity and urban proximity. In particular, smoking represented a male threat to the susceptibilities of women and health of women who were in any case more widely at risk from the aggressive street presence of men.

Against all this anxiety, one further image of dustmen and the tobacco habit offered an interestingly alternative version of the social structure of fads and fashions. One of Seymour's *Sketches*[14] called *Snuffing* is organised not at a street panorama of disparate types brought together by the accident of their physical proximity but rather as a densely packed circle of heads representing an extremely broad range of social types – a dandified courtier, a bewigged lawyer, an eccentrically caped figure with a walking stick, a young woman in décolletage. Despite their close proximity to each other in the tight grouping used by Seymour, none of the assembled snuff takers are looking at each other except for two bluff-looking dustmen on the right of the image, who are sharing a paper twist of snuff, the epitome of genial and freely offered exchange. The whole image is more genial and less obviously satirical than most of the caricatures in this chapter, and offers a kind of cosy inclusiveness as the outcome of a shared habit rather than exploiting the cross-class tensions that structure the images of the tobacco habit reproduced above.

## The dustman as consumer – eating, drinking and shopping

As with the images of such dustman activities as smoking and courting, the caricature representation of dustmen as consumers is rendered ambiguous by the contradictory artistic claims of documentary reportage and iconographical or metaphorical complexity. Such contradictions are immediately apparent in images of the eating and drinking habits of dustmen. Perhaps unexpectedly, dustmen are shown drinking tea or other non-alcoholic beverages nearly as often as they are shown drinking gin or beer. Less surprising, given that these depictions form rather gentle images of legitimate moments of refreshment and relaxation on the street, is the high level of apparent naturalism shown in them. Even in the highly emblematic images in *Real Life in London* that formed the cultural moment when dustmen emerged into prominent social scrutiny, a relatively naturalistic dustman can be found delineated in Drury Lane 'at five in the morning' taking a dish of tea at a street stall managed by a kindly looking, if short-sighted, matron (fig. 11). Surrounded by a characteristic assembly of early morning street people – a sweep's boy, a drayman, a hod-carrier and other building workers, two of whom are eyeing up a prostitute – the dustman is caught at a brief moment of pause in his work. The appearance of the two dandified young men, Tom and Bob, on their way home from a night of revelry (alluded to by the watchman in the background), does surprisingly little to interrupt this serene and picturesque street panorama. There are several other more or less picturesque images of street tea stalls, invariably presided over by elderly ladies, that included thirsty dustmen. One, by Egerton called 'Street Breakfast', assembles a line of rogues and ne'er-do-wells along the stall, with a dustman, drawn rather out of scale and isolated at the left of the image, attempting to light his clay pipe.[15] Another comparably tranquil image combines more or less the same elements – a group of passers-by pausing for refreshment and brought together at a stall run by a muffled-up woman accompanied by a yapping dog and a steaming tea urn.[16] Even when the picturesque naturalism of Egerton is replaced by William Heath's satirical energy, dustmen at tea stalls come across as more genteel than threatening – no. 3 of the *Scenes in London* shows a picky dustman pulling away from a tea stall while berating the stall-holder for her failure to provide lump sugar.[17] Similar images of gentle, mundane and peaceable street scenes depict dustmen eating at street stalls, although these are mainly drawn from the illustrated weekly papers of the 1840s., which were generally eager to suggest that London streets were essentially orderly and harmonious. A wonderfully naturalistic *Illustrated London News* image shows a raggedly heroic dustman at a pineapple stall (fig. 37).[18] The *Comic Almanack* has

**37** 'Dustman at a pineapple stall'

a Cruikshank etching of a dustman at an oyster stall standing quietly amidst a frenzy of surrounding street activity (fig. 38).[19] Even when the dustmen are shown with a pot of 'heavy wet' or porter in their hands on the streets, there are images that show them as peacefully refreshing themselves – though again these images come largely from picturesque or naturalistic representational traditions.[20]

Yet, of course, writers from Pierce Egan to Mayhew and caricaturists from Robert Cruikshank to C. J. Grant endlessly associated dustmen with drunkenness and with the sociability and violence that drinking creates. Egan created the low East End tavern as the natural habitat for Nasty Bob, and few later commentators disagreed, certainly not Mayhew, who insisted that his investigations only confirmed the closest of links between dustmen and their local pub. For Mayhew, love of alcoholic liquor was one of the defining characteristics of dustmen. Similarly, caricature dustmen turned up with monotonous frequency

AUGUST.

in various stages of often violent inebriation in bars, taverns and gin palaces. In the metaphorical codes of caricature dustmen were thus often represented as animalistic victims of their appetites and hedonistic desires, and therefore as drunks and gluttons. A number of these images have already been discussed in Chapters 2 and 3 as the product of the *Life in London* frenzy of the 1820s and 1830s. But there were plenty of later images of drunken and sottish dustmen. One of Bonner's wood-engraved vignette illustrations to George Smeeton's *Doings in London* shows a dustman looking very much at home in a gin shop among 'the wretched motley group' that haunted the establishment.[21] A tiny image from McClean's *Looking Glass* in 1830 forms a punning version 'City Intelligence', which shows a capering and obviously inebriated dustman announcing that 'Spirits is up' to a sprawling companion with a tankard who opines 'And beer fallen'.[22] A Robert Cruikshank wood engraving has a dustman in one of his favourite retreats, a noisy tavern, pouring the contents of a bottle of spirits down his throat with casual insouciance.[23] William Heath, a man with a ready eye for the grotesqueries of dustman behaviour, shows a completely drunk dustman, waving his fantail hat, being wheeled home by a scarcely more capable companion.[24] Never one to be charitable to the habits of the working classes, C. J. Grant has numerous images of drunk or drinking dustmen among his multi-image plates – three dustmen share out a jug of spirits in 'Division (short)' for example, one of many tiny images that made up Grant's travesty title page for *Arithmetical Terms*.[25] So permanently fixed has the idea of drunken dustmen become that when W. Henderson put together a collection of Victorian street ballads in the 1930s he inevitably illustrated two of his chosen songs about drinking with wood-engraved vignettes of dustmen, even though these were not the original illustrations to the texts.[26]

*opposite*
**38** George Cruikshank, 'August'

Of course it is possible that dustmen could have been both peaceable customers of street refreshment stalls by day and rowdy denizens of bars, dives and taverns by night – indeed, it is likely that this was often the case. But it is the dialogue between the literal and the figurative, the actual and the stereotypical, the banal and the exaggerated that gives these images much of their interest, investing the ordinary with a heavy freight of inherited iconographical meanings which were, at best, in problematic relationship to social realities. It seems highly probable that many dustmen, as urban working men who needed little education to do their job and who undertook hard and dirty physical work at relatively unsociable hours and in some isolation from convivial colleagues, would have turned to the attractions of taverns in their leisure hours, and that many of them would have been hardened drinkers. But it is equally probable that caricaturists would have wanted to exaggerate the degree of drunkenness among urban working men partly for comic effect but more substantially as part of the narrative of threat and danger which they constructed for their middle-class customers, who were always willing to have their perceptions of appetites of the lower orders confirmed. It is interesting that in the case of their eating and drinking habits, a more obviously naturalistic counter-narrative also exists within the graphic record which represented dustmen as peaceful, even contemplative, street figures, relaxing briefly from their labours for a moment of reflection. But of course these apparently naturalistic images were also to some extent the product of the representational tradition in which they were produced – in this case the urban picturesque. In the dialogue between the grotesque, the naturalistic and the picturesque which informed the making of images of the metropolis in the period between 1820 and 1840, not all the power lay with caricature.

The eating and drinking habits of dustmen, so vividly represented in caricature of this period, led inevitably to the somewhat troubling further recognition that dustmen were able to consume on a considerable scale – the world of pineapples and oysters (admittedly a food of the poorer classes in the period), beer and gin was open to them. Dustmen had evidently become significant consumers. Accordingly they were beginning to be represented as purchasers, pursuing their needs across previously taboo limits by entering genteel shops. One of Henry Heath's *Sketches in London* shows an uncharacteristically abashed dustman digging into his pocket for change in a tobacconist's shop presided over by an elderly matron. 'Give a penorth of bake missus' is his hesitant request.[27] Seymour's *Sketches* show a much less intimidated dustman, puffing on his pipe and looking decidedly disreputable, asking for a popular street ballad in a genteel stationer's shop, much to the consternation of the fashionably dressed shopkeeper, whose alarm is evident.[28] In this they were often depicted using the tropes of a 'world turned upside down', thus partaking in a trangressive travesty of genteel habits and activities. The wide range of images of dustmen shopping clearly advertised the class politics of early Victorian consumption by concentrating on images of irruption, transgression and social aggression with dustmen invading the genteel spaces of shop interiors in pursuit of vulgarised versions of available goods. Such images shaded into the even more important account of *cultural* consumption that will be examined in the next section of this chapter – the increasing association of dustmen with books, education, art works and music that linked them precisely to discourses about the politics of the 'march of intellect' and new conceptualisations of class mobility.

*opposite*
**39** Robert Cruikshank Frontispiece to W.T. Moncrieff *The March of Intellect*

## The cultured dustman – learning, reading and improving

It was the frequent appearances of the figure of the 'educated dustman' in the many caricatures of the march of intellect that first alerted me to the potential complexity of the representational history of dustmen. They appeared in the full range of images through which the march of intellect was formulated as an important subject for public discussion between 1820 and 1850: the intricate and complex

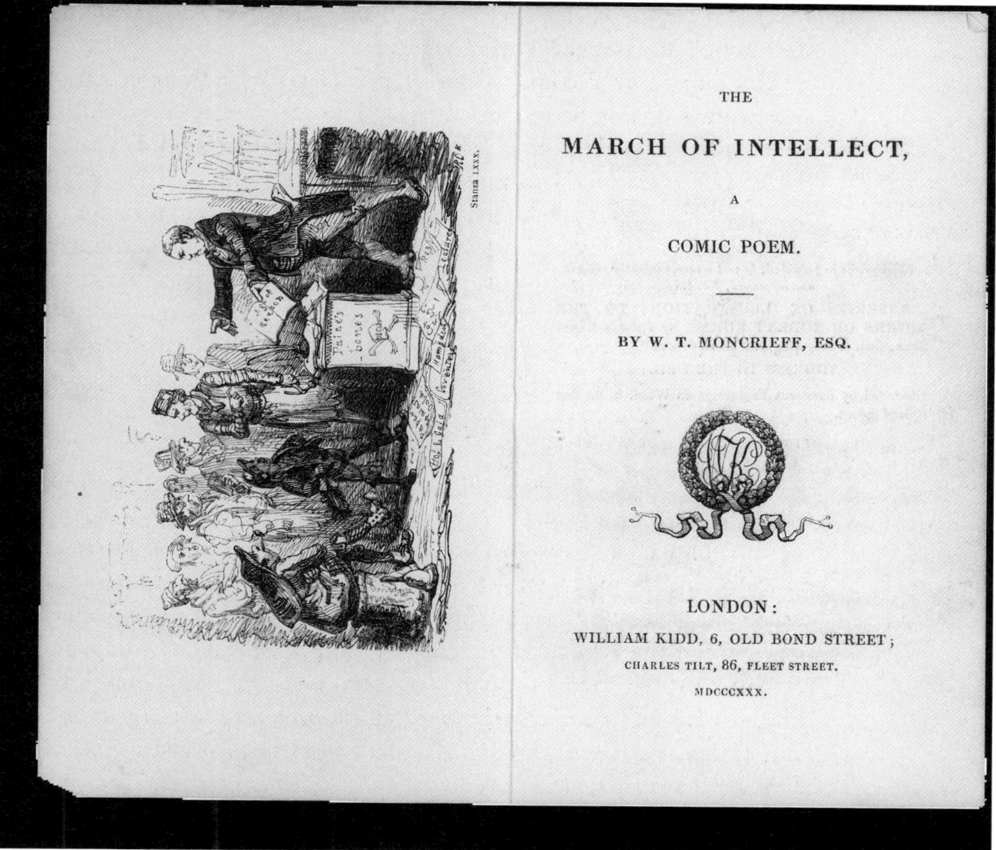

THE

MARCH OF INTELLECT,

A

COMIC POEM.

BY W. T. MONCRIEFF, ESQ.

LONDON:

WILLIAM KIDD, 6, OLD BOND STREET;

CHARLES TILT, 86, FLEET STREET.

MDCCCXXX.

etchings and engravings which showed the interconnections between 'progress' and social transformation;[29] the group of travestied title pages of the *Penny Magazine* and self-help journals scornfully produced by C. J. Grant and other caricaturists in the 1830s; the illustrated songs and ballads which followed Moncrieff's comic epic *The March of Intellect* in making popular education a topic of humorous interest (fig. 39);[30]

the many plates produced by jobbing caricaturists like Seymour and the Heaths, who were always willing to exploit any topic which had caught the print-buying public's fancy; and, perhaps unexpectedly, the considerable number of parodies of the Mulready envelope which had been introduced in 1840 to celebrate the cultural opportunity represented by the inauguration of the penny post.[31] I have already published two substantial discussions of the importance of these issues, both of which drew a range of the available images on this topic.[32] But it is perfectly possible to find a quite different set of caricatures on which to base the same discussion, and I have tried here to use caricatures which have not previously been discussed in any detail.

The central tactic of caricatures of the march of intellect is to interpellate figures drawn from the 'lowest' social classes into the cultural milieu, conversational exchanges and social activities of the nervously and newly genteel middle classes. At one level this is a classic exposition of 'the world turned upside down' described by Stallybrass and White, a comic and carnivalesque inversion of the normal social order in which hierarchy and status become confused. Such structures might be best thought of as tropes of irruption or invasion, with areas that had been recently established or colonised by the newly genteel bourgeoisie as 'cultural' spaces – such as coffee shops, reading rooms, public lectures, bookshops, music shops, the opera, the stock exchange, garden parties and the like – being increasingly invaded by the unwashed and frequently unlettered urban working classes. In the first ten years of its existence, *Punch*, in particular, made use of these ideas, with seemingly endless variations on the comic idea of dustmen discussing their stocks and shares or visits to the opera with people they had bumped into on the streets.[33] Some of the spaces into which dustmen were beginning to wander or march were feminised ones into which self-evidently masculine figures intruded, thus confirming the increasing aggression and invasiveness of newly aroused proletarian social and cultural ambition. The dustman who insisted that he 'vants a Cobbett' to read brought together in the minds of the print-buying public ideas which not only equated literacy with social unrest but underpinned both with a disconcerting image of brawny masculinity (fig. 40).[34]

But at another level these are not so much images of irruption and threat as satirical comment on the pretensions, follies and ambitions of a newly self-conscious middle class, uneasily aware of their limited grasp of how to behave at the opera or which financial speculations to support. It is this duality between continuing acknowledgement of the threat brought to middle-class serenity by the unwashed and a willingness to poke fun at just that new bourgeois sensibility that gives these images their particular power and complexity.

So the motifs, graphic refrains and figuration which caricaturists used to consider the irruption of the vernacular into the genteel as an aspect of the march of intellect used the coded shorthand of caricature to bring together multiple and diverse anxieties about social change, and dustmen formed a central protagonists in the representation of early Victorian social change. The extent to which such ideas had become codified and available across the range of representational modes can be gauged from the remarkable persistence of one comic idea – a proletarian figure, most often a dustman, waits in a coffee shop for a newspaper to become available while another proletarian seeker after information reads determinedly on. Caught between characteristic aggression and impatience on the one hand and a sense of the good manners required by his surroundings on the other, the dustman negotiates for a chance to read the news. In one of Seymour's widely reprinted and distributed *Sketches*, etched with characteristic delicacy, two dustmen, one distinctly



*opposite*
**40** A. Crowquill, 'Four Specimens of the Reading Public'

Jewish looking, resolved the issue with entirely genteel consideration – 'You shall have the paper directly, Sir, but really the debates are so very interesting', says one, to which his companion replies 'Oh pray don't hurry Sir, its only the scientific notices I care about'.[35] All this took place in 'The Byron Coffee House and Reading Room', clearly a cultural enclave less exclusive than its name might suggest. In the cruder, more simplified vulgar world of lithographed caricature the same idea was discussed in less refined terms. One of Tregear's *Flights of Humour* showed a dustman, in full working gear but with the addition of reading glasses, being approached by a rather desperate if genteel-looking drinker modelled perhaps on a Romantic poet fallen on hard times. 'I'll thank you for the *Times* after you sir' the man asks, but the dustman, proud possessor of the newspaper, replies that 'it is bespoke by the gentleman in black', pointing to a villainous figure with a filthy squashed hat and arms menacingly folded in impatience on his other side.[36] The 'lowness' of the tavern is rendered visible in the notice announcing that 'To prevent mistakes Pay on Delivery' and by the looming presence of a travestied pseudo-classical bust with a scowl on its face. A more genial version of precisely this incident, involving two affable dustmen and a sweep, appeared in a lithograph published by Hodgson.[37] Again it is the contrast between the punctilious pursuit of good manners and the 'low' status of the protagonists that initiates the humour of this image. This is the humour of inappropriateness – the unlikely presence of genteel codes of behaviour in a scenes already rendered full of social meaning by the irruption of the low into the traditional genteel world of cultural capital.

But, despite their mockery of an upside-down world in which dustmen vied with sweeps for a glimpse of the *Times* and the cultural anxiety implicit in such humour, it seems to me that these images are on the whole benign ones, humorously aware of the anomalies of social change. While sceptical about the likelihood of a cultural advance within the proletariat, especially among unskilled trades like sweeps and dustmen, nonetheless images like these seem to fantasise out the idea of the learned dustman as a welcome possibility, and, indeed, evidence of a truly progressive and civilised society. A similar geniality is evident in the several images of dustmen enjoying the processes of self-education in a domestic setting. The most famous of these, Henry Heath's 1828 etching of *The March of Intellect*, shows an absorbed dustman reading *An Introduction to the Pleasures of Science* in front of glowing fire, a glass of port before him on the table and a cheroot in hand (Plate XVI). In this image, the emblems of aristocratic leisure – the lemon and sugar for the port, the bust of Shakespeare on the mantelpiece, the monocle worn by the dustman, his flowered waistcoat and bright neckerchief – are rendered as pauperised travesties of the genteel, a poverty rendered visible in the bare cupboards, ragged cane-seated chair and a candle stuck in a bottle of the dustman's home. Yet, with its contented-looking dog and assembled luxuries, this is an image as much of true contentment as of mocking satire. The dustman here, in however lowly a form, even



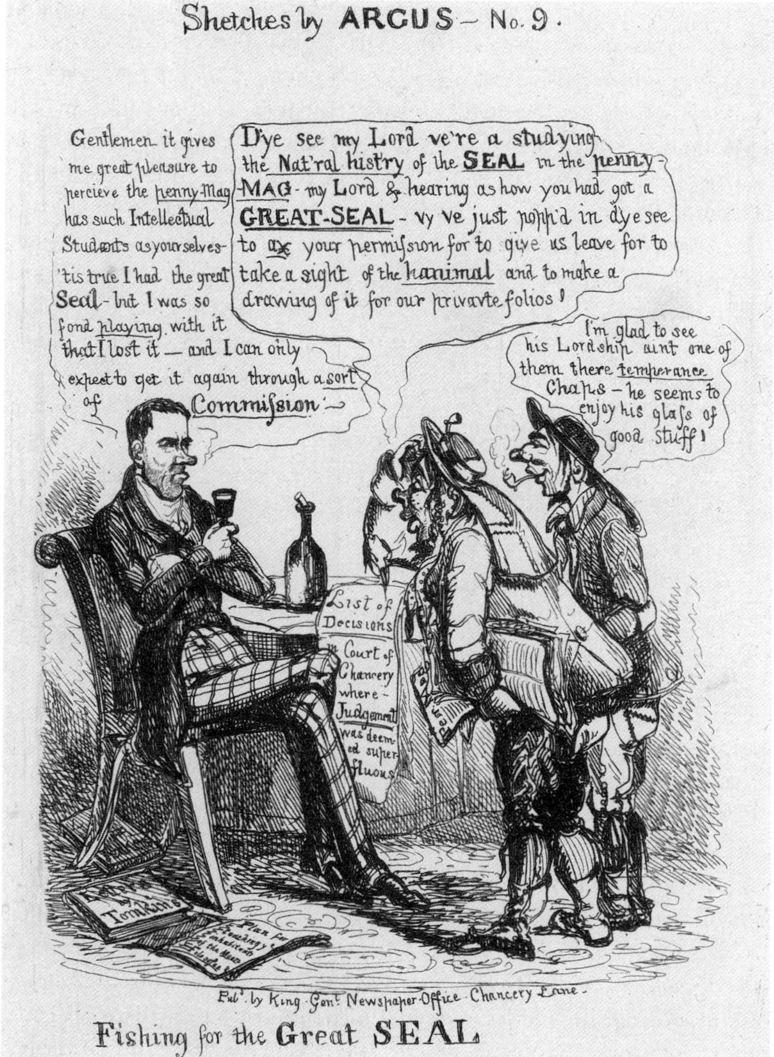


**41** 'Argos' 'Fishing for the Great Seal' King

suggests a certain heroic quality, a talismanic representative of the 'pursuit of knowledge under difficulties'.

Even more at home with the manifestations of cultured leisure is another Henry Heath dustman, this time inhabiting a lithograph from 1834 (Plate XI).[38] The crayony textures of lithography are here used to suggest the lush and rich textures of genteel social life – a crimson velvet curtain fills the left-hand edge of the image, while a Biedermeyer-style lamp and pedestal table are on the right, with the dustman seated in a Regency armchair reading in the centre. The dustman himself is depicted in a rich combination of textures and colours – his plush breeches, red head-band and gold watch chain are picked up in the red morocco binding of the book he is reading, a pair of glasses perched on the end of his nose. There is of course mockery here – no dustman was ever this genteel or socially acceptable. Yet this is also a powerfully realised vision of social possibility, with the dirtiest and most offensive of working men redeemed into respectability, peacefulness and, not least important, self-fulfilment. In Heath's lithograph, the *Penny Magazine* has done its work in rendering the working classes both civilised and contented. More mocking, but still on the side of the heroic potential for working-class cultural advance, is a woodcut image from one of Moncrieff's songbooks, which shows a dustman, at ease in a nouveau riche interior put together in obvious bad taste, supervising the music practice of his young son. This interesting image, reprinted by Louis James in *Print and the People*, which has been extensively discussed elsewhere,[39] both ridicules the dustman's intellectual and social pretensions and celebrates the social transformations being wrought by the march of intellect.

*opposite*
**42** Image from unknown source

As I've suggested here and elsewhere, those images which brought together 'educated' dustmen with that central icon of the march of intellect, the *Penny Magazine* provided some of the most profound and complex available commentary on the issue of popular education and class mobility. Characteristic evidence of the complex of meanings packed into relatively crudely drawn small images is a smallish anonymous etching called *Fishing for the Great Seal* (fig. 41).[40] In this caricature two dustmen, avid enthusiasts for the vision of learning offered to them by the *Penny Magazine*, have decided to visit Henry Brougham, the controversial Lord Chancellor who had also been the founding figure of that great Whig project, the Society for the Diffusion of Useful Knowledge, which published the *Penny Magazine*. One dustman, deferentially inclined towards Brougham and touching his forelock respectfully, explains their difficulty:

*I'm wery sorry Sir to be so werry troublesom, but this 'ere Novel is to cuting, it as such afect on our nurves, so I vonts you to change it for somthing more Mild, for I and my Sal can't stand it!*

Dusty Bob

> Dye see my Lord ve're a studying the Nat'ral history of the SEAL in the penny-Mag – my lord & hearing as how you had got a GREAT-SEAL – vy ve just popp'd in dye see to ax your permission for to give us leave for to take a sight of the hanimal and to make a drawing of it for our private folios.

The obvious joke here is the dustmen's ignorant confusion of Brougham's emblem of office – the Great Seal – with the relentlessly informative *Penny Magazine*'s account of natural history. But a range of other meanings inform this image as well. While the irruption of two archetypical dustmen – pipes, hats, breeches and all – into the Office

**43** Image from unknown source

*What shall I have the honor Gentlemen of selecting for your Evening studies.*

*Let's have any thing wot's short & not werry dry.*

of the Lord Chancellor satirises the dustmen's lack of understanding of traditional hierarchy as well as their disdain for notions of ceremony or appropriateness it also mocks Brougham for his political duplicity.

There are also many images of dustmen failing to cope with the demands of the march of intellect. One dustman, returning a book to a dandified bookseller, commented, tearfully, that 'I'm wery sorry Sir to be so werry troublesom, but this 'ere Novel is to cuting, it has such afect on our nurves. so I vonts you to change it for something more Mild for I and my Sal can't stand it' (fig. 42).[41] The dangers of an advanced sensibility produced by education could hardly have been more clearly suggested. Another aggrieved dustman, in seeking a book for his son, rejected works on travel ancient history and geography for the less demanding pleasures of a *Pickwick*.[42] A third dustman client in a bookshop accompanied by his similarly garbed little boy confronted the enquiry of a cadaverous proprietor, folios under each arm, – 'what shall I have the honour of selecting for your evening studies?' – with the disappointing response of 'Let's have any thing wot's short & not werry dry' (fig. 43).[43] Clearly, not all dustmen had mastered the demands of the march of intellect, nor were they likely to do so.

# 6

# Dust and the early Victorian urban imagination

## Introductory

This chapter and the next, 'Dust commodified and categorised', are centrally concerned with what happens when the potentially multivalent traditional readings of the represented figure of the dustman available in the picaresque, caricature and dramatic traditions of the 1820s and 1830s become overlaid or overburdened by Victorian moral and social perspectives, and, indeed, by nostalgia. These chapters thus look more widely at the ways in which the representational traditions of accounting for the cultural importance of dustmen inherited from the Regency period and described in the preceding three chapters become assimilated into and bent to the will of a variety of differing ideological projects in the writings and graphic images of the early and mid-Victorian periods.

In terms of their scope, these chapters bring together a range of written and graphic accounts of Victorian dustmen. In this chapter the focus is on comic songs, poems and ballads written early in the Victorian period and on the emergence of urban reportage in the late 1830s and 1840s. In these decades the extent of threat posed by dustmen in both social and socio-psychic terms was perceived to be on the wane as the result of both a considerable amount of legislation, described in Chapter 1, and wider efforts to establish urban order.

The first kind of writing considered here comprises comic verse and song, drawn largely from the annuals, song books and joke books presented by the likes of George Cruikshank, Thomas Hood and the *Punch* humourists. The social level of the audience for these songs is difficult to analyse from their form and content. While they are intentionally 'popular', the extent to which they penetrate artisan or working-class culture is open to question. Nearly all of these songs and verse were published before 1850. The second group of writings is drawn from those genres which together might be called 'urban sketches' – brief exploratory and investigative journalistic writings intended for newspapers and periodicals, in which a documentary purpose is offset against a need for vividness, impressionistic colour, and an awareness of an emerging journalistic tradition for writing about urban working people. This tradition drew on pre-existing ideas of the urban picturesque, with its heroic, celebratory vision of variety, idiosyncracy, and distinctiveness, but overlaid these picturesque ideas with a more analytical vision of urban deprivation and alienation. As early exercises in urban reportage, they draw upon new ideas about the nature of social observation (or even surveillance), but submit their urban gaze to some extent to traditional inherited assumptions about dustmen and their social significance. Thus this chapter suggests the beginnings of a shift from the comic to the serious as a mode of urban perception, with traditional meditations and dust and mortality giving way to more characteristically Victorian concerns with wealth, chance, waste and social mobility structured, in analytical terms, by the emergent methods and taxonomies of social investigation. If the songs and poems mainly look back to Regency tropes and motifs, by the 1840s journalists were beginning to embark on a new social project – a detailed and 'scientific' account of the urban proletariat. The next chapter looks in more detail at that account and some of its most celebrated practitioners.



## 'The Apollo Bell' and other obscure songs

Any account of the record of a particular trade, or indeed any other topic, within the popular song and broadside tradition is bound to be both partial and frustrating. The historical dialogue between oral and print culture means that the availability of evidence is always going to be dependent on accidental or erratic survival mechanisms. In particular, only texts which have made their way from the oral tradition into print are likely to have survived. Such texts as have survived are extremely difficult to date, especially when they are published in forms like the broadside, where anachronistic and often irrelevant images were often tacked on to pirated texts, themselves frequently the garbled survivors of older oral/printed versions. Collections of songs seldom give sources and only sporadically acknowledge authors or give tunes. Topical references can be added or deleted, so even references to specific historical events do not offer reliable evidence of date. In these circumstances is not unfair to assume that only songs which were either exceptionally popular, or exceptionally long lived, perhaps by means of association with the theatre or other more visible forms of cultural continuity, were likely to survive into print. The many song books and comic annuals which have survived tend to represent metropolitan tastes and are doubtless in thrall to ideas of respectability as well as popularity. Given the ephemerality and vulnerability to passing whims of fashion of much popular song it is obvious that the surviving record is really only an indication of how much has been lost.

The songs and broadside verses about dustmen studied here, then, are an unashamedly miscellaneous and unrepresentative sample of a vast unrecoverable resource. The volatility of this resource is quickly apparent. The way in which a favourite text might be carried around the varied contexts and discourses of popular culture, and thus achieve considerable visibility and longevity, is shown by 'The Literary Dustman', already discussed in relation both to the discussion of theatrical dustmen and to 'educated dustman' in the previous chapter. Contextually linked to the early 1830s by its references to Lord Brougham, the Society for the Diffusion of Useful Knowledge, and the *Penny Magazine*, 'The Literary Dustman' nonetheless re-appears in a songbook as late as 1854,[1] when much of its topicality must have been dissipated. Louis James reprints a version of the song which comes from one of W. T. Moncrieff's song books, suggesting that the verses had been incorporated into performances and play-texts somewhere in their journey through popular culture.[2] An extremely similar version appears on an undated Cambridge broadside.[3] The ready availability of this text in such diverse sources suggests considerable contemporary familiarity and affection for it, as does the inclusion of its title in a later comic song by W. T. Moncrieff which was entirely made up wittily strung-together titles of popular songs.[4] It is, nonetheless, extremely dangerous to assume too much significance for any single text, however visible in the printed record.

Visibility, in any case, is seldom straightforward in early Victorian popular culture. An article in *The Town* for 1838, for example, discusses the 'great celebrity of Professor Glindon's song' *The Apollo Bell*.[5] Despite its alleged celebrity, I have been unable to unearth a song with this title. The snippet of the text printed in *The Town*, however, *does* belong to a surviving text, a song more commonly known as *The Dustman's Brother*. The popularity of this text is suggested by its appearance on a Seven Dials broadside containing three texts gathered under the title of *Friendly Garland*. The Bodleian Library holds two copies of the *Friendly Garland* in different collections.[6] *The Town* characterises the song as one 'in which the acquirements of an accomplished dustman are described with graphic felicity, and done vast justice to, by the unimpeachable humour with which the Professor invests its execution. The discoveries referred to, in the song in question, would have immortalised a Newton and added freshness to his bays.' Yet the available texts suggest that the song is *not* actually about a dustman at all, but rather centres on a dustman's brother who, after various dubious ventures, ends up as a street seller of ballads. Nor have I found any evidence to link this song to a Professor Glindon, and presumably, beyond the Professor, to the early music hall or the popular theatre. Yet there does exist an American lithographed song cover called *The Literary Dustman* that claimed to be written and sung by Mr Glindon.[7] The text of the song is not available from this cover, so it is not clear which song has been given the totemic title of *The Literary Dustman* here. Again, such confusing evidence points to the ways in which a complex of related tunes, song texts and ballads form a meeting point for a range of allusions and references within contemporary popular culture.[8]

The above description of a comic recitative by (presumably) a spoof professor of music halls and burlesque shows suggests a song that, despite its Victorian date, draws on the traditional carnivalesque visions of a world turned upside down and, in a travesty of a settled social hierarchy, peopled by 'accomplished dustmen'. In several other songs and broadside verses from a similar date it is possible to see the familiar tropes and stereotypes of the late eighteenth-century dustman being recycled to satisfy conservative taste. Nowhere is this process more obvious than in an undated broadside held in the Bodleian Library and called, baldly enough, 'The Dustman':

What tho' a poor dustman, I cry thro' the street,
Great numbers in search too of dust do I meet,
Tho' fa[i]r[e]r their outside to you may appear,
Their inside is blacker than mine I much fear.

CHORUS
With my bell in my hand, and my hamper at my back,
I cry dust, dust O! and my whip it goes smack.

The clergy they read, they do preach, and they pray
You must mind what they do, not mind what they say,
'Tis the dust they can gain is what chiefly they mind,
They know they are mortal, so to dust are inclined.

The doctors of physic examine your case
Then sh[r]ug up their shoulders, put on a grave face,
You must tip them the dust, or no recipe
For deuce a prescription if there is no fee.

The lawyers in Westminster Hall do attend,
And browbeat each other for to gain an end,
They are like two lawyers, whate'er cause they try,
Pull up, or pull down, still the dust it will fly.

When dust-o I cry, ye maidens dust your rooms,
Get ready your mops, and handle your brooms,
And if any cobwebs about your heart dwell,
Ah I cleanse them away, and your insides dust well.

And now to conclude, my song here shall end,
And when I cry dust-o, believe me your friend,
Of dust we are all made, and to dust must return,
We are but living dust in this world's wide urn.[9]

At one level, this ballad is as crude a commodity text as can be imagined, merely a casually assembled sequence of motifs and tropes drawn miscellaneously from the common stock of the well-worn and popular ballad repertoire. But as so often with such unselfconscious collages of favourite bits and pieces, the overall effect, in the context of the previous discussions of the social history of the dustman, is more like a summary of stereotypical possibilities than a tired rehearsal of cliches.

For a start, the dustman is described here in his proto-*flâneur* role – out on the streets, bumping into people from all classes, – 'great numbers in search too of dust do I meet'. Not just meet, of course, but also analyse, so that the litany of traditional ballad versions of 'old corruption' (hypocritical, self-serving clergymen, greedy doctors and eagerly litigious lawyers) that follows is presented as a disaffected social vision rather than a picaresque spectacle. While hardly suggesting that the dustman spectator has anything original to say by way of political commentary, nonetheless he forms here an interesting and unusual addition to the socially marginal speakers of ballad social analysis. Traditionally accoutred with bell and hamper (I read the whip as referring metaphorically to satire rather than literally to an item of dustman equipment) the street presence of the dustman here is enlarged from pleasurable and amazed spectatorship into that of moral commentator – a clear step beyond the role ascribed to the watching dustman by caricature.

The unexpected connection made in the ballad between the dustman and the world of old corruption proves in fact not to be just his street presence or his random pavement collisions with the establishment. It is rather managed linguistically by means of a pun. 'Dust' on the one hand is the by-product or the unwanted effluent of a civilised society. But it is also the slang term for money, and it is this second meaning that links greed and corruption to rubbish. This verbal connection is made with some degree of wit, especially at the end of the fourth verse where spuriously contentious lawyers metaphorically 'make the dust fly' in their unnecessarily adversarial court arguments in order to ensure that 'dust' (that is, money) also flies into their pockets. These are puns which evoke the complex banter and linguistic energy of the dramatisations of *Life in London* and *Tom and Jerry* where many equivocations about the connections between muck and money, waste and wealth are structured with some punning intensity.

Then there is the dustman as a sexual adventurer, despoiling 'maiden' who are both servants and sexual ingenues. Using the conventional sexualised double meanings of ballad tropes, verse five is more explicit about dustmen as sexual predators than other forms of literature were permitted to be. In the cavalcade of foolishly amorous, hopefully courting and sexually threatening dustmen, often rendered foolish and 'unmanned' by their lust, that we have seen, it is interesting to find a text which is quite unequivocal in its description of predatory sexual activity as a form of 'dust'. Once again accommodated as a pun, this time between domestic chores and illicit sexual activity, 'dusting' here brings together more improbably matched social groups.

Finally, and somewhat feebly at the conclusion of the rich vein of punning and verbally derived social contiguities in the bulk of the song, dust serves its traditional Biblically derived metaphorical role as an emblem of mortality. On the whole the connection between Biblical dust and London waste is worked through, in literary terms, in more ambitious literary modes than commodity texts like broadside ballads or comic songs. Hood's ballad pastiche 'Death's Ramble', for example, escorts 'the dreary old King of Death' on his daily rounds, during the course of which he assists into death a broad range of people already tending in that direction through their own follies.[10] A characteristic combination of highly wrought puns, verbal play, grotesque invention and amused if caustic contempt for human folly, 'Death's Ramble' inevitably runs up against a dustman:

He met a dustman ringing a bell,
And he gave him a mortal thrust;
For himself, by law, since Adam's flaw,
Is contractor for all our dust.

It is hardly to be expected that Hood would miss out on a chance to use the punning possibilities of dust in such a poem. The connections between material waste and Biblical dust are, however, much more elaborately figured in the illustration to Hood's poem (fig. 44), in which a skeleton dustman, loosely draped in jacket and breeches, drags along a funereal skeleton horse while ringing his bell for his next customer. Grotesque enough as the image is without any added weight, nonetheless Hood completes the dustman's outfit with a basket rakishly set on his skull. This act of defamilarising a central element of the dustman's kit is extremely effective in subverting the geniality of the poem into something both more sinister and more profound. This little wood engraving may have been lurking in the minds of Dickens and his illustrator Marcus Stone when they came to draw up the title page for the part issue of *Our Mutual Friend*, as a strikingly similar figure appears in miniature in a right-hand panel. Certainly Eliza Cook, in her poem 'Dust', is quite clear of the metaphorical connection between dustmen and death:

DEATH'S RAMBLE.

"DUST O!"

ONE day the dreary old King of Death
Inclined for some sport with the carnal,
So he tied a pack of darts on his back,
And quietly stole from his charnel.

His head was bald of flesh and of hair,
His body was lean and lank,
His joints at each stir made a crack, and the cur
Took a gnaw, by the way, at his shank.

There's a famous old Dustman comes cleaning the way;
He gathers by night and he gathers by day;
He sorts the shroud-rags, he heaps grey bones,
And locks up his stores under marble stones:
When he comes for your ashes you know him full well,
For he carries a scythe instead of a bell:
His name – oh! Whisper it under your breath,
For 'tis he – the immortal, old scavenger, Death:[11]

In its way, Cook's 'Dust' is as genially disconcerting as Hood's ostensibly comic meditation on the same theme. Both manage to be more effective and serious that the Bodleian ballad, however, where the bathetic rhyme between 'return' and 'world's wide urn' disrupts the possibility of the ballad resolving itself into something approaching seriousness in the final couplet. Yet, despite this weak conclusion, the ballad has earlier made, quite wittily, the connection between dust/money and mortality – 'They [the clergy] know they are mortal, so to dust are inclined'. The double meaning is clear – clergymen are well aware of their own mortality because of the nature of their profession, but they are also no more than human themselves and thus are vulnerable to venality and greed.



For all its failings as a literary achievement, I think 'The Dustman' is a text which serves an important purpose in accommodating a variety of stereotypical notions about dustmen within the conventions (not to say the clichés) of street ballads and their audiences. Impossible as it is to date a text of this nature – published without even a publisher's or printer's mark, and paired with an anachronistic woodcut of the Grim Reaper dressed as an eighteenth-century gentleman – nonetheless it serves as further confirmation of the extent to which dustmen were constructed in the public consciousness through a series of stereotypical shorthand characteristics and tropes. In six brief verses, this ballad manages to exploit many of these by wrenching them verbally into alignment with a number of equally well established ballad refrains – the corruption of the professions, the sexual energy of the working man represented through a metonymic extension of his trade language, and the conventional invocation of the short span and vanity of human life.

*opposite*
**44** Thomas Hood wood-engraved illustration to 'Death's Ramble' from *Whims and Oddities*

Another song that reworks familiar stories in genial punning verse is *Polly Cox*, which is to be found among the many urban narratives in *The Universal Songster*, a three volume anthology of popular texts illustrated by woodcut vignettes drawn by the Cruikshank brothers George and Robert and published by S. Jones, the original publisher of *Life in London*.[12] The song describes a contest between a dustman and a coal-heaver for the affections of a young dealer in 'rags and phials' which inevitably results in violence:

To each other they'd not much to say,
As quarrels they were right for,
And so they pitched upon a day,
When Polly they would fight for.

The dustman he had got most length,
    And he bid his foe defiance;
But the coalheaver could boast of strength
    And a goodish bit of science.

It would have done your eye-sights good,
    If you the fight had *seed*, sirs,
The dustman nearly six feet stood,
    Though he was baker-kneed, sirs,
But coaly's fist was near the size
    Of a decent leg of mutton,
And when it caught the dustman's eyes,
    He owned he warn't no glutton.

So coaly proved the better stuff,
    And the dustman's pain was such, sirs,
He not only owned had *enough*,
    But a precious sight *too much*, sirs.
He fighting didn't like at all,
    As dows'd was both his glims, sirs,
He'd stand some gin, but as for Poll,
    She migh go to h-ll for him, sirs.

The dustman he felt nation sad,
    'Cause he had got such a wopping,
And the coalheaver ran off right glad
    And never thought of stopping.
He was thinking what his Poll would say
    To him, her fancy fighter,
When he found his Poll that very day,
    Had married a lamplighter.

This put him into such a funk,
    He ne'er his fate resisted,
He went and got most precious drunk,
    And for a soldier listed.
Ma'am Polly she was put to bed,
    About seven months too soon, sirs.
And the dustman he was transported
    'Cause he *found* a silver spoon, sirs.

As already noted, this song was published in the three volume *Universal Songster* which appeared in volume form in 1825, 1826 and 1828.[13] The appeal of the *Songster* seems to have rested on its ability to translate the well-established genre of the popular songbook or 'warbler', traditionally a down-market, pocket-sized anthology of sometimes suggestive and often vulgar lyrics drawn from the oral tradition, plays and theatrical burlesques, ballad-sheets and broadsides and established lyricists like Thomas Dibdin, into something attractive to middle-class bookbuyers. Apart from the enormous mass of material collected and indexed by categories in the *Songster*, there were a number of other factors which made the book appeal to relatively affluent consumers. First of these was the addition of elaborately designed title pages which located a number of images illustrating songs within a swirling emblematic design. These designs, which drew their inspiration from the famous title pages of *Life in London* and its imitations, and which became translated into the complex images used as part issue covers for the novelists of the 1840s, including Dickens, were etched rather than wood-engraved and linked the *Songster* with the picaresque fictions of urban adventure which characterised the popular literary successes of the 1820s. Secondly, the *Songster* was issued in parts, comprising 84 weekly numbers in all. Each sixteen-page gathering opened with a large wood-engraved vignette, giving the book the classic format of later penny-issue serial fiction, although the Cruikshanks's engravings, with their skilful adaptation of eighteenth-century caricature tropes to the new medium of wood engraving and the more genteel audiences of the 1820s, were considerably more sophisticated than most later comparable book illustration. Thirdly, the vignettes which opened every part of *The Universal Songster* were on a scale and of a quality which turned the book from an anthology of 'low' literature into something worthy of the library table.

*The Universal Songster*, then, seems to have been aimed at the kind of audience opened up by the various fictional adventures of Tom and Jerry, and which was beginning to savour the vicarious picaresque explorations of low-life London emerging in the literature of the 1820s – John Badcock's *The London Guide* (1818), George Smeeton's *Doings in London* (1828) and 'John Bee's' *A Living Picture of London* (1828), which was in fact also written by Badcock.

'Polly Cox' is a song, presumably drawn from some kind of theatrical source, which falls well within the remit of the *Songster*. Classified among the 'Comic' songs, it re-iterates the process by which low-life London is rendered comically accessible to the picaresque armchair adventurer. The *Songster* is full of monologues, patter songs, and recitations which construct a comic account of the habits, adventures and conversation of the metropolitan streets. Needless to say this is done through stereotypes, tropes and refrains drawn from eighteenth-century caricature, the popular theatre and comic journalism overlaid with a new sense of rapid change and consequent dislocation. 'Polly Cox' immediately associates its two protagonists, a dustman and a coal-heaver, with traditional comic tropes – as unwashed and comically ill-matched rivals for the hand of a street trader in rags and phials and as equally unmatched pugilistic rivals. The association of courtship and violence is of course one widely used by the caricaturists. The basic comic device is that of carnivalesque inversion – in a travesty of genteel courtship and rivalry, two equally brutalised and obstinate suitors (both sarcastically described as 'handsome') pursue an unworthy object of affection to the point of a vicious fight. The fight, despite occupying the site allocated to a genteel or honourable duel, travesties all notions of honour and gentility in its brutality and brevity. Although well matched in dirtiness, vulgarity and obstinacy, the two suitors make poor opponents in a fight. The dustman 'had got most length' (it is interesting that his exceptional height should be described as 'nearly six feet'), but was 'baker-kneed' – that is, bandy legged and buckled at the knees after the fashion of all the carrying trades. Such a body shape – the thin, attenuated profile with splayed lower legs – is readily recognisable from many caricature repetitions. His opponent, however, had 'strength', 'a goodish bit of science' and a 'fist … near the size of a decent leg of mutton', so his instant victory comes as no surprise. Less orthodox is the ending of the poem, not so much in the rag woman's rejection of both suitors but in the tidy disposal of the dustman, transported to the colonies as the thief of a silver spoon. Whatever their many faults described in the caricature record, very few dustmen are specifically depicted as criminals – one caricature shows a dustman as the thief of a joint of meat, but basically they are law-abiding within their own aggressively defined social space and confined to trade disputes rather than broader violence. While capable of social disorder and fond of localised affray, they are almost never shown as thieves, muggers or footpads. They may well assert their right to what they find in their dust, but, as penny capitalists, the caricaturists see this as their legitimate right. It may be that the song is merely rehearsing a traditional ending for a comic love song – the protagonists might as easily have been servants, footmen or knife grinders perhaps. What we have here may be often repeated tropes rather than any specific to the particular trades of the combatants. But nonetheless this is an unusual version of the dustman as petty criminal.



Most of the surviving songs about dustmen, then, elaborate one or other of the popular stereotypical views of their significance – their role as improbable protagonists in the march of intellect, their many failures as amorous adventurers, their 'nuisance' value as a source of noise and conflict, and their presence in the travesty spectacle of a world turned upside down. These are the conventional themes, as we have seen, of previous caricature and theatrical representations. But a few of the songs touch on the more complex social ambiguities represented by the dustman. The most interesting of these is 'The Contrast' (fig. 45), a poem accompanied by two wood-engraved vignettes which was published in the *New Comic Annual*,[14] one of the many small format collections of jokes, facetiae, puns and other comic bits and pieces published by the likes of Tilt, Willoughby and Lacey in the 1830s and 1840s and usually aimed at the gift book market. The 'contrast' named by title is between 'The Ball' and 'The Hop' – a formal society dance and an improvised dance in an East End gin shop. The first dance is undertaken by 'Lord Flashpan', an aristocrat ('one of the fooleries imported from the Tuilleries') dressed in black tights, high stiff collar and rigid frock coat, whose main characteristic is a propensity to tell endless stories of his Continental travels. The 'humble HOP', on the other hand, is being danced by a ponderous dustman 'in his Sunday clothes, / Nails in his heels as well as his toes', who enjoins his inevitable porter-drinking partner Sal to 'take a swig o'heavy wet, / Then, down the middle, change, and set'. The poem concludes:

> Though this is vulgar – that refined
> Contrasted like the human mind;
> If Cham-pagne sparkle at the one,
> At t'other flashes – real fun.

This seems to me a poem which, beyond the tropes of travesty, reversal and mockery through which the comic vision of the 1830s operates, shows a genuine acknowledgement of simple, spontaneous (if drink-generated) generous-hearted pleasure – in short, 'real fun'. The transgressive bourgeois fantasy of the 'real fun' to be found beyond the constraints of manners and conduct within low-life spontaneity has been a recurrent theme in the previous chapters, but here recurs in its most wistful terms. 'Sham (pain)' and 'real' need to be added to the binaries through which, in Adorno's words 'the refined are drawn to

## THE CONTRAST.

A VARIED contrariety,
Or contrary variety,
How oft we see, of fooleries
Imported from the Tuilleries.
Some Lord, such as our boroughs send us,
Oh! from such Lords the Lord defend us!
The mark of Cain stamped on his face,
(The marks of cane his back would grace,)
The antique antics which he carries
Bespeak him—just arrived from Paris.
Though, like the monkey, who his tail
Had lost, you'll find him with a tale
Long as a sailor's "long yarn" spinning,
And in the ball-room young hearts winning.
He'll swear, that on his hands and knees
He scrambled o'er the Pyrenees

THE BALL.

THE HOP.



Climbed Pompey's pillar; sat upon't;
And thrice swam o'er the Hellespont;
Peeped down *below*, all black and sooty,
At famed Vesuvius—like old Booty.
No sense, indeed, or stings of conscience,
Fall to his lot; but lots of nonsense.
Then will he vapour (although fighting
He owns he never took delight in)
Of hair-breadth dangers, and hair triggers,
And at A BALL Lord Flashpan figures.
But, for a moment, let us stop
To criticise the humble HOP;
Where, 'stead of her Port, Sal drinks Porter,
And John with malt and hops must court her;
A dustman in his Sunday clothes,
Nails in his heels as well as toes,
Cries, "Dang it, Sal! I think atween us
You beat the famous Med'cin Wenus;
Come, take a swig o' heavy wet,
Then, down the middle, change, and set."
Though this is vulgar—that refined—
Contrasted like the human mind;
If Cham-pagne sparkle at the one,
At t'other flashes—real fun.

the unrefined, whose coarseness deceptively promises what their own culture denies'.[15]

Several songs, including the recurrent 'Literary Dustman', which equated dustmen with social mobility and cultural advancement, in however travestied a form, have been discussed in Chapter 3. Most of these belong to the cluster of texts produced by William Thomas Thomas ('W. T. Moncrieff') as by-products of his many theatrical activities, and list the dustman among the trades of London which Thomas used as a never ending source of punning comedy. 'A Round of Topers?', for example, has the dustman situated, with Egan-like verbal play and energy, among the many tipsy trades –

> The *Tanner* we very well know *soaks his hide*,
> And *Blackstrap* in plenty's the *Shoemaker's pride* –
> The *Dustmen* gets *muddled*, till scarce he can stand,
> While the *Glazier* has daily his *glass in his hand*.[16]

*opposite* **45** Wood-engraved illustrations to 'The Contrast' drawn by W. Brown for *The New Comic Annual*

The allusions to *Life in London* and its linguistic adventure into the demotic are even more explicit in a song drawn from an Adelphi production of another of Moncrieff's farces:

> Slang the current language is, with gentry and nobility,
> Their mother tongue they patter it – the pedant's frown defy,
> The higher classes boast they're up, and young sprigs of nobility,
> Roses, pinks, and tulips, now are regularly fly;
> While Dusty Bob and Afric Sal don't stand upon gentility,
> But swear they're down, and leery coves with just the same facility:
> And as your Toms and Jerrys on their sprees, larks, rambles, pass his way,
> Old watchey swears that he's awake, and knows full well the time of day ...[17]

So the tradition of the urban picaresque – with its transgressive aristocratic low-life adventurers and comic but hearty low-life 'characters', all unified by the use of flash language – is re-animated in the decades after *Life in London* by the persistence of songs and recitations within the printed tradition but still easily available to oral occasion, declamation and sociable performance.

As we will see in a number of different genres of writing, however, Egan's urban picaresque begins to give way to a more socially radical bohemian boisterousness in the 1830s and 1840s. Robert Seymour's sequence of illustrated comic verses, 'The Pugilist's Progress', dating probably from the late 1820s or early 1830s, which reads like Hogarth re-written by Egan, and already discussed in the 'Fighting' section of the last chapter, is a late example of the novelist's influence.[18] The new tradition of comic urban surveillance is characteristically represented by the *Comic Almanack*, which began publication in 1835 and ran on until 1853. The first eight years of the *Almanack*, as already suggested, are teeming with dustmen. While many of these are associated with the re-ordering and re-presentation of traditional caricature tropes and formulations, especially to do with street noise,[19] at least one offers a comic verse narrative more allied to Hood's Victorian grotesque than Egan's breezy heartiness. In 'Manners Make The Man' the mock heroic levee ('That is, to Juggernaut, / Themselves beneath Aurora's car, / With Pagan zeal …') and breakfast ('Though Bob knew nought of Aeolus, / He learnt from all this internal fuss, / 'Twas time for breakfast now') of a 'horny' dustman are described with a jubilant appreciation of the pleasures of vulgarity. Presenting himself at a street stall in all his filthy splendour and asking for bread and cheese, he is fobbed off with an ancient stale bun (a 'musty, antiquated crust') which had become, on account of its antiquity, the residence of a mouse. 'The man of dirt', on starting to eat the bread, discovers its resident mouse, but, in a triumph of insouciance, merely comments 'There's some mistake in this, / I didn't ax you for a sandwich, Miss!' Together with a recognition that dustmen constitute a perpetual 'memento mori', this narrative belongs along with the verses from Hood, Cook and the Bodleian broadside cited above, to a newly charged Victorian comic tradition which brings together the humorous grotesque with something approaching genuine horror. The dustman in this tradition is less a threatening reminder of cultural otherness than a representative of common human frailty. A similar interest in the grotesque informs a 'Letter' in the *New Comic Annual* which purports to offer, in hopelessly ungrammatical and weirdly punctuated sentences and unrecognised puns, a pleasure-seeking trip from London to Gravesend undertaken by Robert Dust and his hapless family.[20] Mocked for his lack of education and worldly knowledge, taken advantage of by everyone he meets and hopelessly out of place both in the country and at the seaside, Robert Dust nonetheless emerges as a vulnerable and well-meaning father, forced by his misadventures to regard pleasure as 'Wanity and Wasting of Spirits'.

In the comic songs and narratives of the early Victorian period, then, dustmen become both emblems of mortality and a source of grotesque delight. Previously the butt of traditional satire derived from the caricature tradition or colourful participants in the urban spectacle surveyed by Pierce Egan and his contemporaries, dustmen, in the comic traditions developed in the 1830s and 1840s, become less funny and more disturbing. Indeed, it is no longer within the comic tradition that they are predominantly represented, as subsequent discussions will suggest.

## The emergence of documentary reportage in the 1830s and 1840s

Just as the history of comic journalism organises itself around the foundation of *Punch* in 1841, the emergence of mass-circulation illustrated news journalism is conveniently characterised by the launch of the *Illustrated London News* in 1842. It might well be assumed that by the 1840s dustmen would have begun to fade into the collective social memory, and thus would have outlived their newsworthiness, given the new social focus on the industrial towns of the north-west. Accordingly, it might seem that the rise of investigative journalism, with its determined focus on urban problems and the industrial system, came too late to include dustmen. Largely this is true – dustmen, while they lurk about in images published in weekly periodicals like the *Illustrated London News*, the *Illustrated Times* and the *Pictorial Times* on into the 1850s, become more and more background figures or metamorphose into the new generation of municipal street cleaners. Yet, as with *Punch*, their prolonged vestigial pictorial afterlife is important in marking their entry into collective nostalgia, a faded remnant of a carnivalesque, even transgressive, picturesque street culture that had been dispersed into a more purposive and managed urban order, an order in which hierarchy and difference is perpetually reasserted. There is some evidence that a few individuals clung on their affection for an urban vision based on a Regency childhood. A contributor to *Blackwood's Edinburgh Magazine* in 1849, for example, showed a sentimental attachment to his childhood reading of London 'Cries' with 'great staring woodcuts'. There he found:

> That dustman – how he rang his bell,
> And yawn'd, and bellow'd "dust below!"
> I knew the very fellow's yell
> When first I heard it years ago.

What fruits of toil, and tears, and trust,
Of cunning hands, and studious eyes,
Like Death, he daily sacks to dust,
(Here goes *my* mite) 'mid London Cries![21]

Thackeray is another for whom a Regency street culture, comic but never threatening, remained a point of reference. Beyond several celebrations of Pierce Egan in his autobiographical essays, Thackeray also produced an admittedly genteel and unmistakeably Victorian re-working of a children's alphabet in a deliberate pastiche of his childhood reading.[22] Andrew Tuer's *Old London Street Cries and the Cries of Today with Heaps of Quaint Cuts*, which appeared in 1885, suggests an even more long-lived attachment to Regency urban sights and sounds[23] as do the reprints of Regency texts and images by the likes of Charles Hindley which are widely cited in this book.

*opposite*
**46** Title page of *Franklin's Miscellany* 1: 4 (Saturday 6 June 1838)

Despite any such tendency towards nostalgia, however, there is a moment, just before the foundation of the *Illustrated London News*, when dustmen become something of a paradigm case for the new investigative journalists, who were looking to describe, categorise and celebrate urban 'characters'. A determined attempt to develop a 'scientific' taxonomy of the urban workforce was, of course, a major refrain in Victorian culture, and is examined a little more closely in the next section of this chapter. But in the few years before 1841 journalists were still caught between analysis and celebration, with the old idea of the streets as an urban spectacle only slowly being overlaid by the naturalistic and detailed modes of description required to inaugurate a better defined categorisation of the urban workforce. Increasingly, of course, categorisation was being linked to social theory and social practice. In order to give some sense of the emergence of the 'new' investigative journalism, this section of the book looks in some detail at illustrated leader articles from the front pages of three metropolitan broadsheet weekly journals, all published in the period when magazines were beginning to develop the characteristic modes of reportage and formats exploited and defined by the *Illustrated London News*.

The first of these dominates the miscellany of short items, ranging from a sentimental poem to a 'Method for Preparing A Liquor That Will Sink Into And Penetrate Marble', that forms the three-column title page of the short-lived *Franklin's Miscellany* (fig. 46).[24] Built round a wood-engraved and relatively naturalistic comic image of a street encounter between a sweep and a dustman, the article comprises a sparring and punning dialogue between the two tradesmen, a dialogue which, in

# FRANKLIN'S MISCELLANY

A CHEERFUL COMPANION FOR THE LOVERS OF SCIENCE AND LITERATURE, Natural History and Useful Information.

No. 4.—Vol. I.] SATURDAY, JANUARY 6, 1838. [PRICE THREE-HALFPENCE.

## THE FIRESIDE.

When the north blast roars,
And the chill rain pours,
And the damps spread far and wide,
Then the scene to please,
With the mind at ease,
Is John Bull's Fireside.

When the blithe-toned horn,
Salutes the morn,
And the huntsman leaves his bride,
Then the joys of home,
While the sportsmen roam,
Is John Bull's Fireside.

When the nights grow long,
And the cold grows strong,
And the ice floats with the tide,
Then the grateful view,
With the friend that's true,
Is John Bull's Fireside.

When the mist-fogs rise,
And the snow-storm lies,
And the hags of mischief ride,
Then the spot most dear,
And the soul to cheer,
Is John Bull's Fireside.

When the fiend-king howls,
And the wolf-dog prowls,
And the stars in darkness hide,
Then the coal's bright blaze,
And the smile to raise,
Is John Bull's Fireside.

When the sharp-tooth'd air,
Strips the trees all bare,
And bites both far and wide,
Then the heart-raised bliss,
Is the love-fraught kiss,
And John Bull's Fireside.

## ANDREW M'CANN, THE ABSENT MAN.

In the town of Ayr lived Andrew M'Cann,
A very worthy, but absent man:—
Andrew once called at a house in town,
And sent up his name—"Mister Peter Brown;"
Held an egg in his hand while his watch was boiling,
And oft was seen toiling
His weary way to the bridge of Ayr,
With one foot booted and one foot bare.

A very odd man was Andrew M'Cann;
And always before he went to rest,
As soon as undress'd,
He roll'd his small-clothes up like a ball,
Then taking his coat, with the greatest care,
He hung it over the back of a chair;
Then laid his head
On the pillow in bed.
One night he came home more absent than ever,
And, as you may suppose, "uncommonly clever;
So taking his garments (what a conceit!)
He tuck'd them up under blanket and sheet,
Then threw himself over the chair, like a sack,
*And broke his back.*

## PENN'S HAT.

George Fox, the founder of the Quakers, first discovered that 'the Lord forbade him to take off his hat to any man, high or low.' But further, as to hat-worship, William Penn, son of Vice-admiral Sir W. Penn, soon became tinctured with Quakerism, which caused frequent family feuds; and he was greatly persecuted in the reign of Charles II. At length, after being imprisoned, he went back to his father's house, where a long disputation took place on the subject of the son's creed. It broke up with this moderate and very loyal proposition on the part of the vice-admiral—that the young Quaker should consent to sit with his hat off in the presence of the King, the Duke of York, and the admiral himself! In return for which slight compliance, it was stipulated, that he should no longer be molested for any of his opinions or practices. The heroic convert, however, would listen to no terms of composition; and, after taking some days to consider of it, reported, that his conscience could not comport with any species of *hat-worship!* Penn was therefore again turned out of his father's house for his pains.

William Penn and another, on being tried at the Old Bailey, 1670, came into court covered, when one by took off their hats, but the court ordered an officer to put them on again. The recorder then asked if they did not know that it was a King's court? and why they did not pull off their hats? Penn replied, he knew it to be a court, and supposed it to be the King's, but did not think pulling off a hat showed any respect. Then the court fined him forty marks for contempt; whereupon he desired it might be observed that they came in with their hats off, and as the court ordered them to be put on, the bench ought to be fined and not him.—*Clarkson.*

Napoleon's Idea of what constitutes a good General.—Napoleon said one day, "that courage was not the first quality necessary in a general officer, particularly in one commanding an army." I did not, at first, seize the true sense of his proposition; but he afterwards developed his idea so clearly, that I comprehended it in all its bearings. "Why," said he, "has the soldier so high a respect for his commanding officer? Because he knows him to be a man of superior information. He follows him with confidence across deserts, over mountains, through countries unknown to himself, but with which he supposes his general acquainted. When courage is united with talent, then the general officer becomes an accomplished soldier. Still this courage must not be rash; it must not lead him to expose the lives of his men for the sake of mere fighting. People are sometimes surprised at the rapid promotion of a lieutenant-colonel, first raised to the rank of colonel, and, immediately after, to that of brigadier-general. It is because the newly-promoted colonel does not answer the expectations which were conceived of him. It is true, that he bravely leads on his regiments in action; but, like a hair-brained boy, to the mouth of the enemy's cannon, so that he returns from every action with one wound more, but with fifty men less. Now such a man is a bad colonel. He is a good soldier; but, as he cannot be put into the ranks, why he is made a general officer, and is very efficient under a commander who knows where to place him. And this is the kind of knowledge necessary to a war minister." Napoleon gave great extension to his idea, and, in illustration, mentioned several names, which it is needless here to repeat. He cited Kellerman (afterwards created Duke of Valmy) as combining talents with the most undaunted courage. Lannes was also mentioned as the most perfect model of an accomplished soldier. He afterwards named one of the most celebrated men in his army, and said, with a smile, "Well! this man has immense talent, and yet he dislikes gunpowder. But what matters that? So long as the soldiers under his command are ignorant of it, I prefer him to a knight errant riding in search of perilous adventures. But, on the other hand, the troops must not know that their general is a coward.—*Madame Junot.*

## A DIALOGUE

BETWEEN A SWEEP AND A DUSTMAN.

Sweep.—I considers that my perfession is a *soot*-able a vun as your'n.

Dustman.—Your vord vont *in-flue*-ence me to think that ere vile mine brings more o' *the dust.*

Sweep.—Arn't we always called *clargymen?*

Dustman.—And arn't ve *angels?* arn't ve *flying* dustmen?

Sweep.—Vel if you belongs to the *fly*, don't ve belong to the *flew?*

Dustman.—Don't ve *bear the bell*, vilst you always *gets the sack.*

Sweep.—Now checky! *who prig'd the spoon?*

Dustman.—Ve never thinks it vorth our vile to take such a *vooden von* as you, ve always leaves such like in the mess.

Sweep.—P'raps you'd jist like to *tast* a bit of my *fist.*

Dustman.—I'd rather not, I dusn't like a *hand of pork* vithout its vell *cured*; so *brush*, my *cure-osity in summer*, my *pet snow-ball.*

Sweep.—(Losing his temper.) Now stupid. Them 'ere neat ancles of yurn seems to be jealous of the close cov'aintance of your knees.

Dustman.—You stole that 'ere *sack* from a fellow clargyman! hean't that *sack-rilige?* Dust ho e! dust! (*exit.*)

Sweep.—S'veep! s'veep! (*exit.*)

Female Courage.—Dr. Warwick, in the course of a lecture which he lately delivered, in Worcester, related the following anecdote:—A common sewer, of considerable depth, having been opened at Noyon for the purpose of repair, four men passing by late in the evening unfortunately fell in, no precautions having been taken to prevent so probable an accident. It was almost midnight before their situation was known, and, besides the difficulty of procuring assistance at that unseasonable hour, every one present was intimidated from attempting to rescue these unfortunate creatures, who appeared already in a state of suffocation from the mephitic vapour. Fearless, or ignorant of danger, and irresistibly impelled by the cries of their wives and children, who surrounded the spot, Catherine Vassent, the daughter of a French peasant, insisted on being lowered without delay into the noxious opening; and, fastening a cord, with which she had furnished herself previous to her descent, round two of their bodies, she restored them to life and to their families; but in descending a second time her breath began to fail, and after effectually securing a cord to the body of the third man, she had sufficient presence of mind, though in a fainting condition, to fix the short end of the rope, which still remained, firmly to her own hair, which hung in long and luxuriant curls. Her neighbours, who felt no inclination to imitate her heroism, had willingly contributed such assistance as they could afford, compatible with safety; and on pulling up the third man's body, were equally surprised and concerned to see the almost lifeless body of Catherine suspended by her hair, and swinging on the same cord. Fresh air, with *eau de vie* soon restored this excellent girl; and I know not whether more to admire her generous fortitude, in a third time exploring that pestilential cavern, which had almost proved fatal to her, or to execute the dastardly cowardice of the bystanders, for not sharing with her the glorious danger. In consequence of the delay produced by her indisposition, the fourth man was drawn up a lifeless and irrecoverable corpse. Such conduct did not pass unnoticed; a procession of the corporation, and a solemn *Te Deum*, were celebrated on the occasion. Catherine received the public thanks of the Duke of Orleans, the Bishop of Noyen, and the town magistrates, together with a considerable pecuniary contribution, and a civic crown. To these were added the congratulations of her own heart, that inestimable reward of a benevolent mind.

Good and Evil Omens.—If a person have his measure taken for new clothes on a Sunday, he will be sorrowful and crying. If on a Monday, he will have ample food and provisions. If on a Tuesday, his clothes will be burnt. If on a Wednesday, he will enjoy happiness and tranquillity. If on a Thursday, it will be good and propitious. If on a Saturday, he will experience numerous troubles and misfortunes. If one put on a suit of new clothes on a Sunday, he will experience happiness and ease. If on a Monday, his clothes will tear. If on a Tuesday, even if he stand in water, his clothes will catch fire. If on a Wednesday, he will readily obtain a new suit. If on a Thursday, his dress will appear neat and elegant. If on a Friday, as long as the suit remains new, he will remain happy and delighted. If on a Saturday, he will be taken ill. If a person put on a suit of new clothes in the morning, he will become wealthy and fortunate. If at noon, it will appear elegant. If at about sunset, he will become wretched. If in the evening, he will continue ill. If a person bathe on a Sunday, he will experience affliction. If on a Monday, his property will increase. If on a Tuesday, he will labour under anxiety of mind. If on a Wednesday, he will increase in beauty. If on a Thursday, his property will increase. If on a Friday, all his sins will be forgiven him. If on a Saturday, all his ailments will be removed. For shaving, four days of the week are preferable to the rest, viz., Mondays, Wednesdays, Thursdays, and Fridays: the other three are evil and inauspicious.—*Musselmann's Code.*

## METHOD FOR PREPARING A LIQUOR THAT WILL SINK INTO AND PENETRATE MARBLE; SO THAT A PICTURE DRAWN ON ITS SURFACE, WILL APPEAR ALSO IN ITS INMOST PARTS.

Take of aqua-fortis and acqua-regia, two ounces of each; of sal-armoniac one ounce, of the best spirit of wine, two drachms; as much gold as may be had for four shillings and sixpence; of pure silver two drachms. These materials being provided, let the silver, when calcined, be put into a vial; and having poured upon it the two ounces of acqua-fortis, let it evaporate, and you will have a water, yielding first a blue, and afterwards a black colour: likewise, put the gold, when calcined, into a vial, and having poured the aqua-regia on it, set it by to evaporate; then pour the spirit of wine upon the sal-armoniac, leaving it also to evaporate; and you will have a golden coloured water, which will afford divers colours. And after this manner you may extract many tinctures of colours out of other metals; this done, you may, by means of these two waters, paint what picture you please upon white marble of the foster kind, renewing the figure every day for some time with some fresh superadded liquor; and you will find that the picture has penetrated the whole solidity of the stone, so that cutting it into as many parts as you will, it will always represent to you the same figure on both sides.

Mr. Bird, a stone-cutter at Oxford, practised this art before the year 1660; several pieces of marble so stained by him are to be seen in Oxford; several others being shown to King Charles II. soon after the restoration, they were broken in his presence, and found to correspond through the whole substance.

The American Locust.—No part of natural history more abounds in wonderful and extraordinary productions, than that portion of it embraced in the study of entomology. Whether we consider the number and variety of insects, or the curious changes they undergo in the progress of their existence, we are led to admire not only their elegant forms and beautiful colours, but also the harmony and order which attends all the operations of nature. Amongst this numerous class, none excites the wonder and admiration of man more than the cicada septendecem The regularity with which they return at the expiration of seventeen years, their simultaneous appearance over a vast extent of country, and the countless myriads of their numbers, equally arrest our attention. They have made their appearance at Marietta, Ohio, at three different periods, since its first settlement; viz., in the year 1795; again in 1812; and now in 1829. With us they have commenced their ascent from the earth the last of May and first days of June, and disappear the beginning of July, two or three days earlier or later according to the temperature of the season. They appeared only in situations which were covered with trees, thereby proving that they had not wandered far in each journey of seventeen years. The earth was perforated like a riddle, with holes about a third of an inch in diameter. In an orchard in this town, I counted twenty-five holes on a foot square; and an intelligent acquaintance told me that in his neighbourhood, he had seen more than double that number in the same space. Where trees were not near each other, the ground underneath them was covered with their skins or cast-off robes, to the depth of two or three inches. These shells retain the exact figure of the insect when it leaves the earth, with a rent on the back, through which the cicadæ creeps as from a coat of mail—and are firmly fastened by the feet to the bark and twigs of trees and bushes, until they are thrown down by the winds or rain. Instinct leading them to seek the nearest tree, bush, or post, as soon as they leave the earth; here they remain until they have left their shells for some hours, or until their wings are dry, and sufficiently strong for flying. A continual scream was kept up by the males during the day, but they were silent through the night. Their flight was short, seldom exceeding eight or ten rods, and their whole lives appeared to be spent near the place of their nativity. I could not discover that they made use of any food; they certainly eat no leaves of trees or plants, as they are not furnished with jaws or teeth. From their being unprovided with organs for eating, it would seem that their whole business during their short visit to the surface of the earth, is to propagate their species and to die. While here they served for food for all the carnivorous and insect-eating animals. Hogs eat them in preference to any other food; squirrels, birds, domestic fowls, &c., fattened on them. So much were they attracted by the cicadæ, that very few birds were seen around our gardens during their continuance, and our cherries, &c., remained unmolested. By the fourth or fifth day after their leaving the earth, the female began to deposit her eggs in the tender branches of most kinds of orchard and forest trees. She generally selected the wood of last year's growth, and commenced her task on the under side of the twig, by slitting the bark with her puncturing instrument, which embraced the properties both of a saw and a punch, the point being lancet-shaped and serrated, and then making a hole in an oblique direction to the pith of the branch, she withdrew the instrument a little way, and deposited an egg through a tube in the punch. This was repeated until from ten to twenty eggs were deposited on each side of the centre of the pith, the centre wood having been previously comminuted and cut up so as to make a soft bed for the eggs, and to afford food for the embryo until it hatched.

rehearsing a series of time-honoured puns on 'dust', 'flying dustmen' and 'clergymen', must have been reassuringly familiar to theatre-goers, caricature connoisseurs and consumers of popular literature.[25] As with the Bodleian broadside discussed above, this early Victorian text and image is an overwhelmingly familiar re-working of traditional material – an image borrowed from the caricature tradition but re-drawn as a crude wood engraving married to a comic dialogue which might have been acted out on any stage in England after 1821. The traditional rivalry between sweeps and dustmen, and the mechanics of how this is negotiated on the streets, is unselfconsciously relocated here from its origins in urban popular culture to the front page of a representative example of the new cheap mass-circulation weekly journals. The extent to which such images retain their currency, and hence their familiarity, may be gauged from the re-appearance of this vignette as an illustration to a Great Exhibition ballad called 'How's Your Poor Feet' published by W. S. Fortey at the Catnach Press in or after 1851.[26] The image is entirely inappropriate for this later sheet ballad, which recounts the doings of a young couple on the spree in London without any mention of dustmen or sweeps. Such a startling example of the de-contextualised re-use of stock wood-engraved blocks (on this occasion at least thirteen years after its original publication, suggest how widely images of dustmen wandered through popular culture, even reaching texts where they had no obvious reason to be present.

The other two texts to be discussed here, though similarly situated in prominent display form in the middle of title pages drawn from cheap weekly broadside magazines, are rather more challenging in their engagement with new modes of purposive documentary reportage. An illustrated lead article in a metropolitan twopenny weekly, the *London Saturday Journal*, published on 13 February 1841 and presumably written by James Grant, one of the co-editors of the magazine, is offered as number 7 in a series called 'Illustrations of Humanity'. Grant was one of the most prolific writers of urban sketches at this time.[27] His 1838 *Sketches in London* was the second in a popular trilogy of books, sandwiched between *The Great Metropolis* of 1836 and *Travels in Town* of 1839, but the only one of the three to be illustrated. Marriott summarises Grant's importance in bringing the traditional interests of Pierce Egan and Smeeton into alignment with a much more rigorous investigative method involving interviews as well as wide reading in periodical literature.[28] All of Grant's writing was informed by his Evangelicism, and his account of the 'lower classes' in the first volume of *The Great Metropolis* is shot through with both moral fervour and disgust.[29] While

Grant seemed not to have any particular interest in dustmen as a group in his more extended writings, two of Phiz's illustrations for *Sketches in London* show dustmen in entirely characteristic places – at the edge of images, turned across the picture plane, and in one instance absorbed in a lurid melodrama at a penny theatre and in the other surveying, in idle contentment, the crowds leaving the Court of Requests.[30]

'Illustrations of Humanity' is a title that seeks to reconcile an anthropological purpose with a redemptive, humanitarian one (fig. 47). The

THE
LONDON SATURDAY JOURNAL.

CONDUCTED BY JAMES GRANT, AUTHOR OF "RANDOM RECOLLECTIONS," "THE GREAT METROPOLIS," &c. AND FRANCIS ROSS, FORMERLY SOLE EDITOR OF THE JOURNAL.

No. 7. New Series.] SATURDAY, FEBRUARY 13, 1841. [Price Twopence.

CONTENTS.



LONDON DUSTMEN.

J. Rider, Printer,] [Bartholomew Close.
Vol. I. H

**47** Title page of the *London Saturday Journal* n.s. 1: 7 (Saturday 13 February 1841) implication is that careful attention to the lives of the urban working classes – begun as a documentary undertaking, also, through a recognition of the social value of the dirty trades – reconciles the observer to the essential humanity and worth of those engaged within them. The result is an uneasy combination of closely observed social detail, an overwrought and rather smug account of the dependence of middle-class comfort on the labour of the street trades, and a hearty, indeed sycophantic, account of the dustman as a loveable rogue. All this is held within a narrative of continuity and survival meant to give London readers a sense of their own urban history and of the ability of the city to withstand momentous civic change through the deployment of persistent, indeed unchanging human decency. While the socially disruptive potential of the dustman is acknowledged, it is carefully managed within a celebratory narrative of picturesque continuity. The dustman's face is marked 'with all that characteristic drollery, that peculiar aspect, a compound of grinning whimsicality and broad good-humour, for which the London dustmen are famed'.[31] However 'roguish' dustmen might be they are essentially good humoured, good natured, even, in their own way, genteel – Grant actually uses the word 'gentlemen' to describe dustmen, although making sure that the epithet is given an ironic twist by inverted commas. They are 'the genuine personification of London common life'. While he acknowledges in a deferential nod to the long traditions of stereotypical dustmen we have seen in the previous chapters, that they might 'moisten the day' and crack 'the broadest and drollest jokes', they are, Grant argues, basically as benevolent towards as they are essential to the London scene. By 1841, it seems, the somewhat menacing figure of the dustman as a belligerent, even threatening street presence, so familiar in caricature of the 1830s, has regressed back into an essentially picturesque and accommodated element of the metropolitan streetscape.

But if the main function of Grant's piece is a somewhat patronising demonstration of the amiable 'humanity' of the London dustman as an urban 'character', the article is also traversed by a number of other narratives. One is, embryonically at least, anthropological and morphological, and concerned with the establishing of urban 'types' through models of affinity and difference. In pursuit of distinctions, Grant uses an interestingly diverse vocabulary and set of conceptual frameworks. Initially arguing that 'labour' is 'divide[d] into ten thousand forms', which might be differently and more poetically described as the 'varied hues and colours of humanity', he then specifically uses the term class, arguing that society is comprised of a 'strange variety' of 'classes'. Taking up this definition, he then elaborates his model of difference. While still found on the street as picturesque presences, the Jewish old clothes dealer is out of place as an 'exotic' (surely a covertly racially abusive term) and the milkman as essentially a symptom of the countryside. But the dustman, perceived in a continuation of racially derived categories, is a 'real cockney aborigine', for whom London 'is theirs, "to have and to hold"'. Dustmen, however, share their origins as 'pure' and 'original' Londoners with other 'tribes', most notably coal-heavers. Grant elaborates this metaphor as both one of appearance and, more fancifully, one of 'function' with both 'tribes' involved in the continuity of coal, fires and ashes which bespeaks middle-class comfort. But dustmen, in an interesting and perhaps hardly conscious manoeuvre in Grant's argument, are, even more than coal-heavers (and, by implication, Jews) 'native, peculiar, and marked' and, even more than sweeps 'London's own natural children'. Within this swamp of anthropological, racial and social metaphor, Grant seems to want to argue that dustmen represent a version of the urban working classes that should be read as both heroic and iconic.

These meditations on who 'true' and 'pure' Londoners might be stimulates Grant to construct another narrative concerned with time, continuity and survival. This narrative is both particular and metaphorical. In surviving legislation against street noise which threatened the continued existence of their trade, Grant argues, dustmen demonstrated their essential and continuing role in maintaining the civic fabric of London. Metaphorically, he asks 'who shall extinguish our Dustmen … [with] their old immortal cry of "Dust Ho"?' Thus he situates dustmen within a clear history which regards them as both 'old' and 'immortal'. As the 'natural children of London', Grants insists, dustmen 'aborigines' predated the increasingly repressive metropolis and its civic legislation, and have continued to contribute their somewhat vulgar but nonetheless essential 'variety of humanity' to the urban fabric. This book has shown, of course, that such a narrative could only be an entirely fabricated historical fantasy, but it is interesting, and entirely characteristic of early Victorian arguments, that Grant should be so willing to attribute such an heroic and ancient role to a trade that the previous generation had both feared and to some extent despised.

But, Grant argues further, dustmen are not just 'old' but also 'immortal', somehow invulnerable to being turned into the 'dust' and 'ashes' which form the purpose of their trade, and thus not just immortal but rather 'immortals', the spirit of London personified. Drawing on the potent connections between dust as a commodity and dust as a metonym for human existence, Grant seeks to give weightiness and significance to dustmen as a 'natural' force, at once both human and commercial, which will direct the future success of the metropolis.

> Marvellous ashes! – these, the last remnant of all this wonderful combination of human labour, are calling into existence another race, and giving life and activity to other groups of humanity ... Who says there is such a thing as annihilation? Let him come to London, and take a lesson from our Dustmen. They will show him a cinder among their ashes which has escaped over the careless kitchen maid's sifter, and then they will tell him that a few more such cinders will not only bake, but buy their Sunday dinner. Annihilation, indeed! the trades of London discarded it, long before science disproved it!

Of course such overblown rhetoric is, on Grant's part, the product of sentimentality and nostalgia for an imagined pre-civic social order, but he has nonetheless mobilised a complex set of concepts and metaphors in trying to construct dustmen as the heroic and life-affirming representation of an anti-authoritarian, good natured and, above all, *continuous* London capable of human resistance to forces of change and misplaced authority.

The discussion of Grant's article has so far concentrated on its allusiveness and figurative energy, but it is important not to lose sight of the considerable documentary element in the piece. Even a casual glance at the large-scale wood engraving which dominates the title page of the *Journal* suggests how central reportage is to Grant's purpose. As a documentary image, this illustration stands comparison with anything shown elsewhere in this book, largely because it is relatively free of both caricature and the crudely heroic. For a wood engraving it is also surprisingly detailed and naturalistic in mode. The image has obviously been composed with an overtly informative purpose in mind – the three figures offer front, side and rear views of the dustman who collectively sit, stand and lounge. The dustmen are physically unexceptional. Neither grotesquely emaciated nor threateningly brawny they are nonetheless substantial and physically imposing. The potentially decadent lounger on the left is offset against the more purposive standing figure. The seated figure, while seated at ease and blowing out a large plume of smoke, nonetheless suggests the immediacy with which basket can be transformed into seat and back again. Indeed the text insists on one of the key themes seen over and again in representations of dustmen – the peculiar closeness of the relationship between work and leisure that characterises their trade. 'The shovel, the basket, the porter-pot, and the pipes, constitute the garnishing of the scene, and tell us that Dustmen can turn from work to play, and from play to work, with all the easy grace of the accomplished gentleman.' The totemic equipment is carefully deployed – basket (doubling as seat) and shovel from the work kit and porter pot and pipe from the leisure equipment. Where there are absences in the image, they are explained by the text. Bells have been subject to legislation, and their absence is fully analysed as part of the argument of the text. The article also defends the absence of horse and cart by insisting that its purpose is with the *human* and not with the animal. There is a large amount of both closely observed detail and wider stereotypical assumption in the article. The detailed description of dustman dress here has already been cited in the previous chapter,[32] and many of the other characteristics attributed to dustmen here are drawn from the common stock of knowledge and belief. Dustmen are humorous, easily distracted, jovial, roguish, fond of beer and tobacco. But here they are also good family men (they 'feed their wife and babies') who 'give life and activity to other groups of humanity'. Even as they are categorised as vulgar aboriginals, dustmen are, beyond all the ironies and rhetorical flourishes, here celebrated as the living embodiment of the commercial energy, social continuity and human resourcefulness represented by a mythicised London. As we shall see, not all early Victorian commentators were prepared to go this far, but most contemporaries of Grant were at least prepared to acknowledge that dustmen were more a topic for sociological and cultural analysis than a source of fear and loathing.

Given the history of *The Town* as a notorious magazine which courted scandal and controversy,[33] the front-page article on dustmen under the title of 'Characteristic Sketches – No. LXII' which was published on Saturday 4 August 1838, is surprisingly uncontroversial, even muted (fig. 48). The article, one of a series which had run throughout the life of the magazine, comprises three elements – a short unattributed poem, a wood-engraved vignette illustration confined within the central column of the three column format, and a prose commentary on the illustration. The context of this group of material in *The Town* is an interesting one for two reasons. The first is Gray's contention that *The Town* might be considered in significant ways to be the heir to Pierce Egan in its construction of the urban scene:

> the principal topic of the *Town* was an idea popular in the generation that was passing: the idea of the Town itself, the London of Pierce Egan's *Life in London* (1821), a metropolis of mostly night-time pleasures and a society of bucks and courtesans, gamblers, brothel-

"TO HOLD AS 'TWERE THE MIRROR UP TO NATURE, AND SHOW THE VERY AGE AND BODY OF THE TIME."—SHAKSPEARE.

No. 62.] LONDON, SATURDAY, AUGUST 4, 1838. [Price 2d.

## WE ARE OUT ON THE WATERS.

"How gloriously her gallant course she goes!
Her white wings flying—never from her foes;
She walks the waters like a thing of life,
And seems to dare the elements to strife."—*Byron's Corsair.*

We are out on the waters, and far from the land,
With the moon shining o'er us invitingly bland;
The breezes are blowing as fresh and as free
As ever they blew o'er a midsummer sea;
Whilst the murmuring waves, as they gallop along,
Seem pleas'd with the sailor-boy's nautical song,
Breaking forth from the shrouds, where, intent on his work,
He heeds not the dangers that under him lurk.

We are out on the waters, remote from the few
To whom we have bade (p'rhaps for ever) adieu;
And whilst from the heavens, so recently dark,
The stars appear watching our tight little barque,
We think of the friends we have left on the shore,
Whose kindness we feel, and whose charms we adore;
And though we are fearless of dangers to come,
The tears will break forth, whilst expression grows dumb.

We are out on the waters, and, like a proud swan,
Our spruce little vessel goes gallantly on,
Which, far from the rage of the eastern monsoon,
Courts the smile of the brilliant and vertical moon;
And whilst we are watching her beautiful traits,
And thinking our friends on her halo may gaze,
We glow with the thought that she'll soon light us back
To the eyes that are tracing our perilous track.

We are out on the waters, and, though far and wide,
No speck like an island or ship be descried,
There are spirits around us whose songs fill the breeze,
And find their bass tones in the murmuring seas:
O'er the shrouds, when the welkin looks dismal and drear,
Those spirits in Love's brightest sunshine appear;
And but for the hope which their presence inspires,
We ne'er should perform what our duty requires.

We are out on the waters, and, twinkling afar,
O'er the hills in the east, shines the bright morning star,
Whilst the moon, going down from the equinox line,
Seems pensive and pale as a nun at her shrine:
Not a whisper is heard—not a breath fills the sails—
And our progress, at last, much resembles the snail's;
Though Aurora is making her way through the clouds,
Where the hurricane wind in his panoply shrouds.

We are out on the waters—the heavens are bright,
For Morning has delug'd them over with light,
Whilst Neptune is laughing, delighted to see
The nautilus scudding much faster than we:
Were it not for the hearts that are yearning at home,
To what brighter sphere could a mariner roam,
Than that which is glist'ning before us, or where
Would his soul find a heaven more tranquil and fair?

We are out on the waters, and, though we are bent
Upon making a profit of so much per cent.,
We can gaze on the scenes that around us expand,
Without scarcely giving one thought to the land;
For what under heaven, for peace and repose,
Can vie with the prospects these waters disclose?
Strip the heart of its homely endearments, and here
You may find that Elysium the poets revere.

We are out on the waters, but nature still calls,
And our spirits, though link'd to these staunch wooden walls,
At the sound of her summons, look forth to the west,
And yield to those feelings that can't be suppress'd;
Ev'ry knot that we go, ev'ry distance we count,
Reduces our toils and our fears in amount;
And we spring from our hammocks enraptur'd to find
That our hopes are before and our perils behind.

We are out on the waters, but still there's a spot
'Neath the glowing horizon that can't be forgot;
As the needle's unerringly true to the pole,
So to that single spot is the mariner's soul;
There the children we love—there the wives we adore,
Are impatient to greet us, and hug us once more;
And brutes must we be could our hearts fail to yearn
For those who are waiting our wish'd-for return.

We are out on the waters, but, crown'd with a smile,
In the distance we trace the white cliffs of our isle,
Those bulwarks which fling back the waves of the sea
With the scorn and contempt that distinguish the free;
And, as we survey them our hearts fondly thrill
With emotions that nought but possession can still:
But, having embrac'd the fond forms we adore,
Those emotions are calm'd, and disturb us no more.

*Holloway Grove, July, 1838.* J. G.

## CHARACTERISTIC SKETCHES.—No LXII.

Hail! hero of the hat fantail,
Coeval with the first man;
When Adam sinn'd, his curse it was
That he should be a dustman.

Thy bell in hand proclaims thy trade,
And sharply does it tingle;
And when thou'rt dead a bell will tell
That dust and thee do mingle.

"Come, Mister *Town*, don't spin a yarn,
Let's try a drop of max, sir;
I knows you vont think worse of me
Because I'm bold to ax, sir.

"The march o' hintellect, you sees,
Wot Master Brougham guv us,
Has made us, sifted like our *breeze*,
Perlite to them above us."

The above sketch represents a familiar personage about town, especially to be met with in the morning portion of the day; his fantail hat, knock-knees, kickséy-casings, white gaiters, and bell, are alike worthy of notice. This class of the community are generally well-conducted men, and pride themselves not a little on their calling; they consider themselves as standing in class number two of the laborious and legitimate out-door cart community. They reckon the top-sawyers to be those employed by the large wholesale houses, in the city especially, and the draymen of opulent brewers. They deem the class scavengers, and those who perform night duty, infinitely below them

The collecting of dust, in former times, was a source of great profit to the principals, who then received a bonus for their duties, beyond the dust; but now they pay for the privilege of carrying it away. The mound of cinder-dust that so many persons must remember to have seen near the site of that frightful stacking of stone, King's Cross, was estimated, previous to its removal, as worth sixty thousand pounds. Many contractors, in those times especially, realised immense fortunes, and even now the business is by no means a bad one.

The dustmen of the present age are many of them intellectually-inclined people. The cheap literature, and their natural love of music, have softened their natures and polished their manners. The Mechanics' Institute and the lectures of Lord Brougham, Dr. Birkbeck, and other eminent philanthropists, have done much to benefit this class of men. The drama has been much patronised, time out of mind, by dustmen. The gallery of a theatre is scarcely a characteristic portion of the house without a sprinkle of the disciples of "Apollo Bell." Talking of the last-named personage, we cannot refrain from noticing the great celebrity of Professor Glindon's song of that name, in which the acquirements of an accomplished dustman are described with graphic felicity, and done vast justice to, by the unimpeachable humour with which the Professor invests its execution. The discoveries referred to, in the song in question, would have immortalized a Newton, and added freshness to his bays. It was left to the dustman of the nineteenth century to unfold secrets that had lain in the womb of night for ages. As an illustration, we have the following invaluable discovery:—

"The *Pilgrim's Progress*, writ by Boz,
And Bunyan's *Tristram Shandy*."

Those callings which custom has associated with the use of a bell, seem to have escaped the restrictions of legislative enactments. The act which denied to the poor slip-shod sweep the use of his tongue, as a notification of his "whereabout," left the dustman, the errand-cart man, and the cozey domestic-looking crumpet lad, the free use of their bells. We cannot account for this; for, in our estimation of a nuisance, the shrill piercing vibrations of the dustman's bell are a positive infliction, compared with the old-fashioned cry of the sweep, which often excited statutary impressions of sympathy on a bleak and wintry morn. The fraternity of dustmen, like the coal-porters, are strict observers of dress; both these classes sport a clean shirt and gaiters on a Monday morning, and, by a strange rule of taste, or the lack of it, the gaiters are usually lily-white. If a mate is discovered buttoned up near the throat, he is immediately investigated as to the condition of his linen; and, should he be detected cultivating a foul shirt, a gallon of porter is the penalty of his crime. There is no remission from this rule, which applies equally to the gaiters.

In conclusion, we must observe, that the calling of a dustman, which we have lyrically affirmed to have been the *first* profession, must necessarily, by the laws of nature, be the last; for the poet has truly said, in talking of the last enemy of man, Death, that—

"He is by law, since Adam's flaw,
*Contractor* for all our dust."

## DOCKS.—THE LONDON.

### THE CUSTOMS.

Before entering this magnificent and extensive establishment, you perceive a building to the left called the Customs. On entering and proceeding to the first floor, you will find on the left a door, on which is written "wet goods;" on entering which door you will perceive a great many little boys, with sample-baskets and bottles, crying out for their orders. At the further end of the office, you behold an infinite number of carmen's puppies, and a good sprinkle of brandy-faced gents, asking very calmly for their orders.

On the right your eye reposes upon an obliging little personage, who is screened from too close a contact with the vulgar, by a railway of small wooden balusters. This gentleman's name is Beeston; he is decidedly one of the most obliging persons in the office.

A gentleman advanced in life, and known in the establishment as Old Munro, delights in blowing up any poor devil who does not understand his business. His excitement lasts for a long time after the jobation, and is exhibited by divers mutterings and half-suppressed cursings.

Then we have Mr. Whiskered Allerton, who has a prevailing taste, during any disturbance, for suggesting a stand-up fight, as the best means to suppress it. In addressing a knot of people, he frequently says, "I'll have no noise here, nor stand any of your impudence. I'll take the best man of the lot, and settle it by a fight; but I won't have a thundering row here, I can tell you."

There is a gentleman in this department who sits in state, with a sort of demi-court dress on. His shirt-frill is illustrious from its whiteness and size. In the centre of it is embowered a shirt-pin, the size and colour of a raspberry tart. Our friend's name is Schilling, but he is by no means a *hog*. The duties of this gentleman consist in delivering out the exports, &c., and instructing those who are *green* at their business.

On looking round to the left of the aforesaid, you may perceive a *werry* nice-looking young man, of the name of Huntley, who is seated near to our illustrious friend Long Walker, who boasts of his intimacy with Miss Lock and Mrs. Bacon. The latter he enjoys at breakfast—the former he devours in the evening, in the Whitechapel-road, at her papa's lush-crib.

The last person we notice is Little Ryder. This gentleman is so unfortunately small, that, at a distance, his nob looks like a large inkstand sliding off the desk. Like all little men, he is fond of little things—such as wearing a sun-flower in his coat, and carrying a chaise umbrella in his hand.

We shall continue the subject in a future number.

keepers, sportsmen, policemen, pickpockets, confidence men, and cadging beggars.[34]



The immediate description in this article of the dustman as 'a personage about town' very precisely underlines Gray's argument. The second is a sense of a changed or changing audience for urban sketches in the first years of Victoria's reign, an audience beyond the concerned middle classes or traditionally genteel spectator. As Gray puts it, 'the primary audience was made up not of young and middle-aged gentlemen enjoying or remembering the pleasures of the town, but rather of apprentices, shop assistants, clerks and other young men of common station who were coming of age in the first Victorian decade of manifest political and social changes and chances to ride them to new social identities.'[35] But if, as Gray concludes, 'the *Town* is interesting because it tells us something about the London of pleasure and exciting risk in which these readers wanted to participate',[36] the account of dustmen offered here is surprisingly sedate and accommodating, stressing not so much a 'town' of illicit pleasure but rather one of working-class worthiness, deference and social advancement.

*opposite*
**48** Title page of *The Town* No. 62 (Saturday 4 August 1838)

Tellingly, *The Town* identifies dustmen as successful protagonists in the march of intellect:

> HAIL! Hero of the hat fantail,
> Coeval with the first man;
> When Adam sinn'd his curse it was
> That he should be a dustman.
>
> Thy bell in hand proclaims thy trade,
> And sharply does it tingle;
> And when thou-rt dead a bell will tell
> That dust and thee do mingle.
>
> 'Come, mister *Town*, don't spin a yarn,
> Let's try a drop of max, sir;
> I know you vont think worse of me
> Because I'm bold to ax, sir.
>
> 'The march o' intellect, you sees,
> Wot master Brougham gav us,
> Has made us, sifted like our *breeze*,
> Perlite to them above us.

This little poem provides an interesting counterpoint to previous ones – the equation of dust with ideas of mortality recalls both the Bodleian broadside and the *Franklin's Miscellany* dialogue cited above, and the notion of the dustman as 'coeval with the first man' sharply underlines the claims made in the *London Saturday Journal* that the dustman is the original, even the aboriginal, Londoner.[37] The almost habitual punning on trade terms, characteristic of much popular verse derived from Egan's Regency verbal inventiveness, survives here in the pun on 'breeze'. But otherwise the 'town' in this poem is startlingly Victorian. Peopled by deferential working men grateful for the reformist zeal of Whig social policy and conscious of their own mortality, the streets suggested in this poem are hardly specimens of the 'pleasure and exciting' risk that Gray ascribes to Nicholson's vision of London. The march of intellect described here is not a bitter battle between vulgarity and ignorance on the one hand and respectability or social advancement on the other but rather a triumphant progress towards social usefulness and conformity, with only the odd 'drop of max' to remind the reader of the dustman's traditional role in Egan's pre-Victorian urban picaresque.

Nor is there anything else in either image or text to contradict this account. Indeed, the article is largely dedicated to sober facts about dustmen – the details of their appearance (stressing the cleanliness and neatness of their dress as well as its uniformity), the financial organisation of the trade, the impact of street noise legislation, and their leisure pursuits (notably the theatre). These facts accumulate into a vision of 'well-conducted' men who 'pride themselves on their calling', 'many of them intellectually inclined people'. Thus the satirical narrative of the caricaturists of the previous two decades, which had mocked the appearance, social aspirations and intellectual pretensions of dustmen as part of a threatening world turned upside down, is here accepted not just as true but also as socially cohesive, even heroic. Dustmen are even accorded here the dignity of a 'calling' as if the dirty trades have been transformed by an early Victorian consciousness keenly aware of social necessity into an altruistic vocation rather than a vulgar trade. Even the wood-engraved vignette, unusually showing the dustman in apron and smock rather than thick overcoat, suggests a more feminised and countrified figure than usual. Despite the full-face pose and considerable physical presence this dustman is a quieter, more self-contained figure than many of his depicted contemporaries. Hemmed in by the narrow column and rounded arch of the vignette, not to mention the sketchy background railings, he fills an urban space without ever threatening to transgress beyond it.

This article in *The Town* suggests a further characteristically Victorian tendency. As we have seen, the leader in the *London Saturday Journal* on dustmen began to suggest an interest in comparison and categorisation in its account of London trades. Such a tendency becomes more pronounced in *The Town*. Dustmen, the article asserts, position themselves continually 'as standing in class number two of the laborious and legitimate out-door cart community', second only to the 'draymen of opulent brewers'. Their contempt for scavengers is also emphasised. A later discussion of the impact of street noise legislation forms the basis for further categorisation of the variety of street trades – sweeps were silenced while the errand cart man, the crumpet man and the dustmen (surely the aristocrats of this ill-matched assembly. Like coal-porters, dustmen, the article insists, supported a strict dress code which was enforced by peer pressure. Here, then, is the beginning of a Mayhew-like social structure in which dustmen, who are all at once 'proud', 'laborious', 'legitimate', 'intellectually inclined' and 'well conducted', emerge as perfect examples of a labour aristocracy. Even the old urban myths about the wealth of dustmen is turned to their advantage – in acknowledging that the trade no longer was 'a source of great profit to the principles' that it had once been, nonetheless 'even now the business is by no means a bad one'. Their fabled idleness had turned into laborious legitimacy. The aggressively profiteering dustmen of Regency caricature have metamorphosed into useful, productive and modestly successful tradespeople, representatives of a new polite civic order. In the emerging Victorian sociology of urban types, dustmen had left their violent and threatening past behind them and were rapidly being assimilated into the progressive and productive fabric of a post-picaresque metropolis.

As already suggested, despite the increasing incorporation of London dustmen into civic employment with an accompanying loss of their distinctive street identity and social threat in the 1840s, they enjoyed a cultural afterlife in such places as *Punch* and the *Comic Almanack*. They also appear sporadically in the new illustrated weeklies as part of the drive towards documentary reportage. Some of these appearances merely transpose old caricature formulations into a more documentary mode. The *Illustrated London News* and the other weekly illustrated papers occasionally depict dustmen in the traditional street locales beloved by caricaturists but replacing the satirical mode with the observational. The dustman at a pineapple stall, already described in Chapter 4, for example, takes the old joke about the ignorant and unmannered dustman gate-crashing the genteel world of luxurious consumerism and but renders his presence with documentary accuracy, accompanied by an informative and unironic text.[38] If, by and large, dustmen have been incorporated without conflict into the urban landscape of documentary reportage by 1850, they are nonetheless becoming of increasing interest to the social analysts and theorists of the Victorian city. It is this shift of focus that forms the central concern of the next chapter.

7

# Dust commodified and categorised: Mayhew, Dickens and the investigative impulse, 1840–1900

## Mid-Victorian dustmen and social theory

James Grant's 1838 *Sketches in London* has already been mentioned as a clear example of a text where journalistic excitement and subjective observation were beginning to be overlaid by more formal investigative methods such as individual interviews and statistics. Grant lays considerable stress on the authenticity of his descriptions as 'the results of a very extensive intercourse on the part of the Author, with the inhabitants of this modern Babylon, and of an intimate acquaintance with many of its most interesting institutions'.[1] In attempting to bring together the intense personal experience of urban life found in Egan with the more sober accumulation of fact to be found in Smeeton's work, Grant prefigures some of the characteristics and, indeed, some of the tensions to be found in the descriptions of the urban poor which dominate mid-Victorian literature. This chapter will look at a range of urban writing which specifically focuses on dustmen – the journalistic account of waste and dust in *Household Words*, Mayhew's *London Labour and the London Poor* and James Greenwood's illustrated account of *Mr Dodd's Dustyard.* It will conclude with late Victorian journalistic pieces, the first from James Burnley's *The Romance of Modern Industry* from 1889 and the second from the illustrated temperance journal *The British Workman.*

From its first 1850 volume on, *Household Words* showed a consistent interest in dust and waste. Apart from R. H. Horne's celebrated 'Dust; or Ugliness Redeemed' in the first volume in 1850, there are four other articles which consider waste and dust.[2] The central concern of these articles, apart from broad discussions of public health issues, was to show 'how art and science have been brought to bear upon things thought worthless'.[3] *All The Year Round* was similarly preoccupied.[4] Such new and sustained interest in the reclamation and transformation of waste, as well as in the precise scientific description and analysis of dust, were entirely characteristic of the mid-Victorian period.[5] The central importance of Horne's article, however, lies in his clear shift of attention away from the repeated depictions of the street collectors of dust familiar from the caricaturists of the previous three decades. His focus was instead on the dust yard and its varied denizens and activities. It was the contractors and the sifters who interested Horne, just as they were to interest Dickens a decade later. To some extent this changed focus was away from the dustman as a male proletarian street character to the dustman as successful entrepreneur, whose work-force, now perceived largely as sifters and sorters rather than collectors, were increasingly rendered as an oppressed and socially marginalised female group. Horne's view of dust was fundamentally economic, and he accepted the heroic and startling narrative of the transformative commodification of dust mediated through the sifting and redeployment processes that take place in the dustyard. Much of his article comprises interpolated statistics and lists, including an exhaustive (and by this time entirely traditional) categorisation of the varieties of dust to be found in a heap.[6] But, like the mid-Victorian 'social problem' novelists, Horne was also deeply concerned at the human implications of this economic miracle, at the poverty which sustained and characterised the wealth to be found in dust, and, especially, at the degradation and squalor endured by the sifters in the course of their work and the effects that such deprivation had on the moral and emotional life of the sifters. It is this concern that determines his subtitle 'Ugliness Redeemed', a phrase that, in seeking to make a connection between the trade in dust and the idea of redemption, prefigured one of the central concerns of *Our Mutual Friend*.

Horne's article is an extraordinary combination of statistics, anecdote, popular mythology and fiction. It centres on three individuated sifters: a one-legged 83-year old-woman, Peg Dotting, a bent 97-year-old man called Gaffer Doubleyear (the soubriquet of 'gaffer' of course resonating with Gaffer Hexham in *Our Mutual Friend*) and a 'poor deformed lad' called Jem Clinker, who collected cat skins from the 'very large and very valuable' 'dusky mountain' of a suburban dust heap. With their advanced age – Horne calls Peg Dotting and Gaffer Doubleyear 'patriarchal labourers' – emblematic names, and the dramatised melodrama of their workplace, Horne turns his dust sifters into something approaching Hardyesque 'Ancients'.[7] A distressed gentleman – 'a scholar, a man of wit, of high sentiment, of refinement' – whose documentary claim on his property has been lost, walks solemnly past on the canal path that skirts the dustheap, very much in the manner that presages a suicide attempt.[8] However, the suicide is postponed to allow the author both to offer his readers detailed information about dust and to let the three named sifters tell stories in turn about the semi-magical allure of the dustheap – Doubleyear recounts a visionary moment when he saw the sun dropping a bit of itself on the heap as a kind of blessing, Dotting tells of finding at night a 'shining star' with 'a soft blue mist' round it which turned into a 'red shell of a lobsky's head' on reaching her home, and Clinker, after musing on his time as a sweep's boy, describes a Blakean vision of an angel, glimpsed momentarily on the dust heap, and figuring in his mind all the available treasure hidden in the heap.[9]

These metaphorical glimpses of the redemptive treasures available, if only fleetingly, in the dust heap are given substance in the narrative (after a lengthy digression on soot) by the quick-eyed discovery by Jem of a gold-mounted miniature and some half-destroyed documents. Before deciding what to do with this 'real' treasure, the sifters are diverted by the sight of a 'drownded man' floating by in the canal. At considerable risk, the grotesque trio pull the 'corpse' ashore, and, drawing on dustheap lore which stated that cats and kittens shallow buried in the dust often came to life, dig a trench and cover the body with ashes. As Dotting puts it, 'he'll lie very comfortable, whether or no'.[10] The 'unfortunate gentleman' recovers 'by various kindly attentions and manoeuvres such as these poor people had been accustomed to practise' – as Dotting comments 'We're only your good angels like – only poor cinder sifters – don'tee be afeared'.[11] Clinker is instructed to run off to sell the miniature to get brandy, cordial and a blanket. The narrative unravels in proper fairy-tale mode – the recovering gentleman finds enough documentary evidence in the parchment round the miniature to restore an adequate portion of his fortune (but, pointedly, not all of it), and, as a reward, fulfils the three sifters' hearts' desire by building them a cottage near the dust heap. Even this redemptive closure is not enough – in visiting the 'great Dust-Contractor' who owned the dust heap at his home in Manchester Square in order to secure the land for the sifters' house, the gentleman met and subsequently courted the contractor's 'very accomplished' daughter. The contractor offered a marriage settlement of either £20,000 or the dust heap, and the couple, declaring that, while the dust heap was probably the more valuable gift, nonetheless 'did not understand the business' and settled for the money. As a final gesture in confusing the genres invoked in his piece, Horne concludes with what might be described as an authentic fairy-tale statistic: 'This was the identical Dust-heap, as we know from authentic information, which was subsequently sold for forty thousand pounds, and was exported to Russia to rebuild Moscow.'[12]

Horne's extraordinary article is significant on a number of counts. It has often been used, perhaps improbably given its dominantly fictive mode, as a prime source of information about dust and soot.[13] It brings together a range of urban myths and beliefs about dust heaps – that they comprised a unique landscape which offered a very particular aesthetic and emotional experience; that they were wealth producing on a massive scale even if that wealth seldom reached the sifters; that they contained hidden treasure (sometimes of a documentary kind); that they could miraculously revive half-dead animals. However, there are new elements here. The first is the belief that dust heaps were, among much else, a field of dreams, the stuff of fairy tales, and thus provided a focus for the visions and longings of the poor. The second is the insistence on the redemptive effect of a life lived within the ambit of a dust heap. Not only, through an economic transformation, is the suicidal gentleman redeemed into solvency and charitable benevolence, but the sifters too miraculously construct a modest competency for themselves through the power of their unthinking decency, generosity and compassion. Horne's argument is clear – as well as rehearsing the well-known mid-Victorian narrative of the economic miracle through which waste, dirt and dust become important and valuable commodities, it might be possible also to figure, admittedly through the conventions of the fairy tale or the fable, dust and dirt as a source of *moral* value, a kind of emotional and spiritual manure. In this way the widely visible poverty, degradation and despoliation generated by the dust trade might be accommodated within middle-class consciousness as a redemptive opportunity. In binding together the economic and the moral in this way, Horne grasps one of the central dynamics of Victorian middle-class ideology.

Henry Mayhew's *London Labour and the London Poor* was, of course, an extraordinary adaptation of the part issue idea used for the publication of extended fiction to a work of social investigation. Begun as an extension of his *Morning Chronicle* articles published in 1849–50, *London Labour and the London Poor* 'inflates like a balloon'[14] as Mayhew's project sagged under the weight of his 'limitless curiosity' about street folk, thus subverting his wider goal of a survey of the broad range of working people, and became 'finally unmanageable'.[15] Initially published in serialised parts between 1851 and 1852, the extended four-volume version was published between 1861 and 1865. Such an improvisational method and local intensification of his work was only made possible by the opportunities of serial publication, and it is this fascination with the local and particular, Humpherys argues, that denies Mayhew's work any theoretical coherence as well as confusing the reader with misleading announcements, fictional title pages and misplaced illustrations. More positively, to use Eileen Yeo's formulation, 'Mayhew was a sophisticated empiricist who had no mystical faith that all the facts when collected would automatically suggest their relationship to each other but interpreted his material as he went along', thus allowing a 'subtle interplay between facts and hypotheses in Mayhew's mind'.[16] Central to Mayhew's method was the individual interview, often reported at length and with some attempt to represent the speech patterns and idiosyncrasies of the interviewee, and Mayhew's account of dustmen includes several of these.

Mayhew's dustmen appear in volume II of *London Labour and the London Poor* among a group of trades comprising 'Dustmen, Nightmen, Sweeps and Scavengers', a group which is itself sandwiched between the self-employed street-finders of everything from dogs' dung to cigar ends on the one hand and 'London Sewerage and Scavengery' on the other. They were, as Humpherys notes, the product of Mayhew's 'last major expansion' of his text, and do not appear in the *Morning Chronicle* letters. 'Mayhew extended the category of "street finders and collectors" to a group who only vaguely fit the label ... These groups were not treated in this order in the following text, again showing his changing plans ... This time the loss of control over the direction of his work resulted from the plethora of available statistical information'.[17]

**49** 'The London Dustman' from Henry Mayhew's *London Labour and the London Poor*

THE LONDON DUSTMAN.
DUST HO! DUST HO!

'Of the Dustmen of London', despite sounding like an eighteenth-century philosophical discourse, occupied fourteen close-printed pages of double-columned text,[18] and any casual reader wading through them might well agree with Humpherys that 'the subject of street cleaning proved to be a debilitating one for Mayhew's survey'.[19] The text on dustmen was accompanied by two illustrations, one of a dustman crying out his trade (originally published in a part issue at the end of volume I; fig. 49) and the second, an image of sifters at work in a dust yard, accompanying the main text (fig. 50).[20] More important still than these structural juxtapositions was Mayhew's quasi-anthropological description of street people as 'wandering tribes'. As Humpherys notes, by 'wandering tribes' Mayhew meant those outside settled domesticity and, by implication, the law, whose trade required a considerable amount of wandering the streets.[21] He was not suggesting that dustmen and their ilk were nomadic or unsettled – in fact his description implies quite the

VIEW OF A DUST YARD.
(From a Sketch taken on the spot.)


**50** 'View of a Dustyard' from Henry Mayhew's *London Labour and the London Poor*

opposite – but rather that they were 'of the streets'. In this assumption he followed the caricaturists and urban sketch-writers in associating dustmen primarily with their visible outdoor presence, although his relentless curiosity also forced him to inquire about their domestic arrangements and even their sex lives.

The long tradition of lists that categorise and break down rubbish into its component elements, – a tradition as much concerned with literary bravado as with analytical method – emerged in Mayhew as a metaphorical as well as a literal obsession with 'sifting', with evidence rather than explanation. Whereas writers as various as Wight, Horne and Sala offered lists as a central element in their literary method, Mayhew's listing and sifting extended to every element of the dust trade – its hierarchies of workers, its economic base, its complex relationship to other trades within his general category of 'Street-finders or Collectors'. He included a list of current dust contractors in London, detailed statistics of the numbers employed in the trade, and of the amounts of rubbish collected before launching into the classic exposition of what the various elements of the dust heap are re-used for.[22] Mayhew's own investigations were further informed and authenticated by information offered by a contractor with twenty years experience in the trade. An account of a dust yard 'lately visited' and 'far from uninteresting' follows, which stressed the personal authenticity and thoroughness of Mayhew's visit, shifted the focus of his interest on to the sifters, and then on to several pages which describe categories of labourers involved in the trade, their functions, their wages and their appearance.[23] The first of several reported interviews follows, in this case a dust contractor who insists that the notion that dust heaps might be unhealthy is contradicted by the vigour and longevity of those who work in the trade. (In this context it is interesting to recall the considerable age of two of the central characters in Horne's *Household Words* article.) Mayhew then proceeded to describe the personal characteristics, social lives and morality of dustmen, using interpolated interviews with a contractor (berated parenthetically by Mayhew for his refusal to take responsibility for the welfare of his workforce) and with two dustmen. The first of these interviews ended badly. Mayhew went to visit a dustman praised by his master for his intelligence, but who took fright when Mayhew produced his notebook and fled the room. Mayhew noted phlegmatically that 'one of the most difficult points in my labours is to make such men as these comprehend the object or use of my investigations', a difficulty acknowledged in making generalisations about personal relationships, which had to be based solely on 'from all I could learn on the subject'.[24] The second interview proved more useful.

Leaving aside Mayhew's intensely detailed account of trade practices, an account which provided – even with all its deficiencies and inaccuracies, both acknowledged and unacknowledged – the most detailed available account of dustmen at any point in their history, he has much of interest to say about the moral, domestic and social lives of dustmen. Eileen Yeo has noted approvingly of Mayhew that he 'never treated the poor simply as economic men or considered them only at work … his mind never stood still … his understanding of the social life of the poor developed and deepened'.[25] Such comments construct an interesting dialogue with the assumptions of previous commentators, especially the caricaturists. In essence, and largely without any symptoms of moral judgement, Mayhew confirmed the view of the caricaturists that dustmen represented some of the most morally depraved, drunken, ignorant and socially alienated members of the metropolitan proletariat, yet his account is curiously without either the reformist impulses of the mid-Victorian social conscience or the sense of powerfully grotesque challenge to the social order which informs the caricatures of the previous decades. Indeed, what is unique and extraordinary about Mayhew's account of dustmen is his refusal of all the narrative possibilities traditionally available to him – narratives of contempt at the unredeemable brutality of dustmen, narratives of attempts at social inclusivity which might bring dustmen back into social usefulness, narratives of moral redemption in which the contemplation of dust might lead to a better world, narratives of pleasurable spectatorship in which dustmen might make a picturesque contribution to the spectacle of the urban scene. While the curiosity noted by Humpherys as Mayhew's dominant motive for writing *London Labour* is everywhere apparent in his account, it is drained of narrative meanings of the kind which had structured the versions of dustmen in previous literature and graphic discourses. In Mayhew's description, dustmen drink and smoke, but they are long-lived and healthy, and to some extent their drinking is understandable as a response to their heavy daily labour. Dustmen become noisy in their cups, which sometimes results in 'a general quarrel', but this involves only dustmen and is forgotten by the next morning. Dustmen are seldom married, but they are faithful to their partners, if only for economic reasons to do with the earning power of women engaged in the trade. Dustmen beat their wives when drunk, but no more so than other labourers. Dustmen are generally illiterate and totally ignorant of politics, but they are partial to songs and to elaborate forms of 'chaffing' and coarse humour, which passes for their cultural life.

Mayhew also offers a version of dustmen as a traditional, self-enclosed, relatively prosperous group of labourers, socially and culturally isolated from society at large, and therefore a group unlikely to trouble the wider social order. They have evident faults – as well as their drunkenness they are untrustworthy, ignorant, improvident and brutalised – but then what could be expected given their education and experience, which was entirely limited to the dust yard? Mayhew's dustmen could even be rather dull and orthodox – 'some of the dustmen are prudent well-behaved men and have decent homes' he commented, citing their roots in rural labour as an important factor.[26] They are also shown as simple men with simple pleasures – as one of Mayhew's informants puts it 'You see, ven I'm not out with the cart, I digs here all day; and p'haps I'm up all night and digs avay again agen the next day. Vot does I care for reading? … I tell you vot I likes, though! vhy, I jist likes two or three pipes o' backer, and a pot or two of good heavy and a song, and then I tumbles in with my Sall, and I'm as happy as here and there von.'[27] So if there is any narrative here, it is that of the construction of dustmen among the urban working class as self-enclosed, unambitious, improvident, pleasure-seeking but essentially both *harmless* and *useful*. Mayhew offers dustmen little emblematic or representative significance of the kind we have seen in previous chapters. What is so startling about Mayhew's description of dustmen, then, is the way in which he reduced them from semi-mythological combatants in the culture wars of early Victorian society into a classic representation of working-class self-absorption, apathy and small-scale hedonism. For Mayhew, a man of universal curiosity, the organisation of the dust trade, its hierarchies and sub-divisions, and the nature of the dust itself turned out to be of more interest than the lives and cultural significance of those employed within it.

James Greenwood was a campaigning journalist described by Jeffrey Richards as 'at once the most famous and the most representative of the post-Mayhew generation of social explorers'.[28] Notwithstanding this judgement, Greenwood's work remains relatively little studied or anthologised, and he is principally remembered as the first of many investigators who dressed down in pauper clothes in order to investigate the lives of the poor.[29] *Unsentimental Journeys: or, Byways of the Modern Babylon*, published in volume form in 1872, comprised a series of newspaper reports written several years previously and here republished with double-page illustrations.[30] 'Mr Dodd's Dustyard' appears as chapter X, and forms an authentic Mayhew-like personal visit to a dust yard, on this occasion one of the largest and best-known establishments, Mr Dodd's yard on the banks of the Regent's Canal. Greenwood is shown round by the yard foreman, and, again like Mayhew, bases his account on both empirical observation and detailed conversations with the workforce. But the tone of Greenwood's account, – facetious and prolix, even flippant – is very different, as are his interpretations of what he sees. The first few pages offer a view of the women sifters which stresses their healthfulness and cheerfulness along with their ungainliness and poverty. Greenwood accepts without question that this heartening vision, despite the viciously cold wind and freezing temperatures, is the product of wholesome open-air working and confirms various authorities who have claimed that the trade is a healthsome one. He is immediately impressed by the dexterity and rapidity of the sifters. Taken further into the yard, Greenwood is exposed to yet another exposition of the varied contents of a dust heap, their value as re-cycled material and their varied uses. Mr Dodd seems to have mechanised these processes to some extent, as Greenwood glimpses an indoor sorting room for abandoned footware, paper and bread to be used as pig-swill, before confronting a furnace and a rag-washing vat and drying room.

Greenwood, unlike most other literary visitors to dust yards, acknowledged himself to be rather appalled than fascinated – 'I was

MR. DODD'S DUST-YARD.

anything but sorry when Mr Scorch announced that he had nothing more to show me'.[31] Yet his piece assumes a jovial optimism that, despite the harsh weather, still declared that 'Every one was fat, every one was rosy, and laughing and singing as though it were capital fun to grovel among the refuse of the town out in the open air – a Siberian air, bleak and withering'.[32] The accompanying illustration (fig. 51), while unwilling or unable to depict such revelry, is nonetheless carefully organised to show a well-managed set of industrial activities, with horses being tended at the left, and workers shown talking, smoking and leaning on shovels as well as hard at work. The long line of women sifters offers some evidence of hunched postures and hard labour, but offsets this with images of women smoking, chatting, or even sat at ease with folded arms. Light falls on the workers held within the darker profiles of various mounds of dust. Crammed in by housing, with the spars of a canal barge also just visible, the dust yard assumes the status of a community rather than a factory. Rather than the bleak wind-swept wastes of Siberia, Mr. Dodd's dustyard evokes homeliness, shelter and only moderate expenditure of human energy and labour. In comparison with the fantastic redemptive optimism of Horne and the obsessive categorisation of Mayhew, Greenwood seems to have little interest in constructing a social meaning from what he sees. Despite Greenwood's reputation as a 'campaigning' journalist, Mr Dodd and his dust seem barely to have ruffled the surface of his interest, and then only to produce a series of banal and superficial responses.

*opposite*
**51** 'Mr Dodd's Dust-Yard' from James Greenwood's *Unsentimental Journeys: or, Byways of the Modern Babylon*

Alongside the reasonable and, on the whole, socially confident readings of dustmen to be found in this range of investigative, if mildly sensationalised journalism, it is interesting to posit the perfervid rhetoric and alarmist moral outrage of one of the most popular urban investigators of the mid-nineteenth century, George Augustus Sala, whose series of sketches *Twice Round the Clock* ran in an illustrated weekly, *The Welcome Guest*, during the later half of 1858.[33] At first glance *Twice Round the Clock* seems to replicate many of the characteristics of the urban picaresque described in previous chapters. Sala makes little effort to organise his text as anything more than a series of 'scenes' which happen to take place concurrently. As Bernstein notes, he is less an explorer of the urban scene than a passive witness to it.[34] His verbal sketches are interdependent with a series of wood engravings by W. McConnell which were dropped into the text most frequently as paired illustrations which could be viewed simultaneously, but which were sometimes presented as discrete single images.[35] The visual organisation of these individual images was crucially non-narrative. Both images and text refer back directly to the picaresque readings of the streets offered by the caricaturists of the 1820s and the 1830s. Similarly, Sala's descriptions depend on a detached, seemingly invisible observer for whom the street lays itself out as unending scroll.

'Twice Round the Clock' is a literary formula and structure which is used by Sala not to suggest sequence or continuity but rather as a means of identifying hourly points at which the observing author and artist can take a snapshot of the urban scene. As Rick Allen notes in his comments on the sub-genres of urban description, the focus is 'both spatial and temporal'.[36] Or, as Nead remarks, 'Sala's contribution was to write a temporal geography of London' through the use of a 'litany of locations'.[37] Unlike so many Victorian genre paintings of the urban scene, these representations, both linguistic and graphic, incident-packed as they are, depend as much on contiguity as interconnectedness, on the coincidence of simultaneity as much as on any principles of social interdependence or economic interaction. Such crowdedness is directly represented in Sala's literary style to a level which is almost febrile. This linguistic density and profusion has led both Bernstein and Nead to regard Sala and McConnell's work as something close to incoherence.[38] Sala's response is for Bernstein 'inundated with language' so that 'words and objects are held in uneasy suspension on the edge of linguistic and social chaos'. Class and gender, in individual images at least, are not crucially differentiated but rather elided into the seamless visual plane of the urban scroll. Those represented are perceived as 'types' and not as men and women. Rather than constructing any sense of crowdedness, activity or urgency, both the text and individual images in *Twice Round the Clock* offer a version of London as a scene of either chaos (as Bernstein and Nead argue) or of the picaresque notion of accommodated difference, a theatre in which independent actions occur on the same visual plane without any disturbance to the surface texture of, or anxiety at, the social disconnectedness constructed by text and illustration.

*opposite* **52** W. McConnell, 'Nine O'Clock P.M.' from G.A. Sala *Twice Round the Clock*

But if these traditional mechanisms for organising the urban spectacle, drawn from Regency precedents, inform Sala and McConnell at one level, they are overlaid by increasingly urgent early Victorian compulsions, compulsions which led towards modes of classification and differentiation which, in Sala's case, derived explicitly from the imperatives of moral evaluation and judgement. Sala also revealed, in contrast to the social confidence expressed elsewhere in the writing considered in this chapter, what Nead describes as the 'urban uncanny', a fear so pervasive that it required Sala to construct a 'containment and stylization of the more disturbing associations of the city at night'.[39] Such a London becomes 'solemn, ghastly, unearthly'.[40]

Two dustmen appear in the illustrations to *Twice Round the Clock*. In the illustration to '5 o' clock p.m.: The Prisoners' Van',[41] a dustman is clearly visible at the left of a crowd of loungers that has gathered to see the evening's collection of prisoners loaded into police vans in order to be taken away from Bow Street magistrates' courts to jail. Or, in Sala's fevered rhetoric, 'a choice assembly of the raggedly, ruffianry, felonry, misery, drunkardry and drabbery' watch a 'brazen courtesan in tawdry finery' getting into the van and throwing her hat defiantly into the crowd.[42] The watching dustman is in the classic lounger pose learnt from the mass of caricature images from previous decades, a lit pipe momentarily forgotten in his hand because of his abstracted, solitary absorption in the scene. Here, then, is the familiar spectating dustman – in, but apart from, the urban crowd, at leisure, at ease, at home and yet self-absorbed and unsociable in his pleasurable connoisseurship of the urban incident. Yet this familiar graphic motif is to be contrasted against Sala's fervent interpretation of the scene as one of prurient spectatorship in which urban variety and street good humour give way to a debased scene in which criminality is celebrated by the depraved as a boisterous spectacle.

NINE O'CLOCK P.M.. HOUSE OF CALL FOR THE VICTORIA AUDIENCE.

In this image, McConnell is able to accommodate the traditional spectating dustman within his representation of the urban crowd. But Sala is elsewhere unwilling to leave the dustman to his peaceful pleasures, and insists on making him a central figure for moral outrage. In 'Nine o' clock p.m.: House of Call for the Victoria Audience' (fig. 52) a dustman is depicted doing a number of traditional dustman things – dancing, courting, drinking – in traditional dustman places, both literal and metaphorical – the right-hand edge of a depicted urban 'frieze' and a gin shop. He is, as usual, partially turned away from the viewer looking in at the urban scene. Although apparently coupled with a young woman who is leading a small child and dancing to the music of a banjo played by a black entertainer, the dustman seems self-contained, wrapped up in a world of his own. Dressed in classic dustman garb, his posture is angular and awkward almost to the point of deformity. His physiognomy seems rough, even brutal.

If this image of a dancing dustman came from a caricature of the 1830s, it could be read in any of the traditional ways described in Chapter 3 – as an exercise in the comic grotesque, as a depiction of fantasised transgression and pleasure, as an exploration of low-life customs, as a picturesque account of urban diversity. None of these approaches could prepare us for Sala's reading of the scene:

> In the cartoon accompanying this essay, you will find a delineation of the hostelry – the tavern – bah! It isn't a tavern; it is an unadulterated gin and beer palace – whither takes place the rush at half-price for malt refreshment. I have kept you lingering at the door a long time; I have digressed, parried, evaded the question; discoursed on transpontine drama ... I have been discursive, evasive, tedious, bery probably, but purposely so. I was bound to show you the place, but it is better that the pen should leave the fulness of the representation in this instance. It is humorous enough, brilliant enough, full of varied life and bustle enough. I could make you very merry with accounts of the mock Ethiopian serenaders at the door, with facetious remarks on the gentleman in the sou-wester, knee-shorts, anklejacks and gaiters who is instructing the lady in the mob cap in the mysteries of the celebrated dance known as the 'Roberto Polveroso,' or, 'Dusty Bob and Black Sal.' I might be eloquent upon the subject of the sturdy sailor who is hobnobbing with the negro, the Life Guardsman treating the ladies, like a gallany fellow as he is, and the stream of honest, hard-working mechanics, their wives, and families, who have sureged in from the 'Vic' to have their 'drop of beer.' But the picture would still be incomplete. In graver pages – in tedious, solemn journals only – could be told (and I have told) the truth about a gin-shop in the New Cut. I will not mar my welcome as a 'guest,' and descant upon the crime and shame, the age made hardened, the very babies weaned on gin. Let us

take the better part, and throw a veil over this ugly position of the night side of London.[43]

This is, of course, an extremely irritating piece of writing in its self-conscious reliance on euphemisms to try to hint at the 'truth', its declaration of its own evasiveness, and its final withdrawal behind the 'veil' of inarticulacy. Sala *could* have been facetious or made merry about dustmen, he declares, but he won't do this. But of course he does – the term 'gentleman' is nothing if not facetious, and 'sou'wester' and 'knee-shorts' do make merry with the dustman's appearance. The grandiloquent term 'Roberto Polveroso' for the famous Bob and Sal dance is also facetious, and links the dustman ineluctably with ideas of prostitution and miscegeny – indeed, with the whole transgressive Bob and Sal narrative further represented by the presence of 'negroes' and 'Ethiopeans' elsewhere in the scene. Sala could have read the scene as a comic spectacle, as an example of respectable working-class leisure – the scene is 'humorous enough, brilliant enough, full of varied life and bustle enough' to be rendered as a celebratory narrative. But in truth, he declares, the full moral ramifications of this scene lie beyond language altogether. They are literally unspeakable, and, he maintains, best left to the representations of the pencil, especially if the author is to maintain his place as a 'welcome guest' among respectable readers. Yet what the 'pencil' represents is, to my mind, entirely open to a variety of readings which have to negotiate between vivid urban pleasure on the one hand and total debauchery on the other. In Sala's London at least, the dustman has lost none of his Regency power to shock, threaten and outrage genteel sensibilities. While for many of Sala's contemporaries the dustman can be accommodated easily enough into the social geography of the city and understood, even admired, for his social and economic functionalism, for Sala he remained an exemplar of the morally and socially dangerous underclass. By implication if not by direct statement, the Regency agenda of anxiety and outrage rises up again in Sal's overworked imagination – miscegeny (the product of 'hobnobbing' with Ethiopeans and negroes), prostitution ('the lady in the mob cap' is no lady), and the 'mysteries' of sensual pleasure manifested in dancing and drinking. Even if it can only be constructed in euphemisms, this is indeed 'the night side of London'.

In the later Victorian period dustmen continued to appear in Victorian journalism and social reportage, but with a less urgent and compelling presence. The focus, too, has shifted almost entirely from the street presence and collecting activities of dustmen to the dust yard where dust is sifted, categorised and re-cycled. It is the social conditions of the sifters and the economic ramifications of their trade that preoccupy later spectators, most of whom rely one or other of the available generic traditions to structure their accounts. The sifters feature, for example, as the 'dust wharf people' in J. M. Weylland's 1884 history

**53** 'Group of Rubbish Sifters' from James Burnley *The Romance of Modern Industry*

of the London City Mission, which recounts at some length the heroic work of a Mrs Ranyard in bringing religion to the Paddington Dust Wharf district.[44] An accompanying illustration shows a clergyman, bible at the ready, expounding his faith to sceptical and harassed dust-sifters, both male and female. James Burnley's 1889 *The Romance of Modern Industry* has a long chapter under the self-explanatory title of 'Wealth in Rubbish' which rehearses the long-established taxonomy of dust and its disposal, albeit in considerable depth and with a particular emphasis on the chemical transformation of detritus.[45] Among recently invented uses for rubbish, Burnley cites seaweed, cotton and silk waste as examples of ways in which chemistry has begun to retrieve value from the previously worthless.[46] He also provides a simple but informative image of 'A Group of Rubbish Sifters', dressed rather in the manner of exotic outlaws, but clearly working at the will of the sketched masters lounging in the background (fig. 53). As if to confirm this image, Burnley comments that 'there is a touch of romance in the repulsive occupation of sifting', although he has been at pains to stress the heavy and degraded nature of the work undertaken in the dustyard.[47]

In a different, but perhaps equally partial, idiom, the temperance weekly *The British Workman* provided a late century account of a perfect redemptive dustman: clean and well turned out ('a man need not be a dirty man because he had dirty work'), sober and thoughtful ('some are too fuddled with beer to think much'), charitable and thrifty (deserving recipients on his rounds are offered not just the leavings of his own table, but even the re-cycled waste chicken legs from Lord Purple's), and, inevitably, a devout family man who seeks to do his level best to keep his family from poverty and want.[48] *The British Workman*'s account of this paragon slides from the literal into the figurative in its closing paragraph, drawing first on the elision between the meanings of 'dust' and 'snuff' – 'I'd rather have you [the dust that clogs his nose] than that dirty dust they call snuff, for that fuddles a man's brain, and you can't'. Snuff here, of course, stands not just for the tobacco taken by the rich in an affected manner but also for money, a commodity noticeably lacking in the mile-long stretch of the Albert Road where the dustman operates. But then in the last few sentences the mid-Victorian narrative of re-cycling and transformation becomes explicitly moral and exhortatory as well as metaphorical – 'good reader, hook out the blessings from the dust-heaps of life. See what use you can put things to for God – for your poor neighbour ... what you consider to be no better than a dry dust-heap, contains within it, if you will look for it, the opportunity of blessing others and being blest yourself'.[49] To underline the qualities which an ideal dustman should have, *The British Workman* provides a massive woodcut image of a sturdy, curly-headed dustman, his wicker basket ready for use in one hand, calling out his famous cry of 'Dust Oh!'. His dress by this time has abandoned breeches and white loose coat for sturdy cords and a smock, although the fantail has survived down the years. He looks for all the world like Mayhew's dustman turned preacher, yelling 'Dust Oh!' as a reminder to the world of its Christian responsibilities.

## 'Down with the dust': *Our Mutual Friend*, Dickens, dust and redemption[50]

When Nicodemus Boffin, the Golden Dustman, remarked to his secretary Rokesmith 'it'll look but a poor dead flat without the Mounds', he might have been describing the whole novel, such is the level of both symbolic and picturesque importance that the dust heaps bring to the text.[51] Indeed 'Dickens and Dust' is an entirely imaginable book-length topic. Such a book would of course encompass a detailed reading of *Our Mutual Friend* with its Golden Dustman and its townscapes of secretive and ominous dust heaps. It would engage with the long-standing literary controversy over exactly what dust heaps comprised and thus the extent to which Dickens's urban vision might properly be described as excremental.[52] It would examine in detail the extended genesis of the illustrated title page of the part-issue, which features a kind of dustman memento mori located at the right-hand margin of a complex emblematic drawing (fig. 54).[53] It would offer explanations for the absence of graphic images of dust heaps among Stone's illustrations for the novel, and look at later editions where these have been added.[54] It would argue that the narrative of Nicodemus Boffin, who inherits a fortune in the form of an estate which is literally built on dust, has had insufficient attention in critical discussion of

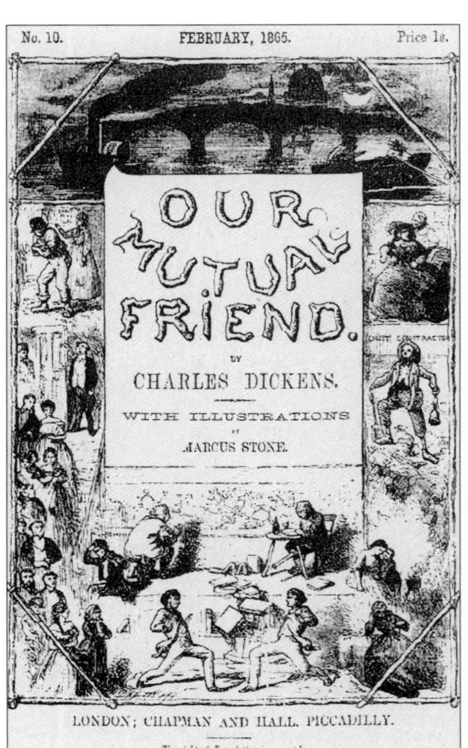


**54** Marcus Stone, title page to the part issue of Charles Dickens *Our Mutual Friend*

the novel, largely because the tale of his journey from spontaneous, open-hearted generosity and simplicity into suspicion, secretiveness and greed turns out to be as much an element of plot mechanics as it is a sustained figuration of the dirt/corruption/wealth complex at the centre of the novel. As Stephen Gill puts it, 'it is a shock to find that all of this is deceit, that open, friendly Noddy Boffin has never changed at all'.[55] Thus the narrative of the Golden Dustman might be read as finally denying the reader the redemptive trajectory that would have fully underwritten the novel's closure. It would look again at the theatrical sources for the novel,[56] and argue that, despite the widespread acknowledgement of the importance of contemporary plays as sources for the novel, critics have concentrated on Bella Wilfer and Lizzie Hexham at the expense of the Boffins and the implications and consequences of their potentially corrupting inheritance.[57] More broadly, it would relate *Our Mutual Friend* to the considerable discussion of dust, waste, wealth and commerce in Dickens's periodicals, especially *Household Words*, where the psycho-pathology as well as the social implications of dirt and waste form, as we have seen, a recurrent topic[58] and fully acknowledge Dickens's likely debts to Mayhew.[59] The idea of re-cycling and re-making is clearly one pre-occupation to be found here, which in turn would link these discussions to a vast range of recent scholarship on ideas of mess, dirt and dust in Victorian culture. These links were briefly discussed in Chapter 1. Such ideas are as amenable to psychoanalytic theory as they are to empirical scholarship, and it is tempting to think of ways in which the connections between dirt, wealth, purity and redemption might be articulated in any such study, which would form a complex gloss on those clichés through which British society has traditionally accommodated these anxieties in phrases like 'filthy lucre', 'dirty money', 'where there's muck there's brass' and so on.

It is not, however, the purpose of this chapter to offer a full re-reading of *Our Mutual Friend* of the kind that has just been described, although it will be apparent that many of the themes that preoccupied Dickens have already been discussed. I am more concerned here to read the novel in terms of its relationship to the complex of stereotypes, representational possibilities and urban myths which have formed the substance of this book. Such a reading will offer some thoughts on the idea of redemption in the novel and suggest at least one major overlooked source for the novel.

One argument immediately follows from this declared purpose of reading the novel as an act of both homage to and re-invention of the popular mythographic repertoire relating to dustmen. Dickens's appropriation of the idea of the dustman in *Our Mutual Friend*, brilliantly realised and complex as it is, is, like much else in his work, essentially retrospective, even outdated. Nicodemus Boffin is constructed out of an astonishingly detailed and comprehensive gathering-up and exploitation of the 'urban myths' and stereotypes associated with dustmen, which are re-ordered and re-formulated to act as a means of examining London in the mid-1860s. However successful this act of appropriation may have been as a fictional strategy, it is also evidence of Dickens's profound debts to notions of urban organisation that not only pre-date the novel but that are also dependent on a wide range of pre-existing literary and graphic tropes. In short, the novel evinces a particularly Dickensian, and particularly compelling, form of cultural nostalgia, which acts as a matrix for his discussions of the deviancies and obsessions that construct the contemporary urban world gone wrong.

Dickens used a number of familiar tropes and motifs, which had almost attained the status of urban myths, to construct the narrative of the Golden Dustman. The first concerned the effects of a sudden chance accession of wealth on the moral life and behaviour of poor, barely literate recipients – or, in Dickens's own description of the Boffins, 'two ignorant and unpolished people'.[60] In Boffin's case, such wealth arrives through his somewhat reluctant inheritance of the Harmon dustheaps, reluctance described in detail in Chapter VIII of the novel through the mechanism of Boffin's 'consultation' with Mortimer Lightwood. Lightwood insists that one of the central virtues of the Harmon inheritance is the extent to which it is free and unencumbered. Yet the Boffins see their new wealth as 'Care and Complication'.[61] As Boffin ruefully, or perhaps bitterly, remarked, while showing his new secretary Rokesmith the 'particular mound which had been left him as his legacy under the will before he acquired the whole estate', 'it would have been enough for us'.[62]

The effects of chance or unexpected inheritance on the moral and material lives of those who benefit is a common enough fictional idea, and Dickens used this familiar narrative structure to relate Boffin to the central examination of the redemptive power of (eventually) manifested worth in a world governed by chance as well as by greed and secrecy. Wegg, in particular, driven by a smouldering sense of jealousy and injustice, insists that understanding of the Harmon inheritance involves a continuing dialogue between chance and worth. 'Here is an immense fortune drops from the clouds upon a person that shall be nameless. Here is a weekly allowance, with a certain weight of coals, drops from the clouds upon me. Which of us is the better man?' forms Wegg's analysis of the nature of inheritance.[63] In spite of Wegg's world view, Dickens bases *Our Mutual Friend* on a perceived, if somewhat optimistic, belief that chance is the product of worth. Thus an unasked-for inheritance might, in the right hands, be used to redeem the origins of the Harmon fortune in the soiled, indeed literally dirty, money accumulated through the avarice, meanness and exploitation of Boffin's former employer. This belief forms a moment of outspoken authorial assertion in Chapter IX of Book I of the novel:

> These two ignorant and unpolished people had guided themselves so far on their journey in life, by a religious sense of duty and desire to do right. Ten thousand weaknesses and absurdities might have been detected in the breasts of both ... But the hard, wrathful and sordid nature that had rung so much work out of them as could be got in their best days, for as little money as could be paid to hurry on their worst, had never been so warped but it knew their moral straightness and respected it. In its own despite, in a constant conflict with itself and them, it had done so. And this is the eternal law. For, Evil often stops short at itself and dies with the does of it; but Good, never.[64]

But why choose a dustman as the central protagonist in such a narrative, especially given that comic or brutalised dustmen had been much more common than moral heroes within traditional representations of the trade? The previous chapters provide some obvious answers. Dustmen, in all their ignorant dirtiness and irredeemable vulgarity, provided a representative, although perhaps extreme, example of a vulgar and brutalised proletarian culture. The onset of wealth for such people is played off against their potentially comic inadequacy in using wealth effectively in the pursuit of self-realisation or happiness. Indeed, as we have seen, the usual consequence is either satirical – the doomed pursuit of gentility – or tragic – a self-destructive orgy of consumption aided by the duplicity of hangers-on and fortune-hunters. Further, popular mythology gave some credence to the idea that a dustman *might* daily come into money through chance discoveries in the heap. The choice of a dustman as the central protagonist in this narrative, indeed, gave plausibility to the idea that chance was a more powerful social and moral agent than individual worth. Dustmen in popular literature at least did sometimes find self-realisation and happiness in the unexpected largesse of the dust heap – Horne's *Household Words* essay, crucially with the word 'redeem' in its title, had seen sifters rewarded for their honesty and compassion albeit with a modest competence rather than a fortune. But it was the more general belief in the chance opportunities dustmen had of acquiring wealth (sometimes in the form of legal documents, again as in Horne's article) that forms the centre of this idea. Accordingly it is not surprising, especially given the other themes of the book – literacy and power, for example – that Dickens picked on a dustman to represent the moral centre of his novel especially given his knowledge not just of Horne's article but also of other contemporary writing, such as the journalism described above, which took a more heroic view of the inner life of the dustman than previous generations had done. It is no accident that James Grant's series of characteristic sketches of urban types in the *London Saturday Journal* was called 'Illustrations of Humanity', as his theme was not only human variety but also 'humanity' in its wider sense.

But there is a more specific reason to think that Dickens would have been familiar with popular versions of the corrupting effects inheritance might have on a fundamentally genial and well-intentioned figure of a dustman, especially given his frequently cited reliance on theatrical sources for other plot elements in *Our Mutual Friend*. One theatrical dustman, who first appeared on the stage in the summer of 1846, offered an interesting if largely comic comment on those ideas of inheritance, concealment, corruption and redemption which come to comprise the central structure of *Our Mutual Friend*. The dustman was ingeniously called Ned Windfall, and he appeared as the central character in a short farce called *The Dustman's Belle*, written by Charles Dance, which had a brief metropolitan theatrical life in the late 1840s.[65] While Dickens is extremely unlikely to have seen this play, he knew its author, and *The Dustman's Belle* was widely noticed in the metropolitan weeklies like the *Illustrated London News* and the *Pictorial Times*.[66] Dickens had become closely associated with the theatrical company brought together by the Keeleys, which performed the play in both its first performances and its later revival.[67] Both the Lyceum and Keeley's company were important elements in Dickens's dramatisations of his works, and he collaborated with the Keeleys both on the 1845 Christmas production of *The Cricket on the Hearth* and the 1846 dramatisation of his Christmas story *The Battle of Life*. Despite Dickens's continual scepticism about the quality of the production and endless resigned complaints in his letters, he acknowledged in private that the company had done a good job in both instances.[68] His theatrical collaborator Albert Smith, who remained impervious to the clash of interests caused by his role as drama critic of the *Illustrated London News* and his activities as a playwright, wrote extensively for the Lyceum along with Dance.[69] The many burlesques presented at the Lyceum during these years, A. E. Wilson notes, were 'mostly the works of Planche, Charles Dance, Albert Smith and Mark Lemon'.[70] Given that the text of the play was promptly published[71] it is not far-fetched to believe that Dickens, one way or another, had some knowledge of the existence of *The Dustman's Belle*. Even if this was not the case, the play still serves as an important indication of the ways in which ideas about the corrupting force of inherited wealth and the redemptive power of individual human goodness might be readily and particularly associated with dustmen. The title wittily brings together the traditional amorous proclivities of London dustmen with a reminder, through the reference to bells, of the street activities particular to the trade.



This 'play' is in reality more a pantomime or an 'extravaganza' and served originally as one element in a triple bill of equally ephemeral summer diversions. Despite its occasional and opportunistic origins as a filler in a triple holiday bill of burlesques and farces, *The Dustman's Belle* was accorded a considerable amount of space and even some respect by the illustrated journals, especially the *Illustrated London News*. It may be that new theatrical experiences were in short supply during summer holidays, but it is tempting to argue that, as previous chapters have suggested, dustmen bore an accumulated weight of interest and social significance which ensured public attention. Certainly the account of the genesis and the narrative of the play given in the *Pictorial Times* at some length offers the play a seriousness beyond the usual measure of a burlesque:

> The sudden accession to great wealth of a very humble individual, who regaled his former boon companions and fellow labourers, cannot have been forgotten, especially by the denizens of the locality so long disturbed by the orgies of the fortunate master of the revels. The author of last night's production borrows his hero from the circumstances we have averted to. *Ned Windfall* (Mr Keeley), an honest dustman, and the betrothed of *Sally Broomley* (Mrs Keeley), the Dustman's Belle, is unexpectedly called to succeed a miserly uncle in the possession of his property, to the amount of 16,000*l.* His wealth attracts the cupidity of a reckless man about town, *Morgan Rattler* (Mr F. Vining), who, aided by a hypocritical scoundrel of the Cantwell school, *Jacob Goodman* (admirably acted by Mr Meadows) seeks to "victimise" the unsuspecting child of fortune. Allured by them, he forgets his plighted troth to *Sally* and enters a life of wild folly and debauchery. When under the influence of wine *Rattler* seeks

> to induce his victim to marry his (*Rattler's*) sister (Miss Villars), but this project meets the disapproval of his accomplice *Goodman*, who himself seeks the hand of the fair *Susan Rattler*, to whom *Goodman* discloses the scheme. S*usan* appears to humour her brother's project, and in an interview with the *Dustman* unfolds to him all, and urges on him a return his old and early love. The heart-stirring appeals of the devoted and attached *Sally*, and the exposure of the villany [sic] plotted against his welfare and happiness, fail to induce the dupe to retrace his steps, but the change is effected by the melody of his once-favourite ditty, 'Sally in our Alley,' played by a passing street minstrel. He returns to love and reason, villany is exposed, and, as usual, the true lovers made happy.[72]

*opposite* **55** A performance of *The Dustman's Belle* from the *Illustrated London News* (28 August 1847), 139

As a further testimony to the surprising significance given to what was, by this account, an unpretentious, conventional and farcical piece of holiday entertainment, *The Dustman's Belle* was revived for another run by the Keeleys in August 1847, this time at the Surrey Theatre. Despite the new venue, the company remained the same, and the revival was again noticed in the *Illustrated London News*, this time accompanied with an engraving of Ned Windfall (Keeley) and his partner, inevitably named Sally (Mrs Keeley; fig. 55).[73] This illustration depicts the newly gorgeous dustman at the redemptive moment when his sweetheart's faithful love is recognised and acknowledged, and Ned renounces if not his new wealth then at least the corrupted self produced by 'filthy lucre'. The farce's central narrative – the corruption by wealth but ultimate redemption by female intervention of a fundamentally decent and good-hearted dustman who undergoes an unexpected accession to wealth – closely prefigures the central ideas of *Our Mutual Friend* and suggests how firmly a narrative which associated dirt, wealth, corruption and redemption had become lodged in early Victorian sensibilities. Further weight is given to the perceived social significance of the 'Golden Dustman' idea by contemporary suggestions that this narrative was not just an urban myth, a necessary dramatic projection of widespread social anxieties, but rather a true, if conveniently emblematic, story. The *Pictorial Times* suggests that 'The incident on which the sketch is based, is drawn from a drama which was enacted in real life some months back in the neighbourhood of Islington'.[74] While I have failed to unearth any such incident from contemporary papers, this assertion provides further evidence of the interpenetration of myth and fact in anything to do with dustmen. Nonetheless, the existence of performances of *The Dustmen's Belle* as an event that may have lodged in Dickens's mind suggests how far early Victorian culture had incorporated dustmen into urban narratives regardless of truth or exaggeration. Nicodemus Boffin, it might be claimed, had lived out his moral crisis in north London, in comic dramatic terms, long before the publication of *Our Mutual Friend* in 1864–65.

A similar refinement of crude stereotypes and folk narratives occurs in Dickens's second major area of engagement with the idea of the dustman

*Sally.*—"Well, come; you're a good old fellow, after all."

MR. KEELEY, AS "NED," AND MRS. KEELEY, AS "SALLY," IN "THE DUSTMAN'S BELLE," AT THE SURREY THEATRE.

in *Our Mutual Friend.* Nicodemus Boffin is, of course, an *educating* rather than an *educated* dustman. He becomes, as a result of his inheritance, both socially and culturally ambitious, and it is his anxieties about the value of literacy and the supposed benefits of education that drives the Venus/Wegg sub-plot in the novel. Boffin represents a powerful equation between illiteracy and vulnerability. Dickens's view of literacy had always been complex or even ambiguous. In some novels, gaining literacy is regarded as a 'fall' into a compromised print culture which is assembled out of hidden knowledge and repressed desire. *Hard Times*, for example, has at its centre an examination of articulacy, and comes to the conclusion that power over language is only gained at the expense of right feeling and compassion. It is the inarticulate and the unlettered – Sissy Jupe and Sleary (a man with a speech defect) in particular – who retain the moral purpose to oppose the contaminated half truths and downright lies of the articulate. Indeed, over-articulacy is one sustained theme in the novel, with Bounderby's bullying eloquence revealed as both cliché and untruth, and Harthouse's insincere utterances trailing off into ennui and silence. In *Bleak House*, Jo the crossing sweeper's inability to read off meanings from the world around him or to articulate his experience in language does not preserve him as an 'innocent', and he proves to be the key to the knowledge which unlocks the 'secrets' about origins at the centre of the novel. Implicit in both these novels is an account of the 'fallen' nature of print culture. The entry into the world of language and letters is also entry into a world of secrets, deceptions and hidden meanings. On the other hand, Dickens offers elsewhere more conventionally optimistic readings of the shift from illiteracy into print culture, most obviously in the case of Sam Weller in *Pickwick Papers*. Sam is mocked by his father for scratching away at a Valentine's card (which the older Weller characterises as 'the pursuit of knowledge under difficulties' in a witty allusion to G. L. Craik's book), but he is well aware of the importance of literacy as a form not just of social but more particularly of economic advancement. Dickens's novels, especially *Our Mutual Friend*, offer a broad depiction of a just or newly literate society where the value of print, while understood as a key characteristic of modernity and social change, remains nonetheless open to debate.

The ambiguous consequences of entry into literacy pervade *Our Mutual Friend*, a novel that persistently alludes to both the opportunities and dangers of print. The opportunities made available by print include the possibility of both social advancement in the case of Tom Hexham and Silas Wegg and of financial gain for Gaffer Hexham and Rogue Riderhood, who live in a world of half-deciphered reward posters and public announcements. Yet in all these instances, knowledge of print culture, especially inaccurate or inadequate knowledge, causes only misunderstanding, conflict and eventual downfall. Animal cunning and instinctive self-interest are proved to be morally damaging, especially when they are exposed to the 'mysteries' of print. Tom Hexham, in living out his sister's recognition of the interrelatedness of education and social advancement, fails to learn anything about tenderness or compassion, and becomes implicated in the terrible verbal battles between Bradley Headstone and Mortimer Lightwood, where the traditional genteel language of contempt and self-control proves more powerful than hard-earned Board-school articulacy. Silas Wegg's literacy causes both his rise and his fall. Wegg's proximity to the printed word as a street seller of popular 'literature' leads Boffin, deluded by his own vulnerabilities, to employ him as a kind of cultural life-style coach. Wegg, unwilling to accept his subservient role and driven by ignorance as well as avarice, is perpetually deceived by his belief in the power of the written word as a form of treasure, and is ultimately destroyed by his relentless poking and prodding in the Mounds in pursuit of secrets. Gaffer Hexham and Rogue Riderhood never manage to cash in the secrets and rewards they suspect are encoded in the posters displayed on Hexham's walls, read off by appearance and memory rather than through any grasp of the significance of letters. In these ways, literacy is represented in *Our Mutual Friend* as a corrupting possibility for the unlearned, a place which promised wealth and understanding but which in practice only offered misunderstanding, corruption and defeat. Lizzie Hexham, powerfully convinced of the value of literacy as a form of social mobility, nonetheless retains her moral weight by her continuing self-exclusion from the fallen kingdom of letterpress. Boffin himself, a rich illiterate with a shrewd, calculating knowledge of his own business, but with a less discerning, if entirely laudable, knowledge of human motive, offers the most sustained development of this theme.

As the previous chapters have shown, the assimilation of the specific and particular figure of the dustman into debates about the cultural and educational progress of the urban working classes was one of the central manoeuvres in the cultural and political dialogue that ensued. In his conception of Boffin as an illiterate dustman, then, Dickens appealed to one of the most powerful stereotypes through which the politics of literacy had been debated. Within that debate, the two extreme positions were represented by those who believed that dustmen were (as Mayhew seemed to believe) too deeply sunk into ignorance, complacency and social ostracism ever to be redeemed into anything approaching social inclusion and those who believed that, however improbable it might be, even the most repulsive fringes of society might be made aware of the benefits and possibilities not just of economic advance but of progress towards education and civility as well.

But Dickens refuses these traditional polarities in favour of a much subtler line of argument – that, while literacy is essential for economic and civil intercourse, it is also a dangerous and corrupting possibility that encompasses secrets as much as understanding, and also one that morally compromises its exponents. Boffin's cautious approach to the acquirement of literacy is extremely carefully managed. His initial approach to Wegg on the street is described in terms of secrecy, guilt and anxiety despite Boffin's bluff acknowledgement of his literary shortcomings. Boffin remains extremely troubled by the prospect of literacy, and accordingly deflects his true cultural aspirations obliquely on to the more frivolous but perhaps less deeply troubling world of 'fashion'. Indeed, he never seeks literacy for himself, and remains anxious about the effects it would have on his moral and economic life. Instead, he seeks to appropriate literacy through the employment of Wegg rather than through becoming literate himself. While the ability to read might have value as a form of fashionable accomplishment or as a commodity, Boffin refuses to acknowledge its potential as a form of self-realisation, a means of opening up the world of knowledge. Although he comments to Wegg that 'print is now opening ahead of me' he immediately qualifies the remark by denying the possibility of self-transformation through education – 'This night a literary man ... will begin to lead me to a new life'.[75] Boffin's 'learning' is to be conducted entirely by proxy. His confession of the limits of his reading skills – he can recognise that 'B' stands for Boffin – is met by Wegg's sly response that 'perhaps it's not as much as could be wished by an enquiring mind' but in reality Boffin clings obstinately to the belief that the world of letters is best left unvisited by people such as himself.[76] Unlike the massive emphasis on social mobility and the world-turned-upside-down in the caricature representations of educated and educating dustmen, Dickens consistently argues in *Our Mutual Friend* that access to print is a potentially dangerous and morally compromising accomplishment, an aspect of the fallen nature of Victorian urban culture. Boffin knows this – at Wegg's first reading, even leaving aside the comic confusion over Roman names and the precise empire that was being declined and falled, Boffin recognised that 'I'm in for it now'.[77] While Wegg sees literacy as a 'secret' that confers economic power and psychological authority on its practititoners, Boffin sees it only as a worryingly necessary accomplishment for a family of fashion. He also regards print as dangerously complex and ambiguous, – in short, a 'mystery' – leading its consumers away from self-evident moral imperatives towards corrupting misreadings and inflexions of events and motives. Neither man sees the acquisition of literacy, as the ideologues and caricaturists of the 1830s had done, as a form of self-realisation or self-transformation allowing its owner to participate fully in the cultural and political life of the nation. In a novel where Rokesmith is also Harmon, and where a single dust yard might be figured in such conflicting terms as 'Old Harmon's', 'Boffin's Bower', 'The Mounds' or 'Harmony Jail' (the latter a complex wordplay on Harmon's name and character), it is hardly surprising that Boffin prefers the impulses of his kindly nature and the knowledge learnt by experience of his trade to the complexities of written discourse.

One further aspect of Dickens's dialogue with the world of dust in *Our Mutual Friend* is worth brief mention – the metaphor of sifting drawn from the range of documentary accounts of dust collecting and disposal that Dickens had available to him. Sifting is of course achieved by riddling, and sifting and riddling are both aspects of the forensic method of investigation. Mr Venus, the articulator of bones and skeletons, brings together ideas of traces and remains as a form of evidence, and is perceived by Wegg to be a specialist at sifting, bringing to his own methods of 'scooping' and 'poking' a level of anatomising and dissecting skills appropriate to the complex remnants that comprise a dust heap. Their joint dissection of the Mounds becomes a form of anatomising, an attempt at reconstructing the secretive and the evasive from their remains, and it is brilliantly theorised in a discussion which takes place, entirely appropriately, over a sequence of glasses of 'mixed' liquor. Wegg seeks a proper method through deduction from binaries – is the top or the bottom of the heap the place to start? Prodding or Scooping? Sorting or Sifting? – thus drawing Venus into his world of deluded secrets. By the time of *Our Mutual Friend* in the 1860s it was widely understood that the value to be found in dust heaps was less likely to be discarded teaspoons than re-cycled breeze or fabrics. An economic understanding of the nature of waste had replaced a superstitious belief in lost or hidden 'treasure'. But in recurring back to the old mythology of dust, Silas Wegg draws on a strand of credulity that goes back a long way in the popular imagination.

The account of dust and dustmen in *Our Mutual Friend* is thus both contemporary and backward-looking. In his conception of Boffin, Dickens undoubtedly had plenty of contemporary sources to draw on, Mayhew and Horne's article in particular, to say nothing of the celebrated Mr Dodd. In these sources the dustman is represented in his late entrepreneurial guise as the manager of a landscape of carefully priced dust heaps with their serried ranks of attendant sifters and sorters. Dickens's concentration on Boffin's domestic arrangements and the absence of the street aspects of dustmanship confirms Boffin, like the avaricious and mean-spirited Harmon before him, as a mid-Victorian entrepreneur. But Dickens also had access to older and more complex renditions of dustmen which linked them to narratives of sudden wealth and cultural advancement. These were more troubled narratives about social change and the fear of contamination, injustice, chance and the power of documents and the written word. In particular, he had available tales and texts like *The Dustman's Belle*, drawn not from the mythology of industrial and entrepreneurial progress but from the oral traditional and urban mythology of dustmen – their sudden access to hidden or lost wealth, their supposed cultural and social aspirations (both ridiculous and heroic at the same time), and their shrewdness, itself the outcome of their distrust of letters and documents. More original, indeed entirely Dickens's own contribution to the continuing dustman narrative, is Boffin's redemptive kindness. Even here, however, Dickens followed available trends and conceived a dustman who embodied in absolute form the redemptive possibility that was beginning to become apparent in mid-Victorian narratives. As we have seen, in the journalism of the 1840s the dustman was increasingly figured as a receding trace of a kinder, stouter hearted, London which was being swept away. Dickens, in short, adapts a cultural nostalgia for the 1840s and 1850s for his own purposes. I believe *The Dustman's Belle* gave him the narrative he needed to assimilate all these ideas into the narrative of Nicodemus Boffin, where a dialogue between wealth, corruption and the human heart is played out in a way that meant that industrial Britain might still be redeemed into something approaching generosity of spirit, and where social aspirations could be expressed through kindness and self-awareness rather than ambition and greed.

# Conclusion

Despite its title, *Dusty Bob*, and its ostensible subject, the late eighteenth- and nineteenth-century dustman, this book is not only, or even centrally, concerned with 'low' or proletarian culture. Rather it is a study of those many writers and artists who made images of dustmen, and of the ways in which these images were understood and consumed. The precise social locale of these makers and consumers of texts and graphic representations is difficult to establish or describe. If one overarching narrative of this book is a shift from 'genteel' to 'bourgeois' representational codes (from *Life in London* to *Punch*, as it were) nonetheless the range of cultural production considered really belongs to some less precisely defined 'middling' part of society. Next to nothing studied here can be confidently ascribed to 'popular' let alone 'working-class' culture. While the latter half of the book has concerned itself with describing the ways in which an increasingly confident and self-aware bourgeoisie formulated and confronted some of its many anxieties about the city through various documentary, comic and fictional genres and textual strategies, even here the term 'middle class' seems too exclusive to describe the variety of songs, magazine articles and fictions gathered here. Perhaps the potential inadequacy of traditional categories – 'low', 'polite', 'genteel', 'middle class', 'shabby genteel', 'bourgeois' and their ilk – might be avoided by invoking the unscholarly but powerful term 'middle brow'. This book, then, is essentially concerned with middle-brow culture – the range of early nineteenth-century urban cultural production that draws on a combination of the kind of genteel traditionalism represented by single-plate caricature, the vernacular energy of the theatre and the musical saloon, and the emergent discourses of social concern.

The three more or less chronological phases used to structure the book – late eighteenth-century urban picturesque and picaresque, the vigorous new genres of visual culture from the 1820s and 1830s, and Victorian discussions of urban themes – subsume a history of representational modes and forms that, if not entirely congruent, nonetheless does serve to reinforce such a chronology. In making this connection between chronological phasing and the history of representational modes a number of issues emerge, not all of them entirely to be predicted. The energy of 'middle-brow' visual culture in the 1820s and 1830s suggested here, for example, does not coincide with a general critical consensus that caricature and comic art reach a low point between the virtual demise of political caricature in the 1820s and the emergence of self-consciously ambitious book and periodical illustration in the early 1840s. Other conclusions are more to be expected – the importance, indeed centrality, of periodicals to the development of early Victorian self-understanding, for example, or the persistence of Regency male bonhomie as a mode of social apprehension on into the early Victorian period, or, even more obviously, the slow transition from reading the streets as comically and diversely theatrical to apprehending them as sites of anxiety, threat and economic endeavour.

The unexpectedly varied and sustained interest in dustmen among the artists, print-makers, dramatists, journalists and novelists across at least the first half of the nineteenth century is a unique cultural phenomenon. While sweeps' boys attracted considerable attention, and other street tradesmen like coachmen and draymen became to some extent mythologised within print culture, dustmen remained a uniquely widespread focus of representational activity. While this book has tried to give an overview of such activity, it has been necessary to exclude at least as much as has been included.

But at least the main reasons for such 'over-representation' should be clear. The dust trade was early understood as a classic formulation of the economic phenomenon usually called 'penny capitalism', and as such it represented an immense challenge to early Victorian peace of mind. Dustmen were ostentatiously in control of their own economic destiny, needed few skills and relatively little equipment, and had the potential to become quite wealthy despite the degraded and despised nature of their work. Their trade practices, including their propensity towards combining work and leisure, suggested both their freedom from what might be called 'line management' and their lack of social accountability. Only later in the nineteenth century were they subject to legislation and municipal control, a shift which diverted the attention of writers like Mayhew and Dickens away from their street presence towards their broader entrepreneurial activities. In refusing any equation between wealth and respectability, in blurring the lines between labour and leisure, and in creating a connection between dirt and money, dustmen challenged traditional Victorian perceptions of economics.

More troubling still was the psycho-social significance of dustmen. Their street presence formed an unremittingly public reminder of the waste, detritus and even (by implication) ordure produced by an urban society. The effects that daily contact with such materials might have on people was repeatedly represented in a wide range of images of hideous, dirty, violent, lecherous and sometimes drunken dustmen grotesquely rendered through the conventions of caricature. Implicitly, the awfulness of dustmen might even be connected with ideas of sexuality, where their swaggering and aggressive masculinity was often, in practice, undermined by their social ineptitude. Yet such troubling apprehensions of the disgusting and the repulsive were also shot through with a sense of potentially more liberating otherness represented by the freedom dustmen had to be diverted, to lounge and observe, and to work when they pleased. The social space accorded to dustmen, while the product of their potentially contaminating or violent presence, let alone their noisiness, was to some extent a mark of grudging respect. Dustmen were represented as connoisseurs of street pleasure, and it is through their amused and fascinated gaze that the Victorian urban spectacle was repeatedly rendered.

More challenging still, dustmen reflected back, in gloriously travestied form, to the respectable and genteel world something of their own social aspirations, pretensions and foibles. As the emerging artisan and middle classes fretted over the niceties of social behaviour, entered the daunting world of consumer choice and sought to establish their right to cultural capital, there, in comic representations at least, was the dustman mocking their aspirations through his own parallel if perverse interest in learning, self-improvement, social-climbing and even fashion. In constructing a debased proletarian pastiche of middle-class manners, dustmen served to remind society in general, and comic artists and writers in particular, of the potential absurdity of their beliefs, habits and manners. The dustman, as his perpetual presence in *Punch* suggests, formed a powerfully carnivalesque riposte to the gentility of early Victorian society.

One further reason for the preoccupation of early nineteenth-century society with dustmen is aesthetic. Dustmen were visually interesting in a range of ways that intrigued and entertained both graphic artists and their customers. Their body shapes, emphasized by their extraordinary dress, re-iterated and sustained the Regency interest in the grotesque human form, and their distinctiveness, especially their fan-tail hats, made them extremely useful to caricaturists looking to give energy and variety to those urban scenes which had become the predominant subject of comic prints in the 1820 and 1830s. Dustmen were (and are) a visual delight. When such aesthetic appeal was combined with their wider socio-political importance it is hardly surprising that they formed a constant reference point for all those interested in the urban scene.

A concluding word on sources. In the attempt to give a broad overview of the topic and to relate representational history to more traditionally conceived social history this book has found its way to many obscure and little-regarded corners of Regency and early Victorian cultural production. In particular, it seems to me that caricature in the 1820s and 1830s has been largely ignored as a rich historical resource. To take a single instance, Robert Seymour's serialised sequence of tiny lithographs *New Readings of Old Authors* contains several hundred street scenes of immense interest and sophistication, yet it is hard to find even fleeting reference to it anywhere in recent scholarship. There is as yet no overview of the key commercial and artistic developments of caricature in the Regency period. Song-books from that period, too, offer much to the attentive reader, and are often illustrated by an extraordinary inventive range of wood-engraved vignettes. Periodicals and magazines, many of them still unexplored, remain a central resource. If there had been space, this book would certainly have spent more effort on constructing a detailed history of comic representations between 1820 and 1850 – and on thinking more precisely about the sociology of cultural production within 'middle-brow' visual culture. The greatest of many pleasures realised in the writing of this book has been that of discovering the diversity, energy and comic delight of the texts, images and performances to be found memorialised in the more obscure and remote stacks of scholarly libraries and collections. I hope this book gives some sense of that pleasure.

# Notes

## Notes to Chapter 1: Dustmen real and imagined

1 James Grant *Travels in Town*, 2 vols (London: Saunders and Otley 1839) I, 29.

2 *Leigh Hunt's London Journal* 67 (11 July 1835), 217.

3 William Heath *Dust O* (Thomas McClean 1 August 1835); fig. 1.

4 John Wight *More Mornings in Bow Street* (London: J. Robinson 1827), 261–2.

5 See Nancy Aycock Metz 'The Artistic Reclamation of Waste in *Our Mutual Friend*', *Nineteenth-Century Fiction* 34:1 (June 1979), 59–72; Ellen Handy 'Dust Piles and Damp Pavements: Excrement, Repression, and the Victorian City in Photography and Literature', in C. T. Christ and J. O. Jordan (eds) *Victorian Literature and the Victorian Visual Imagination* (Berkeley: University of California Press 1995); Kate Flint *The Victorians and the Visual Imagination* (Cambridge: Cambridge University Press 2000); Joseph A. Amato *Dust – A History of the Small and Invisible* (Berkeley: University of California Press 2000).

6 Flint *The Victorians*, 59.

7 David Trotter *Cooking with Mud – The Idea of Mess in Nineteenth Century Art and Fiction* (Oxford: Oxford University Press 2000), 20–1.

8 Linda Colley *Britons: Forging the Nation 1707–1838* (New Haven, CT: Yale University Press); Roy Porter *Enlightenment: Britain and the Creation of the Modern World* (Harmondsworth: Allen Lane 2000); John Brewer *The Pleasures of the Imagination: English Culture in the Eighteenth Century* (London: Harper Collins 1997).

9 J. Marriott (ed.) *Unknown London – Early Modernist Visions of the Metropolis, 1815–1845* 6 vols (London: Pickering and Chatto 2000).

10 J. C. Reid *Bucks and Bruisers – Pierce Egan and Regency England* (London: Routledge & Kegan Paul 1971); Roger Sales 'Pierce Egan and the Representation of London', in P. W. Martin and R. Jarvis (eds) *Reviewing Romanticism* (London: Macmillan 1992), 154–69; Greg Dart '"Flash Style": Pierce Egan and Literary London, 1820–1828', *History Workshop Journal* 51 (2001), 180–205.

11 I. B. Nadel and F. S. Schwarzbach (eds) *Victorian Artists and the City* (New York: Pergamon Press 1980); Dana Arnold *Re-presenting the Metropolis: Architecture, Urban Experience and Social Life in London 1800–1840* (Andover: Ashgate 2000), especially Chapter 2: 'The Art of Walking the Streets'; Deborah Epstein Nord *Walking the Victorian Streets: Women, Representation and the City* (Ithaca, NY: Cornell University Press 1995).

12 Carol Bernstein *The Celebration of Scandal: Towards the Sublime in Victorian Urban Fiction* (University Park: Pennsylvania State University Press n.d.); Celina Fox *Londoners* (London: Thames and Hudson 1987); Lynda Nead *Victorian Babylon: People, Streets and Images in Nineteenth Century London* (New Haven, CT: Yale University Press 2000); Judith Walkowitz *City of*

*Dreadful Delight: Narratives of Sexual Danger in Late-Victorian London* (Chicago: University of Chicago Press 1992).

13 J. Butt and K. Tillotson *Dickens at Work* (London: Methuen 1957), 38; P. Stallybrass and A. White *The Politics and Poetics of Transgression* (Ithaca, NY: Cornell University Press 1986), 191.

14 Sander L. Gilman *Difference and Pathology: Stereotypes of Sexuality, Race and Gender* (Ithaca, NY: Cornell University Press 1985).

15 Frederick Jameson *Signatures of the Visible* (New York and London: Routledge 1990).

16 The main sources for secondary discussions of the march of intellect, such as R. K. Webb, R. D. Altick and P. Anderson have been more recently augmented by the work of A. Rauch and J. Rose, and are listed in the bibliography.

17 See Brian E. Maidment *Reading Popular Prints 1780–1870* (Manchester: Manchester University Press 1996), Chapter 3.

18 Theodor Adorno *Minima Moralia: Reflections on a Damaged Life* (London: Verso 2005).

19 P. Stallybrass and A. White *The Politics and Poetics of Transgression* 5th paperback edn (Ithaca, NY: Cornell University Press 1995), 191.

20 Stallybrass and White *Politics and Poetics*, 128.

21 Stallybrass and White *Politics and Poetics*, 129.

22 Partridge, while giving *Cranford* (1853) as 'an early example', fails to give a clear date for the origin of the phrase. It also notes that 'filthy rich' is a relatively modern coinage. Eric Partridge *A Dictionary of Slang and Unconventional English*, ed. Paul Beale, 8th edn (London: Routledge & Kegan Paul 1984), 391.

23 James Greenwood *Unsentimental Journeys: or, Byways of the Modern Babylon* (London: Ward Lock & Tyler), 66.

24 Henry Mayhew *London Labour and the London Poor*, 4 vols (Griffin, Bohn & Co. 1861–62) II, 175. All subsequent references to Mayhew will be to the four-volume Dover facsimile reprint, ed. J. D. Rosenberg (New York: Dover Books 1968).

25 Charles Dickens *Our Mutual Friend*, ed. Stephen Gill (Harmondsworth: Penguin 1971), 897.

26 Mayhew *London Labour* II, 172.

27 Stephen Wall 'Review of Penguin edition of *Our Mutual Friend*', *Essays in Criticism* 221 (July 1971), 267–8.

28 H. P. Sucksmith 'The Dust Heaps in *Our Mutual Friend*', *Essays in Criticism* 23(2) (April 1973), 206–12.

29 Sucksmith 'Dust Heaps', 211.

30 The publishing history of Henry Mayhew's *London Labour and the London Poor* is a complicated one. The work was substantially published in part-issue form in 1851 and 1852, and then in two volumes with a third appearing in 1856. These volumes incorporated some of the material published in Mayhew's *Morning Chronicle* letters from 1849–50. But the most familiar version of *London Labour and the London Poor* is the four-volume one published between 1861 and 1862, and re-issued in as a facsimile paperback by Dover Books in 1968. Chapter 5 contains my own consideration of this material alongside much else.

31 See Chapter 7 for a full list of articles about dust and waste in Dickens's periodicals *Household Words* and *All the Year Round*.

32 Mayhew *London Labour* II, 166–81.

33 P. Quennell (ed.) *Mayhew's London being Selections from 'London Labour and*

*the London Poor'* (London: Spring Books n.d.), 335–50. This extremely useful volume is one of three Quennell edited for a publisher who specialised in cheap mass-circulation reprints.

34 Mayhew *London Labour* II, 172–3.

35 M. Cotsell *The Companion to Our Mutual Friend* (London: Allen and Unwin 1986), 30–3, 55–7.

36 The piece was written by the campaigning journalist James Greenwood, and was reprinted in 1872 in a volume made up from Greenwood's urban investigations on behalf of the magazine. James Greenwood *Unsentimental Journeys Through Modern Babylon* (London, Ward, Lock and Tyler 1872).

37 The undated trade card of Joseph Waller of Islington, for example, advertises the firm as 'Chimney Sweeper and Nightmen' with chimney cleaning undertaken by 'boys of all ages'. His card also advertises the fact that he puts out chimney fires, and keeps carts and horses for emptying 'Bog-houses, Drains and Cesspools with the utmost expedition'. James Steers is another who classes himself as a 'Chimney Sweeper and Nightman'. Sweeps also advertised their services widely as general carters, although the nature of their carts might have put off many needing transport for their goods. All these examples are taken from the collection of undated trade cards in the Guildhall Library, London, but similar evidence is available from the collections in the John Johnson Collection at the Bodleian Library, Oxford.

38 Robert Stone, for example, who announced on his trade card that he 'Decently performs all he undertakes', noted that his business was 'now carried on by his Daughter Mary Burnet'.

39 Mayhew *London Labour* II, 175.

40 T. L. Busby *Costume of the Lower Orders* (London: Baldwin, Craddock and Joy n.d. [c. 1820]). Busby's work is considered in detail in Chapter 2.

41 Brick dust was widely used for cleaning masonry and doorsteps in the late eighteenth century and brick dust sellers are widely represented in the later decades of the eighteenth century in series of trade images.

42 Charles Hindley *A History of the Cries of London: Ancient and Modern*, 2nd edn (London: Charles Hindley n.d.), 363. Hindley gives an undated *Cries of London* published by Goode Bros. as his source.

43 For 'Cries of London', see Sean Shesgreen *Images of the Outcast: The Urban Poor in the Cries of London* (Manchester: Manchester University Press 2002); for costume books see Sam Smiles *Eye Witness – Artists and Visual Documentation in Britain 1770–1830* (Aldershot: Ashgate 2000), Chapter 4. See also Chapter 2 of this volume.

44 Busby *Costume of the Lower Orders of London.*

45 John Wight *Mornings in Bow Street* (London: Charles Baldwyn 1824), 262–3.

46 Mayhew *London Labour* II, 175.

47 Henry Heath *No Genius* engraving (London: T. McClean n.d.).

48 Hindley reprints an undated series of *Cries of London* published by Goode Brothers of Clerkenwell which includes a crude image of a dustman who has 'got a mighty cinder heap/ Somewhere near Gray's Inn Lane'. C. Hindley *A History of the Cries of London, Ancient and Modern*, 2nd edn (London: Charles Hindley 1884), 363.

49 This couplet is taken from a provincial educational chapbook in the Osborne Collection in Toronto. See http:/collections.ic.gc.ca/Osborne/cries/cries.html.

50 Dickens takes some pains to point out in *Our Mutual Friend*, that the illiterate Nicodemus Boffin can, nonetheless, estimate the value of a dust-heap to within a halfpenny.

51 Dickens *Our Mutual Friend*, 95.

52 Henry Heath 'Vot have you von all they! Vy blow your luck', *Sketches in London* 29. Reprinted in Henry Heath *The Caricaturist's Scrap Book* (London: Robert Tyas ?1840).
53 Mayhew *London Labour* II, 171.
54 *BMC* 7444.
55 Mayhew *London Labour* II, 173.
56 James Greenwood *Unsentimental Journeys; or, Byways of the Modern Babylon* (London: Ward, Lock & Tyler 1872), 67.
57 Greenwood *Unsentimental Journeys*, 67–8.
58 R. H. Horne 'Dust; or Ugliness Redeemed', *Household Words* 1 (13 July 1850), 379–84.
59 Ellen Handy 'Dust Piles and Damp Pavements', 111–33.
60 T. P. Prest (ed.) *The London Singers' Magazine and Reciters Album* 1:67 (London: John Duncombe n.d.).
61 Prest (ed.) *The London Singers' Magazine* 1:23, 181.
62 *George Cruikshank's Omnibus*, 2 vols (London: Tilt and Bogue 1842). As well as the part-issue format and the initial two-volume publication, this work was extensively reprinted during the nineteenth century – for example by Bell & Daldy in 1870 – and suggest the extent to which Cruikshank's work was made available to several generations of readers. See Albert M. Cohn *George Cruikshank – A Catalogue Raisonné* (London: The Bookman's Journal 1924), 65–6. The two New Police Act images appear opposite pages 33 and 34.
63 J. Picker *Victorian Soundscapes* (Oxford: Oxford University Press 2003), 44.
64 Picker *Victorian Soundscapes*, 49.
65 Picker *Victorian Soundscapes*, 43.
66 Prest (ed.) *The London Singer's Magazine* I, 181.
67 'City of London Rakers' Duties and Districts, for the year ending at Midsummer Day 1838.' Guildhall Library C46–43.
68 Guildhall Library C46.33/T 1845.
69 *Pictorial Times* (9 May 1846), 296.
70 *BMC* 11820. The image was published as a print in c. 1811, but the print was reworking of an earlier drawing.
71 Peter Sinnema's *Dynamics of the Printed Page – Representing the Nation in the 'Illustrated London News'* (Aldershot: Ashgate 1998) contains some interesting and provocative readings of the full-page spread of the weekly illustrated journal.
72 *Bell's Gallery of Comicalities* (n.d. 1834?). Guildhall Library C21.2/p. 1832.
73 *Punch* 6 (1844), 65.
74 A photograph in the Guildhall Library dating from around the time of the First World War shows an automatic road sweeper in action. Guildhall Library C46.33/c. 1918.
75 There is some evidence that the National Philanthropic Society's schemes were at least partially implemented. See Guildhall Library C46.33/T 1845 and C46.33/T 1851.

## Notes to Chapter 2: Picturesque and educative dustmen: the urban scene and its dirty denizens, 1790–1821

1 Shesgreen *List* E 26, E 28, E 31, E 33, E 36, E 38, E 40, E 43, E 44, E 45, E 56, E 58 and E 61. Copies of Shesgreen's typescript can be found in the Guildhall Library, London, and the Lewis Walpole Library, Farmington, Connecticut.

2 For the 'Cries of London', especially in their eighteenth-century manifestation, see Sean Shesgreen and David Bywaters 'The First London Cries for Children' *Princeton University Library Chronicle* 59:2 (winter 1998), 223–50; and Sean Shesgreen *Images of the Outcast – The Urban Poor in the Cries of London* (Manchester: Manchester University Press 2002).
3 'Cries as books made their debut in England during the second half of the eighteenth century, when a constellation of forces reframed images of hawkers for a new audience then shifting from the periphery of social scrutiny to its centre – children.' Shesgreen *Images of the Outcast*, 150. See also Joyce Irene Whalley *Cobwebs to Catch Flies – Illustrated Books for the Nursery or Schoolroom 1700–1900* (London: Elek 1974), which has a chapter devoted to street cries and occupations.
4 Shesgreen links these shifts to a movement from the social to the private. 'The rise of modern domestic life and the debut of Cries configured as small tomes are linked by the fact that, whereas prints are public forms of art, books are personal objects. Prints are linked to sociability ... Books are tied to isolation'. While I see the force of this argument, I think that many of the Cries, as teaching texts, combined sociable and private consumption. Shesgreen also notes the miniaturisation of the image found in these texts. The shrinking size of printed images in the 1830s and 1840s is something discussed in Chapter 4.
5 Shesgreen *Images of the Outcast*, 152.
6 I. Opie and P. Opie *The Nursery Companion* (Oxford: Oxford University Press 1980).
7 Shesgreen *Images of the Outcast*, 152.
8 C. Hindley *A History of the Cries of London, Ancient and Modern*, 2nd edn (London: Charles Hindley 1884). See also J. St John *The Osborne Collection of Early Children's Books 1566–1910 – A Catalogue*, 2 vols (Toronto: Toronto Public Library 1958).
9 John Johnson Collection Trades and Professions Alphabets 1. A good reproduction of the entire Harvey and Darton alphabet which contains this image can be found in J. A. Lambert *A Nation of Shopkeepers – Trade Ephemera from 1654 to the 1860s in the John Johnson Collection* (Oxford: Bodleian Library 2001), 133. The image is dated 1837.
10 Percy Muir *Victorian Illustrated Books*, revised edn (London: B. T. Batsford 1985), 16. Muir's book attributes this illustration to an undated *Cries* by Luke Limner.
11 Edwin Pearson *Banbury Chapbooks* (London: Seven Dials Press 1970), 56.
12 Opie and Opie *The Nursery Companion*, 105 and 127.
13 Anon. *Sam Syntax's Description of the Cries of London as they are daily exhibited in the streets with appropriate engravings* (Baltimore, MD: Lucas Fielding Jr. n.d.).
14 While the image I have used here is from an 1818 edition of *City Scenes*, the publication first appeared in 1808, and was written by Jane and Ann Taylor. It was reprinted on numerous occasions, with designs after ink and watercolour sketches by Isaac Taylor. See Lawrence Darton *The Dartons – An Annotated Check-list of Children's Books Issued by Two Publishing Houses 1787–1876* (London: The British Library 2004), 247–9.
15 L. de Vries *Flowers of Delight – An Agreeable Garland of Poetry and Prose* (London: Dennis Dobson 1965), 170. De Vries's anthology is drawn from the Osborne Collection.
16 De Vries *Flowers of Delight*, 170.
17 Anon. *The New London Cries: Or Humorous Alphabet* (London: printed by

T. Richardson for O. Hodgson n.d. [c. 1830?]). Yale Centre for British Art DA 688/N 48/1820Z.

18 John Johnson Collection Trades and Professions 3 (18). For the particular history and significance of scraps as a graphic tradition see A. Allen and J. Hoverstadt *The History of Printed Scraps* (London: New Cavendish Books 1983).

19 Ruari McClean *Joseph Cundall – A Victorian Publisher* (Pinner: Private Libraries Association 1976), 9.

20 Shesgreen *Images of the Outcast*, 125.

21 F. J. Mannskirsch *Dustman* (London: R. Ackermann 1797). The same series also contains an image of a scavenger.

22 Even the *BMC* is very cautious in identifying dustmen in images of this date – see for example *BMC* 12505, which acknowledges that the subject might as easily be a coal-porter as a dustman.

23 *BMC* VII, xliii–xliv. See also H. M. Atherton 'The Mob in Eighteenth-Century Caricature', *Eighteenth-Century Studies* 12:1 (1978), 47–54; J. Brewer *The Common People and Politics 1750s–1790s* (Cambridge: Chadwyk-Healey 1986).

24 See, for example, *BMC* 10763, 10966, 11775, 12341, 12505, 13487 and Rowlandson's *Bartholomew Fair*.

25 *BMC* 7444.

26 Such renewed awareness can be attributed to some excellent recent publications, notably Sam Smiles *Eye Witness – Artists and Visual Documentation in Britain 1770–1830* (Aldershot: Ashgate 2000); Sheila O'Connell *The Popular Print in England* (London: British Museum Press 1999). See also the special issue of *Textile History* 33:1 (May 2002) on 'The Dress of the Poor'.

27 O'Connell *The Popular Print in England*, 196.

28 W. H. Pyne *Microcosm* (London: R. Ackermann 1823). The plate is dated 1 August 1823.

29 Anon. *Picturesque Representations of the Dress and Manners of the English* (London: John Murray 1814). There seem to have been a number of different versions of this image distributed in both England and France.

30 Busby *Costume of the Lower Orders of London. The Dustman*, a coloured etching, is dated 15 May 1820.

31 Smiles *Eye Witness*, 95. 'Such detailed investigations of the backgrounds of the subjects are exceptional ... Busby's book was straining the definition of costume book ... Busby's address to his readers is, thus, insisting on a particular engagement with his subjects, in contradistinction to the more generalised presentations offered in rival costume books.'

32 Smiles *Eye Witness*, 93.

33 G. Cruikshank *London Characters* (London: Joseph Robins 1829). See Cohn *George Cruikshank*, 59; R. A. Vogler *Graphic Works of George Cruikshank* (New York: Dover 1979), 140–1.

34 Vogler *Graphic Works of George Cruikshank*, 140.

35 For Cruikshank's contributions to Wight's works (already extensively cited in Chapter 1) see Cohn 238–40; Vogler 140–7; Patten *George Cruikshank's Life, Times and Art*, 2 vols (Cambridge: Lutterworth Press 1992 and 1996) I, 280–3. Patten notes that '*Mornings* was a minor contribution to a burgeoning new journalistic genre, the urban sketch, which shared with the graphic sketch a looser, more immediate, and less inclusive response to urban life' (280).

36 Vogler *Graphic Works of George Cruikshank*, 140.

37 Smiles *Eye Witness*, 91.

38 Philip Cox, in his excellent study of the dramatisation of literary texts in this period, examined the reasons for Dickens's attempts to distance his work from that of Egan. Philip Cox *Reading Adaptations: Novels and Verse Narratives on the Stage, 1790–1840*, 121–4.

39 As well as popular editions from Methuen and John Camden Hotten, there were numerous upmarket reprints.

40 J. C. Reid *Bucks and Bruisers – Pierce Egan and Regency England* (London: Routledge & Kegan Paul 1971).

41 Since Reid's study it has become commonplace, even obligatory, for popular books on Regency social history to make extensive use of *Life in London* as a form of transposed documentary which elides fiction into 'truth'. See, for example, Venetia Murray's *An Elegant Madness – High Society in Regency England* (London: Viking 1998), 57–61, or Donald A. Low's *The Regency Underworld* (London: Dent 1982, reprinted London: Sutton 1999), Chapter 5, which is entirely based on Egan's work. Low at least tries to decide what might have been true and what fictive in Egan's picaresque imagination, but both he and Murray persist in regarding the novel as a major historical source.

42 See Roger Sales 'Pierce Egan and the Representation of London', in P. Martin and R. Jarvis (eds) *Reviewing Romanticism* (London: Macmillan 1992); Gregory Dart '"Flash Style" – Pierce Egan and Literary London 1820–1828', *History Workshop Journal* 51 (2001), 180–205; Nord *Walking the Victorian Streets*, 30–3; Cox *Reading Adaptations*, Chapter 4; and Marriott's Introduction to volume 1 of *Unknown London*.

43 Dart '"Flash Style"', 180.

44 See Eric Partridge *Slang Today and Yesterday*, 3rd edn (London: Routledge & Kegan Paul 1950), 80–108, for a more detailed study of Egan's use of slang. It is worth noting here that all subsequent dustmen are represented as speaking in a kind of imagined London vernacular, pronouncing 'w' as 'v', and showing their lack of breeding every time they open their mouths.

45 Marriott *Unknown London* I, xxiii–xxv; II, vii–viii.

46 See A. Edward Newton *The Format of the English Novel* (New York: Burt Franklin 1971).

47 Marriott *Unknown London* II, 193.

48 Marriott *Unknown London* II, 286.

49 Anon. *Real Life in London* (London: Jones & Co. 1822).

50 It is difficult to give precise page references for these plates, as they tend to be bound in with the text in rather arbitrary ways. My own edition of *Real Life in London* is made up of various editions of both text and plates, using title pages from two different editions and binding in the plates together immediately after the title page. The caption for this plate reads – 'Tom and Bob, in Masquerade, blowing a cloud and taking their heavy wet at the Black Diamond merchant's free and easy King Charles's Crib, Scotland Yard', thus identifying the fantailed participants as coal-whippers rather than dustmen.

## Notes to Chapter 3: Theatrical dustmen, 1820–60: not so Dusty Bob

1 W. T. Moncrieff *Tom and Jerry; or, Life in London*, Dicks' Standard Plays No. 82 (London: John Dicks n.d.), 22. All references will be to this text, and are given in brackets in the text.

2 The phrase is that used by H. Philip Bolton to describe Moncrieff's theatrical version of Egan's novel in his *Dickens Dramatized* (London: Mansell 1987), 23.

3 Philip Cox's study of the dramatisation of literary texts between 1790 and 1840 forms an extremely useful background to this chapter, especially the discussion of the dramatisation of Dickens's early work by Moncrieff and others. Philip Cox *Reading Adaptations – Novels and Verse Narratives on the Stage 1790–1840* (Manchester: Manchester University Press 2000).
4 For accounts of the *Life in London* phenomenon see: Charles Hindley *The True History of Tom and Jerry* (London: Charles Hindley n.d. [1892]); J. C. Reid *Bucks and Bruisers: Pierce Egan and Regency England* (London: Routledge & Kegan Paul 1971), 50–92; Robert L. Patten *George Cruikshank's Life, Times, and Art* (Cambridge: Lutterworth Press 1992) I, 220–31; Donald A. Low *The Regency Underworld* revised edn (Stroud: Sutton Publishing 1999), 99–122, as well as the essays by Dart and Sales already cited. The accompanying lists of play-bills, performances and texts for which I have found documentary evidence is only a small selection of what must be available.
5 Hindley *True History*, 3–4.
6 *Tom and Jerry in France or Vive La Bagatelle* Royal Coburg Theatre, December 1822. Play-bill, Guildhall Library.
7 *Tom and Jerry* Sadler's Wells, April, May, June and August 1822. Play-bills, Theatre Museum. The hundredth night of this production was advertised on 5 August.
8 *The Songs, Parodies and c. in the Burletta of Tom and Jerry* (printed for P. Egan and published by Sherwood, Neely and Jones n.d.). This pamphlet, which the Beinecke catalogue states is one of only two known copies, seems to have been a kind of souvenir programme for performances at the Sadler's Wells Theatre.
9 *Tom, Jerry and Logic's Life in London* Royalty Theatre, April and May 1822. Play-bills, Guildhall Library.
10 Reid *Bucks and Bruisers*, 77.
11 *Tom, Jerry and Logic's Life in London* Royalty Theatre, April and May 1822. Play-bills, Guildhall Library.
12 The description is taken from an undated W. T. Moncrieff version of the play held in the Beinecke Library at Beinecke Plays 1978.
13 Hindley *True History*, ii.
14 Hindley *True History*, 76.
15 Hindley *True History*, 78–81.
16 Charles Dibdin *Life in London, or, the Larks of Logic, Tom, and Jerry* (London: John Lowndes 1822). Beinecke Plays 42.
17 *Life in London* or *Tom and Jerry* appeared in most of the major series through which play-texts were reprinted. It formed no. 33 in Cumberland's British Theatre (48 vols, 1826 on); no. 82 in John Dicks' The British Drama (12 vols, 1866 on); appeared in Williams Wonderful Penny Series (1877–78); and in Lacy's Acting Edition of Plays, Dramas, Extravaganzas, Farces, etc. (165 vols, 1849–1917). Lacy's Acting Edition was bought by French in 1872, and subsequently issued under their name.
18 See Appendix 2. Apart from Hindley, Reid, James and Patten, information about productions of *Life in London* and *Tom and Jerry* has been assembled from Donald Mullin *Victorian Plays: A Record of Significant Productions on the London Stage, 1837–1901* (New York: Greenwood Press n.d.) and E. Fagg *The Old 'Old Vic', or, from Barrymore to Bayliss* (London: The Vic-Wells Association 1936).
19 *Tom and Jerry, Or, Life in London* Astley's, July/August 1822. Play-bills, Theatre Museum.

20 Hindley comments that the actors 'became tired and worn out with the repetition of their characters'. *True History*, 96.
21 *Tothills Field Tournament* Olympic Theatre, 1823. Play-bills, Guildhall Museum.
22 Dibdin *Life in London.*
23 *Life in London* Olympic Theatre, 11 March 1822. Play-bill, author's collection.
24 W. T. Moncrieff *Songs, Parodies, Duets, Chorusses [sic], etc,* (n.p. 1821). This publication is a rare pamphlet of material related to the Adelphi Theatre production, and was found in the Beinecke Library, 1978/1271.
25 David Kerr Cameron *London's Pleasures: From Restoration to Regency* (Stroud: Sutton Publishing 2001) chapter 2 discussed London club culture, and positions Almack's as the most exclusive of the London gambling clubs.
26 'Max' was a contraction of maximum, and Partridge notes that 'properly' it referred to 'very good gin'. Eric Partridge *A Dictionary of Slang and Unconventional English,* ed. Paul Beale, 8th edn (London: Routledge & Kegan Paul 1984).
27 'A rogue assuming the character of a gentleman, or opulent tradesman, who, under that appearance, defrauds workmen', according to Partridge. A mace can also mean a sham loan office. There were also 'mace-men', 'mace coves' and 'macers'.
28 Partridge gives two main meanings for dust – as a noun 'money' and as a verb 'to blind'. But a 'dust' can also be a row or disturbance, and sometimes 'dust' is used to mean semen.
29 Moncrieff *Life in London*, 23.
30 *Tom, Jerry and Logic's Life in London* Royalty Theatre, April/May 1822. Play-bills, Guildhall Library.
31 Hindley *True History*, 82–3.
32 Hindley *True History*, 82.
33 Hindley *True History*, 82.
34 This comment comes from the Sadler's Wells play-bill for *Pierce Egan's Tom and Jerry* for 21 May 1822 (Theatre Museum).
35 Hindley *True History*, ii.
36 For the symbolic significance of dustmen's hats see Chapter 1 and B. E. Maidment '101 Things to Do with a Dustman's Hat: Dustmen, Dirt and Dandyism 1820–1860', *Textile History* 33:1 (May 2002), 79–97.
37 One version of the play uses a song sung to the air of 'Nothing Like Grog' and concludes with the refrain 'by Jingo there's nothing like max'. *Songs, Parodies and c. in the Burletta of Tom and Jerry*, 20.
38 Hindley *True History*, 65.
39 The importance of Pierce Egan and Moncrieff in making cant and slang a topic of general enjoyment has long been recognised, and suggests important ways in which the respectable could engage with the raffish and even the transgressive. Eric Partridge noted over 50 years ago that 'Egan and Moncrieff, although they did not dispel … eighteenth and nineteenth century contempt for slang … did more than anybody to cause slang to become fashionable and general'. Eric Partridge *Slang Today and Yesterday*, 3rd edn (London: Routledge & Kegan Paul 1950), 83. For a recent discussion of Egan's creative use of cant, slang and 'flash' language see Dart, '"Flash Style"'.
40 George Speaight *Juvenile Drama: The History of the English Toy Theatre* (London: Macdonald & Co. 1946), 88 and 214. Speaight (214) describes West as 'the greatest publisher of the Juvenile Drama' and gives a list of his many publications.
41 Speaight *Juvenile Drama*, 104.

42 J. L. Marks *Scenes From Life in London 2 – Tom Jerry and Logic at All-Max in the East* (Guildhall Library).

43 G. Speaight *The History of the English Toy Theatre* (London: Macdonald & Co. 1946), 288.

44 'W.W.' *All Max in the East, A Scene in Tom and Jerry, or Life in London* coloured engraving (S. W. Fores, 24 April 1822).

45 Leslie Shepard *John Pitts, Ballad Printer* (London: Private Libraries Associations 1969), 67–71. See also Reid *Bucks and Brusiers*, 73–92.

46 It is disappointing not to be able to find a play-text or record of a theatrical performance which included *The Literary Dustman*. The existing play-texts do generally print the lyrics of the songs performed in the plays and often give the names of specific tunes drawn from the widely available common stock, both oral and written, of popular airs. But none of the printed texts I have seen includes *The Literary Dustman*, although Hindley includes a verse of it among his medley of associated material. The tentative conclusion must be that *The Literary Dustman* was written some considerable time after 1821, and became associated with the play at some date in the early 1830s where the topical references to the march of intellect and the *Penny Magazine* would make more sense.

47 Louis James *Print and the People 1819–1851* (London: Allen Lane 1976), 149–50, prints both the text of the song and the wood-engraved image from Moncrieff.

48 Philip Ward *Cambridge Street Literature* (Cambridge: Oleander Press 1978), 26–8.

49 *The Quaver or Songster's Pocket Companion* (1854), 257–9.

50 William Thomas Thomas [W. T. Moncrieff] *An Original Collection Of Songs, sung at the Theatres Royal, Public Concerts &c.* (John Duncombe 1850?).

51 Thomas *Collection of Original Songs*, 241.

52 Thomas *Collection of Original Songs*, 205.

53 Thomas *Collection of Original Songs*, 106.

54 R. B. and W. Brough *Alfred the Great or, The Minstrel King* (London: 1859).

55 H. J. Byron *George de Barnwell* (London: 1863).

56 The image forms part of a copy of the play-bill for the 21 May 1822 performance of *Tom and Jerry* at the Sadler's Well's Theatre held in The Theatre Museum, London.

57 Hindley *True History*, ii.

58 James *Print and the People*, 151; T. Gretton *Murders and Moralities* (London: Colonnade Books 1980), 87. James dates his version of the broadside as c. 1828, which seems very late given the apparently specific allusion to the closure of *Tom and Jerry*'s long run at the Adelphi (1821–23). Gretton gives the firm date of 1823 for the broadside he reproduces, which seems right. Gretton only prints a small section from the complete broadside, which is rather misleading given the diversity and complexity of the complete broadside. Hindley gives a detailed account of Catnach's interest in *Life in London* and its subsequent dramatisations.

59 The full text of the play-bill advertising this benefit is interesting enough to be printed at length: 'Royalty Theatre/Though DUSTY BOB and famed BLACK SALLY/May charm the world their charms can't tally/With those who now appear in view,[sic]/To show what Children's will can do;/Strong plaudits they have carried yet,/And more ere long they'll try to get,/But let us hope, our hopes may sit,/Securly [sic] on this BENEFIT./Wednesday July 21st. 1824./FOR THE BENEFIT OF LITTLE MASTER AND LITTLE MISS LINCH/Who most timidly solicits a little of the kind liberality which

the success of their little endeavours have taught them to hope for, and take this method of informing their little circle of acquaintances, that with a little of the Company's aid, and a little of their patron's favors, they are enabled to present to their Friends their little Bill ... And in the course of the Evening they will Dance the Little Pas de deux of Dusty Bob and African Sal'. Mr Linch had appeared as Dusty Bob in *Tom, Jerry and Logic's Life in London* at the Royalty Theatre in April and May 1822. He also re-created the role of Dusty Bob in another Royalty production – *Tothills Tournament, Or, The Chicken Butcher and the Bear* in March 1823. Play-bills for these productions are in the Guildhall Library.

60 Delia Napier 'John Lloyd of Shelton' *The Antique Collector* (October 1989), 48–53.

61 *Punch Almanac* 2 (1842).

62 *Punch* 4 (1843), title page.

63 *Punch* 7 (1844), 172.

### Notes to Chapter 4: Visual culture and the represented dustman, 1820–50: the public dustman

1 While no detailed history of the trade in prints during this period is available, much information can be gleaned from Dorothy George's Introduction to volume XI of *BMC* as well as from the books by George, Kunzle and Donald, and Pound's unpublished PhD thesis, which are all listed in the bibliography.

2 D. Kunzle *The History of the Comic Strip – The Nineteenth Century* (Berkeley: University of California Press 1990), 18–26.

3 For an extended version of this section see Maidment '101 Things'.

4 P. Cunnington and C. Lucas *Occupational Costume in England from the Eleventh Century to 1914* (London: A and C Black 1976); C. Williams Mitchell *Dressed for the Job: The Story of Occupational Costume* (Poole: Blandford Press 1982); Diane de Marly *Working Dress: A History of Occupational Clothing* (London: Batsford 1986).

5 This quotation forms a stage direction in W. T. Moncrieff's *Tom and Jerry*.

6 *The Town* No. 62 (Saturday 4 August 1838), 'Characteristic Sketches No. LXII'.

7 *Dusty Bob*, a large single-plate engraved caricature, was published by S. Gans on 1 June 1829.

8 Cunnington and Lucas *Occupational Costume*, 278–9.

9 This signed watercolour, one of the aesthetically most sophisticated representations of dustmen I have seen, is shown as item 7 in G. J. Saville's 2001 catalogue of *Caricature – Water Colours and Drawings*.

10 See Busby *Costume of the Lower Orders of London*. Busby's image, which is discussed also in Chapter 2, shows a dustman wearing patched and holey trousers (rather than breeches), clogs and a dark, close-fitting jacket. Henry Alken *Involuntary Thoughts* (London: Thomas McClean 1823). LWL 823 0 26.

11 Cunnington and Lucas *Occupational Costume*, 278–9.

12 'Flying Dustman' from J. Thompson and Adolphe Smith *Street Life in London* (London: 1876–77).

13 Heath *The Caricaturist's Sketch Book* (1840). This volume is characteristic of the commercial opportunism of the period in drawing together various previous published miscellaneous plates and short sequences by Heath into a single volume bound in publishers' cloth. Most of the etched plates are formed out of grouping of smaller images loosely bound together by shared comic ideas or topics.

14 This comment appears in chapter 11 of Dickens, *Our Mutual Friend* (1864–65).
15 Flannel is the usually cited material for these jackets, but certainly fustian would account for the exaggerated shapes seen in these images. I am grateful to Barbara Burman for information on this matter.
16 Anonymous vignette wood engraving in *Punch* 10 (1846), 236.
17 Henry Heath *Intellectual – Character: One of the Club at his Studies!* (I. B. Brookes, 1 May 1834). Interestingly, Heath has used lithography for this image, and the subdued palette is important in conveying the assumed gentility of the subject.
18 Published – and perhaps drawn – by J. L. Marks, this print forms one of a pair. The second image shows the interior of a chimney sweep's house, with a fearsomely overdressed sweep and his wife offering advice to their apprentice children. Lounging in his chair with a cigar in his mouth and 'A Treatise on Curing Chimneys' by Dr Birkbeck dangling from his hand, the sweep here offers a grotesque and absurd vision of assumed gentility.
19 R. L. Patten *George Cruikshank's Life, Times and Art*, 2 vols (Cambridge: Lutterworth Press 1992 and 1996) I, 211.
20 *Illustrated London News* (20 October 1855), 484.
21 George Cruikshank *Pit, Boxes and Gallery* (etching: George Cruikshank 25 June 1836). Published as a plate in *George Cruikshank's Sketchbook*.
22 George Cruikshank *Tobacco Leaves No. 1* (etching: David Bogue n.d.).
23 There are many images where the visual distinction between dustmen and coal-heavers is virtually impossible to make except by context. There is, for example, Cruikshank's well-known image of 'Scotland Yard' in Dickens's *Sketches by Boz* which shows a group of fantailed, be-breeched and loose-coated men smoking and drinking by a pub fire. Only the accompanying text makes it clear that the men are coal-heavers rather than dustmen. See M. Slater (ed.) *Sketches by Boz and Other Early Papers 1833–1839* (London: J. M. Dent 1994), 66–7. I have tried only to use images in this book where the internal or contextual evidence makes it clear that the image is that of a dustman. Nonetheless, the odd coal-heaver may well have found himself celebrated here as a dustman.
24 Mitchell *Dressed for the Job*, 74.
25 G. Saville, catalogue of caricature watercolours and drawings, November 2001, Item 7. Rowlandson died in 1827, so this image is a relatively early one.
26 *Punch* 1 (1843), 159.
27 Anon. *Bartholomew Fair* etching and text (London: Laurie and Whittle 1811). Guildhall Library Satires 1811.
28 Henry Morley *Memoirs of Bartholomew Fair* (London: Frederick Warne and Co. n.d.), 370 and 382.
29 F. C. *The Life of John Richardson, Showman* (London: 1919).
30 F. C. *The Life of John Richardson*, 12.
31 Seymour's *Sketches*, first published in the 1830s, was frequently reprinted, but all the editions I have seen retain the original title-page illustration.
32 James Grant *Sketches in London* (London: W. S. Orr 1838), 181. Reprinted in Marriott *Unknown London* vol. 6 with a useful introduction.
33 G. Cruikshank *Pit, Boxes & Gallery* (London: George Cruikshank 1836).
34 George Speaight *Punch and Judy – A History* revised edn (London: Studio Vista 1970), 76.
35 Speaight *Punch and Judy*, 76.
36 W. Heath 'Stanzas to Punchinella' in the *Glasgow Looking Glass* 1:4 (23 July 1825), 3. *BMC* 15040.

37 Speaight, *Punch and Judy*. If Speaight is right in dating this image at around 1810 it forms one of the first distinct images of a dustman amidst an urban crowd, and is additionally a very early example of a wood engraving in this idiom.
38 A similar image can be found in the *Comic Almanack* (1837), 110.
39 *Comic Almanack* (March 1843).
40 C. J. Grant *The Political Drama No. 2 – The Modern Puritan* (London: G. Drake c. 1833).
41 C. J. Grant's *Almanack for 1832* was re-published in 1833 with only the date changed.
42 R. Seymour 'Low Musical Connisseurs' William Spooner (6 June 1839). LWL 839 6.6 1.
43 W. T. Moncrieff *The March of Intellect, a Comic Poem* (London: William Kidd 1830).
44 W. Heath 'Buttercups and Daisies – A Sketch from Low-Life', S. W. Fores (1 May 1822). *BMC* 14461.
45 Henry Heath *Football in the Streets of London*. The image is dated at c. 1820 by the FIFA Collection. See *FIFA Museum Collection – 1000 Years of Football* (edition q 1996), 31.
46 *Northern Looking Glass* 1, 11–13 (November–December 1825). *BMC* 15091, 15095, 15105, 15391.
47 See, for example, C. J. Grant's 'Trades Union' in *Everybody's Album* 6 (15 March 1834). Grant's view of *all* working men and women was however entirely and unremittingly jaundiced.
48 William Heath *Leaving the House of Lords* (London: T. McClean 1829). *BMC* 15694. For a contextual account of the image, see Edward Du Cann *The Duke of Wellington – The Caricaturists View* (Woodbridge: Antique Collectors' Club 2000), 74–80.
49 Anon. *A Meeting of the Trades' Union* in *McClean's Monthly Sheet of Caricatures* No. 35. (London: T. McClean n.d.).
50 Anon. *General Assembly* (n.d.). Photocopy in LWL.
51 I have drawn this sequence from Charles Hindley's later Victorian collection *Galleries of Comicalities* (London: Charles Hindley), which reprints material published in *Bell's Life in London* in the late 1820s. 'The Pugilist's Progress' occupies pp. 28 to 37.
52 Henry Heath 'Nautical Dictionary' plate 4 in *Caricaturist's Scrap Book* .
53 Anon. [Percival Leigh] *The Comic Latin Grammar* (London: Charles Tilt 1839), 65.
54 A classic exposition of this trope occurs in *The Odd Volume*, a miscellany of short narratives with illustrations by George Cruikshank and Seymour. In one story the text comments 'To escape was impossible. – A cart before, and two carriages behind, made us stationary …'. And the accompanying illustration shows, in an exquisitely drawn vignette, the cause of the blockage to be a dustcart with a dustman serenely surveying the chaos from the rear of his cart. *The Odd Volume* (London: W. Kidd n.d.), 268–9. Robert Seymour's 1829 'The March of Intellect' also shows a street in which a dustman's cart has brought through traffic to a halt.
55 *Comic Almanack* (March 1840).
56 *BMC* 16889. Under the title *Democracy and Aristocracy* a snooty aristocrat asks 'How dare you sneeze as I walk by?' to which the unabashed dustman replies 'How dare you walk by as I sneeze?'.
57 Anon. *Comic Latin Grammar*, 140.
58 [H. Heath] 'Fears' S. Gans (1829). *BMC* 15972.

59 [C. J. Grant] source unknown.
60 *BMC* 14590.
61 George Cruikshank *Illustrations of Time* plate 6 'Christmas Time' (George Cruikshank 1 May 1827). *BMC* 15475. *Illustrations of Time* was extensively reprinted in the nineteenth century.
62 George Cruikshank *December* in the *Comic Almanack* (December 1836).
63 This undated and unsigned lithographed image, held in the John Johnson Collection in the Bodleian Library, looks like a part of one of C. J. Grant's multi-image plates, probably from one of his magazines, but I have been unable to find it elsewhere.
64 *Comic Almanack* (December 1835).
65 Guildhall Library C46.32/T 18.
66 Guildhall Library C46.32 and C46.33.
67 Guildhall Library C46.32.
68 *Punch* 20 (1851), 17.
69 *Punch* 24 (1853), 7.
70 *Punch* 28 (1855), 7.
71 William Heath 'Music' (G. Humphrey 25 March 1823).
72 George Cruikshank 'November – St Cecilia's Day' in the *Comic Almanack* (November 1837).
73 Robert Seymour *Sketches* William Spooner (6 June 1839). LWL 839 6.6 1.

**Notes to Chapter 5: Visual culture and the represented dustman, 1820–50: domestic dustmen and cultural challenge**

1 H. Heath 'Prize – A vessel captured from the enemy' *Nautical Dictionary No. 4* from *The Caricaturist's Scrap Book* (London: Robert Tyas n.d.).
2 [Henry Heath] 'Fears' (London: S. Gans 1829), *BMC* 15972.
3 'Monopolise' from an unidentified 'Lexigraphical Dictionary'.
4 W. Newman *Frontispiece to the Musical Books* 1835 (Lewis Walpole 835.0.208).
5 Henry Heath 'Refit' from the *Nautical Dictionary*.
6 'February' from *Punch Almanac* (1842).
7 'Paul Pry' [William Heath] 'The Tender Passion' (London: S. Gans n.d.), *BMC* 15971.
8 Anon. [J. L. Marks] (London: J. L. Marks n.d.).
9 *Punch* X (1846) 96.
10 'The Last Woman', *BMC* 15341.
11 George Cruikshank 'Tobacco Leaves' (London: David Bogue n.d.).
12 Anon. 'Puff, Puff, It is an age of puffing ... Thomas McClean' (25 September 1827), LWL 827 9 25 1.
13 C. J. Grant *Everybody's Album* No. 12 (15 June 1834).
14 Robert Seymour *Sketches* vol. 5, no. 11 (London: G. S. Tregear n.d.).
15 M. Egerton 'Street Breakfast' from Egerton's *Airy Nothings* (London: 1825).
16 Anon. *Genuine Tea Company* (London: S. W. Fores 1825).
17 William Heath *Scenes in London 3* in *The Caricaturist's Scrap Book*.
18 *Illustrated London News* (1846). The association of dustmen with pineapples at first sight seems a relatively simple extension of the tropes of inappropriateness, aspirational incongruity and pretension which have already been identified. But there is a deeper – dirtier – narrative to be told. In a characteristically helpful aside, Dorothy George makes the point that pineapples were first sold commercially on the streets in 1842. There are, however, many earlier images of pineapples being eaten, and it is no accident that a complex William Heath *March of Intellect* print of 1829 shows (among much

else) two dustmen stuffing themselves with a pineapple and an ice respectively, both bought from a genteel lady sat reading at a charity stall under a Moorish sunshade held by a black servant. The dustman clearly has no idea how to eat the pineapple which he is forcing into his mouth whole, unpeeled and untrimmed. George describes the print as combining 'the fantasies of invention with low-life luxury'. Yet even this description has its ambiguities when applied to the vignette narrative of dustman and pineapple within the print. 'The fantasies of invention' are represented here clearly enough – in their pre-commercial phase pineapples could only be produced by those with the combination of wealth, leisure, know-how and curiosity required for successful cultivation in an alien climate and environment. In effect, the cultivation of pineapples was thus confined to the very rich, and it represented the antithesis of a commercial venture. It is here that the ambiguity of the dustman's social status exerts itself. At one level the print is constructed out of difference. Nothing could be better evidence of a topsy-turvy society than the exotic pineapple, the product solely of aristocratic leisure, becoming available as consumer goods to the lewd, fractious, uneducated and irredeemably vulgar dustman. Yet, as we have seen, the dustman is also the 'penny capitalist' incarnate, the self-reliant tradesman who can choose his own work hours and has learnt that the laws of unregulated capitalism allow him to make money from waste without any financial obligation to parish or state. If anyone from the proletariat can afford a pineapple it is likely to be the dustman, his appearance and reputation notwithstanding. The inversions of the march of intellect are economic as well as cultural. The pineapple and the dustman share another narrative beyond incongruous contiguity, however. In their early British manifestation as the product of aristocratic leisure interest in 'cultivation' (both of the mind and of crops), pineapples could only be grown in pits. The intensive method of cultivation required the low spreading plants to be covered in manure or ordure in order to generate, through the rotting process, the heat necessary to nurture the exotic plants to fruition in the hostile British climate. What could be a more compelling analogy to the socio-economic role of the dustman, who created his own 'yield' from the creative redeployment of waste, and (it was generally believed) excrement? This heroic shared narrative between pineapples and dustmen is given graphic substance in this image from the *Illustrated London News* in 1846. In confirmation of George's sense that pineapples were introduced commercially into London in the 1840s, the paper declares: 'The attempt made last year to import into this country Pine-apples, from the West Indies, was attended with such success as to induce speculators to improve the culture.'

19 George Cruikshank 'August', *Comic Almanack* 1 (1835), 25.

20 See, for example, the rough woodcut, perhaps drawn from a broadside, in C. B. Grafton's *Trades and Occupations – A Pictorial Archive from Early Sources* (New York: Dover Publications 1990) 137, and some of the illustrations to journals of the 1840s discussed in Chapter 6.

21 Marriott *Unknown London* III, 17.

22 *Looking Glass* 1:8 (1 August 1830), *BMC* 16511.

23 T. P. Prest (ed.) *London Singers' Magazine and Reciters Album* No. 91 (London: J. Duncombe n.d.), 225.

24 W. Heath 'Omnium Gatherum No. 4', in *The Caricaturist's Scrapbook*.

25 C. J. Grant 'Arithmetical Terms – Being a Frontispiece to the "Tutor's Assistant"' (c. 1833).

26 W. Henderson (ed.) *Victorian Street Ballads* (London: Country Life 1937), 90 and 94. One of Henderson's unattributed vignettes shows a grinning dustman

with a foaming tankard raised to his lips, while the other shows a dustman downing a pot of beer while working on the streets, and comes from *The Comic Offering for 1833*.

27 Henry Heath 'Scenes in London 41', in *A Caricaturist's Sketchbook* (1840).

28 Robert Seymour 'I say, ma-am', in Alfred Crowquill *Seymour's Sketches* (London: n.d.), Chapter 15.

29 See, for example, W. Heath *The March of Intellect* (London: Thomas McClean 1828), *BMC* 15604 and [W. Heath] *March of Intellect* (London: Thomas McClean c. 1829), *BMC* 15779.

30 W. T. Moncrieff *The March of Intellect* (London: William Kidd 1830).

31 The Irish-born artist William Mulready, generally regarded as a pillar of the early Victorian establishment, was, in December 1839, commissioned by Henry Cole to design the first pre-paid postal envelope. (See M. Pointon *William Mulready* (London: Victoria and Albert Museum 1986), 131 and 175; K. M. Heleniak *William Mulready* (New Haven, CT: Yale University Press 1980), 25. Despite the approval of the Chancellor of the Exchequer and the Royal Academy, the design, which was an emblematic representation of letters flowing out from Britannia across geographical divides to unite families and friends, met with enormous popular derision. This derision was rapidly translated into a series of parodies and imitations of Mulready's admittedly rather crassly emblematic celebration of imperial achievement. Several of the leading caricaturists of the time, including John Leech, Hablot Browne ('Phiz'), Henry Heath and C. J. Grant, produced postal envelopes in the immediate aftermath of the introduction of the penny post on 1 May 1840. (See E. B. Evans *A Description of the Mulready Envelope* (London: Stanley Gibbons 1891), 25–36.) These have been listed and described in detail by Evans. Dustmen or coal-heavers appear distinctively in seven of these engravings. They were represented precisely through some of the tropes examined in this chapter. Several showed dustmen or coal-heavers reading or writing, in most cases with some bravura display of effort. The comic point was that letters could now, under the wondrous new system, reach even the most improbable members of society, and that the march of intellect would include even the lowliest members of society. In two of the images the coal-heaver/dustman figure was paired with a comparably vulgar wife, who was represented as a white version of African Sal – an ample, be-aproned and be-bonnetted figure, who was smoking a short pipe in one instance. In these images, the transgressive Bob/Sal pairing drawn from the theatre has changed into an image of vulgar, but sentimental, shared domesticity. There are further nuances of meaning here – in one image the dustman is sat rather sulkily nursing his knees while his partner reads a letter, with the clear implication that he cannot read and is being shown up by his literate companion. In another image, a dustman is sat quietly smoking while his daughter plays the piano. She refuses his request for a popular tune on the grounds of its vulgarity, thus forming another image of the educated children of dustmen turning their newly fashionable backs on the cultural shortcomings of their fathers. The Mulready envelope, designed to represent an establishment vision of legislative, technological and imperial progress, and its many sarcastic progeny serve as a reminder of the extent to which dustmen had become the most easily available form of shorthand for the unreconstituted and vulgar urban working classes. I am extremely grateful to Dr Colin Graham for information about the significance of the Mulready envelope.

32 See B. E. Maidment *Reading Popular Prints 1790–1870* (Manchester: Manchester University Press 1996), Chapter 3 and '*Penny* Wise, *Penny*

Foolish? – Representations of Mass Circulation Periodicals and "The March of Intellect" in the 1820s and 1830s', in Laurel Brake, Bill Bell and David Finkelstein (eds) *The Nineteenth Century Media and the Construction of Identity* (London: Macmillan 2000).

33 See, for example, *Punch* 9 (1845) 25 and 161; 10 (1846) 136, 165 and 224; 12 (1847) 190; and 16 (1849) 42.

34 A. Crowquill *Four Specimens of the Reading Public* (London: J. Fairburn August 1826).

35 Robert Seymour 'You shall have the paper directly, sir', in *Sketches by Seymour.* This particular joke re-appears in various forms. There is a spectacular full page version in *Punch* 9 (1845) 161.

36 Anon. 'The Gentleman in Black', *Tregear's Flights of Humour No. 56* (London: Tregear n.d.).

37 Anon lithograph (London: O. Hodgson n.d.).

38 Henry Heath *Intellectual-Character – One of the Club at his Studies* (London: J. B. Brookes 1 May 1834).

39 See Louis James *Print and the People 1819–1851* (London: Allen Lane 1976), 148. See also Michael Hancher 'From Street Ballad to Penny Magazine: "March of Intellect" in the Butchering Line', in Brake, Bell and Finkelstein (eds) *Nineteenth Century Media and the Construction of Identities*, 93–103

40 'ARGUS' 'Fishing for the Great Seal' (London: King n.d.), no. 9 in the series of *Sketches by Argus.*

41 Image from an unknown source.

42 Anon. 'Useful Knowledge' (London: T. C. Lewis n.d.), LWL 848 0 6.

43 Image from an unknown source.

## Notes to Chapter 6: Dust and the early Victorian urban imagination

1 *The Quaver or Songster's Pocket Companion* (London: For the Bookseller 1854), 257.

2 Louis James *Print and the People 1819–1851* (London: Allen Lane 1976), 149–50 and 349–50. James gives W. T. Moncrieff's 1834 *Songbook* as his source.

3 Philip Ward *Cambridge Street Literature* (Cambridge: Oleander Press 1978), 27. Ward dates this text at c. 1835, and notes that the illustration, a bafflingly irrelevant image of an old man, is used in another of Talbot's ballad sheets produced at roughly the same time.

4 William Thomas Thomas [W. T. Moncrieff] *An Original Collection Of Songs, sung at the Theatres Royal, Public Concerts &c.* (John Duncombe ?1850), 205. The full text of the verse is quoted in Chapter 3 on p. 77.

5 *The Town* (4 August 1838).

6 Bodleian Library Ballads Catalogue: Harding B 11 (1264); Johnson Ballads.

7 This illustration is held in The Robert Cushman Butler Collection of Theatrical Illustrations [No. 1212] at the State University of Washington.

8 A tune associated with *The Literary Dustman* has survived within the English musical tradition, and is still played by country dance bands as part of their repertoire. See for example *The South Riding Tune Book* published by the South Riding Folk Network, which gives the full text of a version of *The Literary Dustman* drawn from the John Pitts version held in the Bodleian Library Broadside Ballad collection.

9 Bodleian Library, John Johnson Collection, Johnson Ballads 2467.

10 Thomas Hood *Whims and Oddities* new edn (London: Edward Moxon 1854), 224–6.

11 *The Collected Poems of Eliza Cook* (London: Frederick Warne & Co. n.d.).
12 *The Universal Songster, or, Museum of Mirth* 3 vols (London: S. Jones 1825–28) II, 75–6.
13 For full publishing information on *The Universal Songster* see A. B. Cohn *George Cruikshank – A Catalogue Raisonné* (London: The Bookman's Journal 1924), 232.
14 *The New Comic Annual* (London: Hurst and Orme n.d.), 254–9.
15 Adorno *Minima Moralia.*
16 Thomas *An Original Collection of Songs*, 241. This song, announced as being 'sung ... at Convivial Parties', typifies the hearty optimism of Moncrieff's picturesque London.
17 Thomas *An Original Collection of Songs*, 106.
18 Reprinted in *Gallery of Comicalities, Embracing Humorous Sketches by the Brothers Robert and George Cruikshank, Robert Seymour and Others* (London: Charles Hindley n.d.).
19 See previous chapter for a discussion of 'March Dust – The Bell Savage', a wonderfully splenetic poem and illustration featuring dustmen as street menaces, from the *Comic Almanack* (1840), 218.
20 *The New Comic Annual* (London: Hurst, Chance & Co. n.d.), 260–3.
21 B. Simmons 'London Cries' in *Blackwood's Edinburgh Magazine* 65 (April 1849), 484.
22 *The Works of William Makepeace Thackeray* Biographical Edition, 14 vols (London: Smith, Elder & Co.) IV (1908), xxi–xxii.
23 Andrew W. Tuer *Old London Street Cries and the Cries of Today with Heaps of Quaint Cuts* (London: Field and Tuer 1885).
24 *Franklin's Miscellany – A Cheerful Companion for the Lovers of Science and Literature, Natural History and Useful Information* 1:4 (6 January 1838). The *Miscellany* was a weekly paper that sold for three halfpennies.
25 The full text runs: SWEEP. – I consider that my perfession is a *soot*-able a vun as your'n./ DUSTMAN. – Your vord vont *in-flue*-ence me to think that ere vile mine brings more o' *the dust.*/ SWEEP. – Aren't we alvays called *clargymen?* / DUSTMEN. – And arn't ve *angels*? aren't we *flying* dustmen? / SWEEP. – Vel if you belongs to the *fly*, don't we belong to the *flew*? / DUSTMAN. – Don't ve *bear the bell*, vilst you alvays *gets the sack.*/ SWEEP. – Now cheeky! *who prig'd the spoon*? / DUSTMAN. – Ve never thinks it vorth our vile to take such a *vooden von* as you, ve always leaves such like in the mess./ SWEEP. – P'raps you'd jist like to *tast* a bit of my *fist.*/ DUSTMAN. – I'd rather not, I dusn't like a *hand of pork* vithout its vell *cured*; so *brush*, my *cure-osity in summer*, my *pet snow-ball.*/ SWEEP. – (Losing his temper.) Now stupid. Them 'ere neat ancles of yurn seems to be jealous of the close cov'aintance of your knees./ DUSTMAN. – You stole that 'ere *sack* from a fellow clargyman! hean't that *sack-rilige?* Dust ho e! dust! (*exit.*) / SWEEP. – S'veep! s'veep! (*exit.*)
26 See M. Twyman *Printing 1770–1979 – An Illustrated History of its Development and Uses in England* 2nd edn (London: British Library 1998), 253. Twyman's illustration is drawn from a photograph in Reading University Library.
27 See Marriott *Unknown London* vol. VI for a reprint of Grant's best known early work *Sketches in London*, together with some useful introductory comments by Marriott. See also Bernstein *The Celebration of Scandal*, 89.
28 Marriott *Unknown London* VI, vii–viii.
29 [James Grant] *The Great Metropolis* 3rd edn, 2 vols (London: Saunders and Otley 1838) I, 266–306.

30 Grant *Sketches in London*, 180 and 328. Phiz [Hablot K. Browne] drew very few dustmen, but these are interestingly classic representations.
31 All quotations from Grant's article are taken from page 74 of the issue of the *London Saturday Journal* dated Saturday 13 February 1841. The illustration occupies the title page (p. 73) of the same issue.
32 See also Maidment '101 Things'.
33 See Donald J. Gray 'Early Victorian Scandalous Journalism – Renton Nicholson's *The Town* (1837–42)', in J. Shattock and M. Wolff (eds) *The Victorian Periodical Press – Samplings and Soundings* (Leicester: Leicester University Press 1982), 316–48.
34 Gray 'Early Victorian Scandalous Journalism', 317.
35 Gray 'Early Victorian Scandalous Journalism', 318.
36 Gray 'Early Victorian Scandalous Journalism', 318.
37 These ideas shape the concluding sentences of the accompanying article – 'In conclusion, we must observe, that the calling of a dustman, which we have lyrically affirmed to have been the *first* profession, must necessarily, by the laws of nature, be the last; for the poet has truly said, in talking of the last enemy of man, Death, that – "He is by law, since Adam's flaw/*Contractor* for all our dust."'
38 *Illustrated London News* (1846).

### Notes to Chapter 7: Dust commodified and categorised: Mayhew, Dickens and the investigative impulse, 1840–1900

1 [James Grant] *Travels in Town* 2 vols (London: Saunders and Otley 1838) I, Preface.
2 The full list is: I (12 July 1850), 379–84 'Dust: or Ugliness Redeemed'; VI (16 October 1852), 97–101 'Penny Wisdom'; XI (19 May 1855), 376–9 'Important Rubbish'; XVIII (10 July 1858), 79–82 'A Way to Clean Rivers'; XVIII (24 July 1858), 121–3 'Dirty Cleanliness'. For Horne's work for Dickens and *Household Words*, see Ann Blainey *The Farthing Poet – A Biography of Richard Hengist Horne* (London: Longmans 1968), 179–91.
3 *Household Words* XI (19 May 1855), 376.
4 See *All The Year Round* I, 515; VIII 184–7; VIII 209–11; VIII 250–6; IX 474; XIII 157– 64.
5 See Kate Flint's chapter 'The Mote Within the Eye', in *The Victorians and the Visual Imagination* (Oxford: Oxford University Press 2000), 40–63, for an account of the scientific interests shown by late Victorians in dust.
6 Horne's list is worth citing in full because of his comprehensiveness. It runs: coal; cinders; breeze; 'soft-ware' (vegetable and animal matter, including the cat skins that one sifter specialised in collecting); 'hard-ware' (pottery, pans, oyster shells); bones; rags; brass and lead; glass; jewellery. Each of these categories is given its own destination for re-cycling.
7 Horne 'Dust; or Ugliness Redeemed', 379.
8 Horne 'Dust; or Ugliness Redeemed', 379.
9 Horne 'Dust; or Ugliness Redeemed', 381–2.
10 Horne 'Dust; or Ugliness Redeemed', 383.
11 Horne 'Dust; or Ugliness Redeemed', 384.
12 Horne 'Dust; or Ugliness Redeemed', 384.
13 In particular, Horne's undocumented assertion that the Marylebone dust heap produced between four and five thousand pounds of annual profits in the 1820s has become a 'fact'.
14 Anne Humpherys *Travels Into the Poor Man's Country – The Work of Henry*

*Mayhew* (Athens: University of Georgia Press 1977), 68. Humpherys's book remains an extremely good introduction to Mayhew, and offers a useful account of the genesis and structure of *London Labour*. See also the Introductions to E. P. Thompson and E. Yeo (eds) *Unknown Mayhew* (London: Merlin Press 1971), which also contains a useful chart showing the elements of Mayhew's *Morning Chronicle* articles which became incorporated into *London Labour and the London Poor*.

15 Humpherys *Travels Into the Poor Man's Country*, 69. See pp. 66–81 for an account of the complex formation of the text of *London Labour*.

16 Eileen Yeo *Unknown Mayhew* (Harmondsworth: Penguin Books 1984), 77.

17 Humpherys *Travels Into the Poor Man's Country*, 81.

18 Pages 166–79 in the second volume of Mayhew *London Labour*.

19 Humpherys *Travels Into the Poor Man's Country*, 82.

20 It is important to note that the illustrations to *London Labour* were drawn from photographs, and thus comprise some of the earliest documentary use of photography for recording working class-life. See also Thompson's image of 'flying dustmen'.

21 Humpherys *Travels Into the Poor Man's Country*, 71.

22 Mayhew *London Labour* II, 170–1.

23 Mayhew *London Labour* II, 172–5.

24 Mayhew, *London Labour* II, 176, 177.

25 Yeo *Unknown Mayhew*, 93.

26 Mayhew, *London Labour* II, 177.

27 Mayhew, *London Labour* II, 178.

28 James Greenwood *The Seven Curses of London*, ed. Jeffrey Richards (Oxford: Basil Blackwood 1981), v. Richards sees this book as a summary of Greenwood's lengthy investigations of the problems of the metropolis.

29 Joanne Shattock (ed.) *The New Cambridge Bibliography of English Literature* Vol. IV *1800–1900* (Cambridge: Cambridge University Press 1999) lists only a few of Greenwood's children's books, and the studies of urban writing by Bernstein, Nord and Nead only mention Greenwood in passing. Neither Peter Keating's anthology *Into Unknown England* (London: Fontana 1976) nor Rick Allen's *The Moving Pageant – A Literary Sourcebook of London Street-Life, 1700–1914* (London: Routledge 1998) includes a substantial extract. Richards's Introduction to Greenwood's *The Seven Curses of London* (Oxford: Basil Blackwell 1981) remains the best introduction to his work.

30 James Greenwood *Unsentimental Journeys; or, Byways of the Modern Babylon* (London: Ward, Lock and Tyler 1872). The articles had originally appeared in the *Saturday Illustrated Paper* in 1866.

31 Greenwood, *Unsentimental Journeys*, 71.

32 Greenwood, *Unsentimental Journeys*, 66.

33 *Twice Round the Clock* ran from 1 May to 27 November 1858, and then was republished in volume form. There is an extremely useful edition of *Twice Round the Clock* edited by Philip Collins (Leicester: Leicester University Press 1971). See also R. Strauss *Sala: The Portrait of an Eminent Victorian* (London: Constable 1942), 132–43.

34 Bernstein *The Celebration of Scandal*, 25.

35 For McConnell see R. Engen *Dictionary of Victorian Wood Engravers* (Cambridge: Chadwyck-Healey 1985), 169–70. Listed as William McConnell, he trained under Joseph Swain, worked (ultimately unhappily) for *Punch*, and moved on to work for the *Illustrated London News* and the *Illustrated Times*. Vizetelly described him dismissively as 'a somewhat

vulgarised imitator of John Leech'. He was a close friend of Sala and worked widely for periodicals in the 1860s.

36 Allen *Moving Pageant*, 2.
37 Nead *Victorian Babylon*, 106.
38 Bernstein *The Celebration of Scandal*, 25; Nead *Victorian Babylon*, 108.
39 Nead *Victorian Babylon*, 106.
40 Nead *Victorian Babylon*, 108.
41 G. A. Sala *Twice Round the Clock* in *The Welcome Guest* (May–November 1858) ed. P. Collins (Leicester: Leicester University Press 1971), 232.
42 Sala *Twice Round the Clock*, 233.
43 Sala *Twice Round the Clock*, 310.
44 J. M. Weylland *These Fifty Years – Being the Jubilee Volume of the London City Mission* (London: S. W. Partridge & Co. n.d. [1884]), 140–1.
45 Burnley is really only echoing what had become commonplaces of Victorian journalism. An article in the *Quarterly Review* in 1868, for example, had exhaustively discussed the ways through which household refuse was being put to socially useful purposes, using the idea that 'in the economy of nature, waste is unknown, and we may be sure that nothing is lost ... only changed in the universal alembic'. *Quarterly Review* 248 (April 1868), 334–57. Increasingly, as in Burnley's case, such descriptions equated the resourcefulness of nature with the usefulness of chemical discoveries.
46 James Burnley *The Romance of Modern Industry* (London: W. H. Allen 1889), 59–78. I am grateful to Dr Steve Wade for pointing out this reference.
47 Burnley *The Romance of Modern Industry*, 61.
48 *The British Workman* (March 1875), 57–8.
49 *The British Workman* (March 1875), 58.
50 'Down with the dust' is one of the mocking insults hurled at Mr and Mrs Boffin by street urchins as they head off in their carriage in search of a child to adopt. The remark is in fact a complex wordplay – as well as 'down with the people associated with dust' the phrase also means 'let's see your money on the table' or 'prove you can pay', and was something that was presumably often asked of dustmen by tavern keepers. In this sense of 'display your wealth publicly' the comment also underlines the problems faced by the Boffins in making good use of their money without ostentatious show of charity.
51 Dickens *Our Mutual Friend*, 186.
52 The bones of this controversy, if I may put it that way, are described in the opening paragraphs of Chapter 1. These debates were provoked by/informed Stephen Gill's 1971 Introduction to the Penguin Classics edition of the novel.
53 See Jane R. Cohen *Charles Dickens and His Original Illustrators* (Columbus: Ohio State University Press 1980), 204–5 for a discussion of Dickens's close working relationships with Marcus Stone in the publication of the novel. Cohen publishes an interesting sketch by Stone for the cover of the part issue which locates the dustman in the central lower panel of the design. By the time of publication, however, the dustman has been moved to the right-hand side. See also R. L. Patten *Charles Dickens and his Publishers* (Oxford: Clarendon Press 1978), 303–7.
54 The Household Edition, for example, has on p. 252 a dramatic image, drawn by J. Mahoney, of Venus and Wegg spying on Boffin's nocturnal diggings in his dust heap.
55 Gill, Introduction to *Our Mutual Friend*, 24.
56 The current edition of the Penguin Classics *Our Mutual Friend*, edited by Adrian Poole, which replaced Stephen Gill's in 1997, offers an interesting

overview of the dramatic sources for the novel in plays by James Sheridan Knowles on pp. xv–xvii of his introduction.

57 The several early dramatisations of the novel concentrate almost exclusively on the dust heaps, and include Henry Brougham Farne's *The Golden Dustman* (1866), C. H. Hazelwood's *The Dustman's Treasure; or Wegg and the Boffins* (1866) and *The Dustman's Golden Mound* (1866). In the popular imagination at least it seems as if the Golden Dustman was placed at the centre of the text. See J. J. Brattin and B. G. Hornback *Our Mutual Friend: An Annotated Bibliography* (New York: Garland 1984) and H. Philip Bolton *Dickens Dramatized* (London: Mansell 1987).

58 As long ago as 1913 Percy Fitzgerald noted Horne's 1850 *Household Words* article as a major source for *Our Mutual Friend*, and Dickens's likely reliance on Horne, Mayhew and Mr Dodd for information has already been described.

59 See Harland S. Nelson 'Dickens's *Our Mutual Friend* and Henry Mayhew's *London Labour and the London Poor*', *Nineteenth Century Fiction* 20:3 (December 1965), 207–22. Nelson argues that, despite the fact that few previous critics of Dickens had acknowledged Dickens's debt to Mayhew, 'it is next to inconceivable' that Dickens was not familiar with his work. He goes on to present internal evidence in the novel that suggests Dickens's familiarity with Mayhew, but pursues only Mayhew's account of dredgermen as a source for Gaffer Hexham. Nelson makes no suggestion that Dickens made use of Mayhew's writings on dustmen in his development of the Boffin narrative.

60 Dickens *Our Mutual Friend*, 105.

61 Dickens *Our Mutual Friend*, 179.

62 Dickens *Our Mutual Friend*, 185.

63 Dickens *Our Mutual Friend*, 296.

64 Dickens *Our Mutual Friend*, 105.

65 Charles Dance (1794–1863) combined his work as a dramatist with various legal jobs mainly in the Insolvent Debtors' Court. *The Dustman's Belle* was first performed at the Lyceum on 1 June 1846 (Whit Monday). It was revived for short run at the Surrey Theatre in August 1847.

66 Dickens was in Italy in May and June 1846, and there is no mention of the play or of visits to the Surrey Theatre in August 1847 in his letters: *The Letters of Charles Dickens*, Vol. 5 *1847–49*, ed. Graham Story and K. J. Fielding (Oxford: Clarendon Press 1981). There is evidence that Dickens dined with Dance in February 1849, *Letters* V 485. The play is announced in the *Illustrated London News* for 30 May 1846 (VIII: 213), 355 and reviewed on 6 June in both the *Illustrated London News* (VIII; 214), 371 and the *Pictorial Times* (VII: 169), 355–6. The 1847 revival was reviewed at length and with an illustration in the *Illustrated London News* (28 August 1847), 139.

67 One interesting continuity between the Keeley's and theatrical versions of dustmen was that a young Keeley had played Jerry Hawthorn in a Sadler's Wells production of *Tom and Jerry* in April 1822. See Anon. *The Songs, Parodies &c. in the Burletta of Tom and Jerry* (London: Sherwood, Neels and Jones n.d.).

68 See *Letters* IV 151; 452–3; 616; 662–3; 680–1 for some account of Dickens's relationships with the Keeleys during this period. Albert Smith later married the Keeleys' eldest daughter.

69 For some details of the relationships between Smith, Dickens and the Keeleys see Malcolm Morley '*The Battle of Life* in the Theatre', *The Dickensian* 48 (1952), 76–81.

70 A. E. Wilson *The Lyceum* (London: Denis Yates 1952), 65.

71 Charles Dance *The Dustman's Belle: An Original Comic Drama* (London: G. Fairbrother and William Strange n.d. [1846]). I have found this text in a number of libraries, which suggests that the play had some currency.
72 *Pictorial Times* VII (1846), 355–6.
73 *Illustrated London News* (28 August 1847), 139–40.
74 *Pictorial Times* VII (6 June 1846), 355.
75 Dickens *Our Mutual Friend*, 60.
76 Dickens *Our Mutual Friend*, 59.
77 Dickens *Our Mutual Friend*, 67.

# Bibliography


**Collections of primary material and unpublished sources**

Beinecke Library, Yale University, New Haven, Connecticut. Play texts, song books, and theatrical material.

Bodleian Library, Oxford. Ballads Collection.

British Museum. Caricatures and prints.

Guildhall Library, London. Collections of trade cards, cuttings and files relating to dustmen and waste clearance, and theatre posters.

John Johnson Collection, Bodleian Library, Oxford. Collections of trade cards, ballads and other printed material.

Lewis Walpole Library, Farmington Connecticut. Collections of graphic images, prints and caricatures.

Osborne Collection, Toronto Public Libraries.

Pound, Richard John 'Serial Journalism and the Transformation of English Graphic Satire', unpublished PhD thesis, University College, London (2002).

Robert Cushman Butler Collection of Theatrical Illustrations at the State University of Washington.

Theatre Museum, Covent Garden, London. Playbills, play texts and theatrical memorabilia.

Yale Centre for British Art, New Haven, Connecticut. Caricatures, prints and albums.

**Playbills showing performances of *Tom and Jerry, Life in London* and related performances**

*Life in London* 17 November 1821 Olympic Theatre (Author's collection)

*Tom and Jerry* 26 November 1821 Adelphi Theatre (The Theatre Museum)

*Tom and Jerry* 6 December 1821 Adelphi Theatre (The Theatre Museum)

*Tom and Jerry* 7 December 1821 Adelphi Theatre (The Theatre Museum)

*Tom and Jerry* 8 December 1821 Adelphi Theatre (The Theatre Museum)

*Life in London* 11 March 1822 Olympic Theatre (Author's Collection)

*Tom and Jerry* 8 April 1822 Sadler's Wells (The Theatre Museum)

*Tom, Jerry, and Logic's Life in London* 29 April–1 May 1822 Royalty Theatre (Guildhall Library)

*Tom and Jerry* 2 May 1822 Astley's (The Theatre Museum)

*Tom, Jerry, and Logic's Life in London* 6 May 1822 Royalty Theatre (Guildhall Library)

*Tom, Jerry, and Logic's Life in London* 9 May 1822 Royalty Theatre (Guildhall Library)

*Tom and Jerry* 9 May 1822 Davis's Royal Amphitheatre (The Theatre Museum)

*Tom and Jerry* 13 May 1822 Davis's Royal Amphitheatre (The Theatre Museum)

*Tom and Jerry* 20 May 1822 Davis's Royal Amphitheatre (The Theatre Museum)

*Tom and Jerry* 21–25 May 1822 Sadler's Wells (The Theatre Museum)

*Tom and Jerry* 21 June 1822 Sadler's Wells (The Theatre Museum)

*Tom and Jerry* 22 July 1822 Sadler's Wells (The Theatre Museum)
*Tom and Jerry* 29 July 1822 Astley's (The Theatre Museum)
*Tom and Jerry* 1 August 1822 Astley's (The Theatre Museum)
*Tom and Jerry* 5 August 1822 Sadler's Wells (The Theatre Museum)
*Tothill-fields Tournament!* 10 March 1823 (Guildhall Library)
*Tom and Jerry* 9 June 1823 Davis's Royal Amphitheatre (Guildhall Library)
*Benefit for Master and Miss Linch* 21 July 1824 Royalty Theatre (Guildhall Library)
*Tom and Jerry* 10 June 1828 Theatre Royal, Covent Garden (Author's collection)
*Tom and Jerry* 11 June 1828 Theatre Royal, Covent Garden (Author's collection)
*Tom and Jerry* 14 June 1828 Theatre Royal, Covent Garden (Author's collection)
*Tom and Jerry* 16 March 1829 Theatre Royal, Manchester (Author's collection)
*Tom and Jerry* 19 March 1842 Adelphi Theatre (The Theatre Museum)
*Tom and Jerry* 26 March 1842 Adelphi Theatre (The Theatre Museum)

## Primary sources

### *Periodicals and serials*

*All the Year Round* (1859–68)
*The British Workman* (1855–70)
*Everybody's Album and Caricature Magazine* (1834–35)
*The Glasgow Looking Glass* (1825)
*Household Words* (1850–59)
*Illustrated London News* (1842–70)
*Illustrated Times* (1855–72)
*The Looking Glass* (1830–36)
*Northern Looking Glass* (1825–26)
*Pictorial Times* (1844–48)
*Punch* (1841–70)
*The Town* (1837–42)

### *Other printed sources*

Anon., *Bell's Gallery of Comicalities* (London n.d. [?1834]).
Anon., 'Improved Street Cleaning in the Metropolis' in *Pictorial Times* (9 May 1846), 296.
Anon., *New Comic Annual* (London: Hurst and Orme, n.d.).
Anon., *Picturesque Representations of the Dress and Manners of the English* (London: John Murray 1814).
Anon., *The Quaver or Songster's Pocket Companion* (London 1854).
Anon., *Real Life in London* (London: Jones & Co. 1822).
Anon., *The Songs, Parodies and c. in the Burletta of Tom and Jerry* (London: printed for P. Egan and published by Sherwood, Neely and Jones, n.d.).
Anon., *The Universal Songster, or, Museum of Mirth*, 3 vols (London: S. Jones 1825–28).
Brough, R. B. and W., *Alfred the Great or, The Minstrel King* (London 1859).
Busby, T. L., *Costume of the Lower Orders of London* (London: Baldwin, Craddock and Joy, n.d. [1820]).
Burnley, James, *The Romance of Modern Industry* (London: W. H. Allen 1889).
Byron, H. J., *George de Barnwell* (London 1863).
Cook, Eliza, *The Collected Poems of Eliza Cook* (London: Frederick Warne n.d.).

Cruikshank, George, *The Comic Almanack* (London: Charles Tilt 1835–53). Reprinted by John Camden Hotten (2 vols, n.d.).
—— *Four Hundred Humorous Illustrations by George Cruikshank*, 2nd edn (London: Simpkin Marshall, n.d.).
—— *Fourteen Illustrations of Sunday in London* (London: Effingham Wilson 1833).
—— *Gallery of Comicalities, Embracing Humorous Sketches by the Brothers Robert and George Cruikshank, Robert Seymour and Others* (London: Charles Hindley, n.d.).
—— *George Cruikshank's Omnibus*, 2 vols (London: Tilt and Bogue 1842).
—— *George Cruikshank's Sketchbook* (London: Charles Tilt 1834–36).
—— *Illustrations to Mornings at Bow Street by George Cruikshank* (London: T. Griffiths 1827).
—— *London Characters* (London: Joseph Robins 1829).
Dickens, Charles, *Our Mutual Friend* (1864–65).
—— *The Letters of Charles Dickens*, Vol. 5 *1847–49*, ed. Graham Story and K. J. Fielding (Oxford: Clarendon Press 1981).
—— *Sketches by Boz* (183), in *Sketches by Boz and Other Early Papers*, ed. M. Slater (London: J. M. Dent 1994).
Egan, Pierce, *Life in London* (London: Sherwood, Neeley and Jones 1821).
—— *The Life of An Actor* (London: C. S. Arnold 1825).
—— *Finish to the Adventures of Tom, Jerry and Logic* (London: C. Baynes and G. Virtue 1830).
Grant, Charles Jameson, *A Political Alphabet* (London: Thomas McClean 1837).
Grant, James, *The Great Metropolis*, 2 vols, 3rd edn (London: Saunders and Otley 1838).
—— (ed.), *The London Saturday Journal* (1839–42).
—— *Sketches in London* (London: W. S. Orr 1838).
—— *Travels in Town*, 2 vols (London: Saunders and Otley 1839).
Greenwood, James, *Unsentimental Journeys Through Modern Babylon* (London: Ward, Lock and Tyler 1872).
—— *The Seven Curses of London* (?1871), ed. Jeffrey Richards (Oxford: Basil Blackwell 1981).
Heath, Henry, *The Caricaturist's Scrapbook* (London: Robert Tyas 1840).
Heath William [Paul Pry] *Parish Characters* (London: T. McClean 1829).
Hindley, Charles, *A History of the Cries of London, Ancient and Modern*, 2nd edn (London: Charles Hindley 1884).
—— *The True History of Tom and Jerry* (London: Charles Hindley, n.d. [1892]).
Hood, Thomas, *Whims and Oddities*, new edn (London: Edward Moxon 1854).
—— *Hood's Comic Annual 1830* (London: Hurst, Chance 1830).
—— *Hood's Comic Annual 1832* (London: Charles Tilt 1832).
[Horne, R. H.], 'Dust; or, Ugliness Redeemed' in *Household Words* 1 (13 July 1850), 379–84.
Hunt, Leigh, *Leigh Hunt's London Journal* (London: Charles Knight 1835).
Leech, John, *Four Hundred Humorous Illustrations by John Leech*, 2nd edn (London: Simpkin, Marshall, Hamilton, Kent & Co., n.d.).
Lisle, Joe, *Joe Lisle's Play Upon Words* (London: Thomas M'Clean 1828).
Marriott, J. (ed.), *Unknown London – Early Modernist Visions of the Metropolis*, 6 vols (London: Pickering and Chatto 2000).
Mayhew, Henry, *London Labour and the London Poor*, 4 vols (London: Griffin,

Bohn & Co. 1861–62).
Moncrieff, W. T. [William Thomas Thomas] *Tom and Jerry, or, Life in London: An Operatic Extravaganza* (London: Dicks' Standard Plays 82, n.d.).
—— *An Original Collection Of Songs, sung at the Theatres Royal, Public Concerts & c.* (John Duncombe 1850?).
[Nicholson, Renton], 'Characteristic Sketches LXII' in *The Town* 62 (4 August 1838).
T. P. Prest (ed.), *The London Singers' Magazine and Reciters Album* (London: John Duncombe, n.d.).
Pyne, W. H., *Microcosm or, A Picturesque Delineation of the Arts, Agriculture and Manufactures of Great Britain* (London: W. H. Pyne and J. C. Nattes 1806).
—— *The Costume of Great Britain* (London: William Miller 1808).
Sala, G. A., *Twice Round the Clock* in *The Welcome Guest* (May–November 1858), ed. P. Collins (Leicester: Leicester University Press 1971).
Seymour, Robert, *New Readings of Old Authors* (London: Charles Tilt 1834).
—— *Sketches by Seymour* (London: Henry Bohn 1841). The *Sketches* existed as various single prints and series before being collected by Bohn. In volume form they were re-issued many times in the nineteenth century.
Sheridan, Lady Henrietta (ed.), *The Comic Offering for 1833* (London: Smith, Elder 1833).
Simmons, B., 'London Cries', *Blackwood's Edinburgh Magazine* 65 (April 1849).
Thackeray, W. M., *The Works of William Makepeace Thackeray*, biographical edition, 14 vols (London: Smith Elder & Co. 1913–14).
Wight, John, *Mornings in Bow Street* (London: Charles Baldwyn 1824).
—— *More Mornings in Bow Street* (London: J. Robinson 1827).

**Secondary sources**

Adorno, Theodor, *Minima Moralia: Reflections on a Damaged Life* (London: Verso 2005).
Allen, A. and Hoverstadt, J., *The History of Printed Scraps* (London: New Cavendish Books 1983).
Allen, R., *The Moving Pageant – A Literary Sourcebook of London Street-Life, 1700–1914* (London: Routledge 1998).
Amato, Joseph A., *Dust – A History of the Small and Invisible* (Berkeley: University of California Press 2000).
Arnold, Dana, *Re-presenting the Metropolis: Architecture, Urban Experience and Social Life in London 1800–1840* (Aldershot: Ashgate 2000).
Atherton, H. M., 'The Mob in Eighteenth-Century Caricature', *Eighteenth-Century Studies* 12:1 (1978), 47–54.
Bakhtin, Mikhail, *Rabelais and His World*, trans. H. Iswolsky (Bloomington: Indiana University Press 1984 [1965]).
Benjamin, Walter, 'The Work of Art in the Age of Mechanical Reproduction', in *Illuminations*, ed. Hannah Arendt (New York: Schoken Books 1969).
Bernstein, Carol, *The Celebration of Scandal: Towards the Sublime in Victorian Urban Fiction* (University Park: Pennsylvania State University Press, n.d.).
Bolton, H. Philip, *Dickens Dramatized* (London: Mansell 1987).
Brewer, John, *The Common People and Politics 1750s–1790s* (Cambridge: Chadwyck-Healey 1986).
—— *The Pleasures of the Imagination: English Culture in the Eighteenth Century* (London: Harper Collins 1997).

Butt, J. and Tillotson, K., *Dickens at Work* (London: Methuen 1957).
Cameron, David Kerr, *London's Pleasures: From Restoration to Regency* (Stroud: Sutton Publishing 2001).
Cohen, Jane R., *Charles Dickens and his Original Illustrators* (Columbus: Ohio State University Press 1980).
Cohn, A. B., *George Cruikshank – A Catalogue Raisonné* (London: The Bookman's Journal 1924).
Colley, Linda, *Britons: Forging the Nation 1707–1838* (New Haven, CT: Yale University Press 1992).
Cotsell, M., *The Companion to 'Our Mutual Friend'* (London: Allen and Unwin 1986).
Cox, Philip, *Reading Adaptations – Novels and Verse Narratives on the Stage 1790–1840* (Manchester: Manchester University Press 2000).
Cunnington, P. and Lucas, C., *Occupational Costume in England from the Eleventh Century to 1914* (London: A and C Black 1976).
Dart, Greg, '"Flash Style": Pierce Egan and Literary London, 1820–1828', *History Workshop Journal* 51 (2001), 180–205.
De Vries, L., *Flowers of Delight – An Agreeable Garland of Poetry and Prose* (London: Dennis Dobson 1965).
Darton, Lawrence, *The Dartons – An Annotated Check-list of Children's Books Issued by Two Publishing Houses 1787–1876* (London: The British Library 2004).
De Marly, Diane, *Working Dress: A History of Occupational Clothing* (London: Batsford 1986).
Donald, D., *The Age of Caricature – Satirical Prints in the Reign of George III* (New Haven, CT: Yale University Press 1996).
Engen, R., *Dictionary of Victorian Wood Engravers* (Cambridge: Chadwyck-Healey 1985).
Everett, G., *English Caricaturists and Graphic Humourists of the Nineteenth Century* (London: Swann Sonnenschein 1903).
Fagg, E., *The Old 'Old Vic', or, from Barrymore to Bayliss* (London: The Vic-Wells Association 1936).
Flint, Kate, *The Victorians and the Visual Imagination* (Cambridge: Cambridge University Press 2000).
Fox, Celina, *Londoners* (London: Thames and Hudson 1987).
George, M. D., *Hogarth to Cruikshank – Social Change in Graphic Satire*, revised ed. (London: Viking 1987).
Gilman, Sander L., *Difference and Pathology: Stereotypes of Sexuality, Race and Gender* (Ithaca, NY: Cornell University Press 1985).
Gray, Donald J., 'Early Victorian Scandalous Journalism – Renton Nicholson's *The Town* 1837–1842', in J. Shattock and M. Wolff (eds), *The Victorian Periodical Press – Samplings and Soundings* (Leicester: Leicester University Press 1982).
Gretton, Tom, *Murders and Moralities* (London: Colonnade Books 1980).
Handy, Ellen, 'Dust Piles and Damp Pavements – Excrement, Repression and the Victorian City', in Carol T. Christ and John O. Jordan (eds), *Victorian Literature and the Victorian Visual Imagination* (Berkeley: University of California Press 1995), 111–33.
Haviland, V. and Coughlan, M. N., *Yankee Doodle's Sampler of Prose, Poetry and Pictures* (New York: Thomas Y. Crowell Company 1974).
Houfe, S., *The Dictionary of British Book Illustrators and Caricaturists 1800–1914*,

revised edn (Woodbridge: Antique Collectors' Club 1981).
Humpherys, Anne, *Travels Into the Poor Man's Country – The Work of Henry Mayhew* (Athens: University of Georgia Press 1977).
James, Louis, *Print and the People 1819–1851* (London: Allen Lane 1976).
Jameson, F., *Signatures of the Visible* (New York and London: Routledge 1990).
Kunzle, D., *The History of the Comic Strip: The Nineteenth Century* (Berkeley: University of California Press 1990).
Lambert, J. A., *A Nation of Shopkeepers – Trade Ephemera from 1654 to the 1860s in the John Johnson Collection* (Oxford: Bodleian Library 2001).
Low, Donald A., *The Regency Underworld*, revised edn (Stroud: Sutton Publishing 1999).
Maidment, Brian E., *Reading Popular Prints 1780–1870* (Manchester: Manchester University Press 1996).
—— '101 Things to do with a Fantail Hat: Dustmen, Dirt and Dandyism 1820–1860', *Textile History* 33 (spring 2002), 79–96.
—— '*Penny* Wise, *Penny* Foolish? – Representations of Mass Circulation Periodicals and "The March of Intellect" in the 1820s and 1830s', in Laurel Brake, Bill Bell and David Finkelstein (eds), *The Nineteenth Century Media and the Construction of Identity* (London: Macmillan 2000).
Meisel, Martin, *Realizations – Narrative, Pictorial, and Theatrical Arts in Nineteenth-Century England* (Princeton: Princeton University Press 1983).
Mitchell, C. Williams, *Dressed for the Job: The Story of Occupational Costume* (Poole: Blandford Press 1982).
Muir, Percy, *Victorian Illustrated Book*, revised ed. (London: B. T. Batsford 1985).
Mullin, Donald, *Victorian Plays: A Record of Significant Productions on the London Stage, 1837–1901* (New York: Greenwood Press, n.d.).
Murray, Venetia, *An Elegant Madness – High Society in Regency England* (London: Viking 1998).
Nadel, I. B. and Schwarzbach, F. (eds), *Victorian Artists and the City* (New York: Pergamon Press 1980).
Napier, Delia, 'John Lloyd of Shelton', *The Antique Collector* (October 1989), 48–53.
Nead, Lynda, *Victorian Babylon: People, Streets and Images in Nineteenth Century London* (New Haven, CT: Yale University Press 2000).
Newton, A. E., *The Format of the English Novel* (New York: Burt Franklin 1971).
Nord, Deborah Epstein, *Walking the Victorian Streets: Women, Representation and the City* (Ithaca, NY: Cornell University Press 1995).
O'Connell, Sheila, *The Popular Print in England* (London: British Museum Press 1999).
Opie, Iona and Opie, Peter, *The Nursery Companion* (Oxford: Oxford University Press 1980).
Partridge, Eric, *A Dictionary of Slang and Unconventional English*, 8th edn, ed. Paul Beale (London: Routledge & Kegan Paul 1984).
—— *Slang Today and Yesterday*, 3rd edn (London: Routledge & Kegan Paul 1950).
Patten, R. L., *Charles Dickens and his Publishers* (Oxford: Clarendon Press 1978).
—— *George Cruikshank's Life, Times and Art*, 2 vols (Cambridge: Lutterworth Press 1992 and 1996).
Picker, J., *Victorian Soundscapes* (Oxford: Oxford University Press 2003).
Quennell, P. (ed.), *Mayhew's London* (London: Spring Books, n.d.).

Reid, J. C., *Bucks and Bruisers – Pierce Egan and Regency England* (London: Routledge & Kegan Paul 1971).

Rickword, Edgell, *Radical Squibs and Loyal Ripostes* (London: Adams and Dart 1971).

Sales, Roger, 'Pierce Egan and the Representation of London', in P. W. Martin and R. Jarvis (eds), *Reviewing Romanticism* (London: Macmillan 1992).

Shepard, Leslie, *John Pitts: Ballad Printer of Seven Dials, London 1765–1844* (London: Private Libraries Association 1969).

Shesgreen, Sean and David Bywaters, 'The First London Cries for Children', *Princeton University Chronicle* 59 (winter 1998), 223–50.

Shesgreen, Sean, *Images of the Outcast: The Urban Poor in the Cries of London* (Manchester: Manchester University Press 2002).

Sinnema, Peter, *Dynamics of the Printed Page – Representing the Nation in the 'Illustrated London News'* (Aldershot: Ashgate 1998).

Smiles, Sam, *Eye Witness – Artists and Visual Documentation in Britain 1770–1830* (Aldershot: Ashgate 2000).

Speaight, George, *Juvenile Drama: The History of the English Toy Theatre* (London: Macdonald & Co. 1946).

St John, J., *The Osborne Collection of Early Children's Books 1566–1910 – A Catalogue*, 2 vols (Toronto: Toronto Public Library 1958).

Stallybrass, P. and White, A., *The Politics and Poetics of Transgression* (Ithaca, NY: Cornell University Press 1986).

Stephens, F. G. and George, M. D. *British Museum Catalogue of Political and Personal Satires*, 11 vols (London: British Museum 1874–1950). Referred to in the text as *BMC*.

Strauss, R., *Sala: The Portrait of an Eminent Victorian* (London: Constable 1942).

Sucksmith, H. P., 'The Dust Heaps in *Our Mutual Friend*', *Essays in Criticism* 23:2 (April 1973), 206–12.

Thompson, E. P. and Yeo, Eileen, *Unknown Mayhew* (London: Merlin Press 1971).

Tooley, R. V., *English Books with Coloured Plates 1790 to 1860 – A Bibliographical Account* (London: Dawsons 1973).

Trotter, D., *Cooking with Mud: The Idea of Mess in Nineteenth Century Art and Fiction* (Oxford: Oxford University Press 2000).

Tuer, Andrew W., *Old London Street Cries and the Cries of Today with Heaps of Quaint Cuts* (London: Field and Tuer 1885).

Turner, M. and Vaisey D. (eds), *Art and Commerce* (London: The Scolar Press 1973).

Twyman, Michael, *Printing 1770–1979 – An Illustrated History of its Development and Uses in England*, 2nd edn (London: British Library 1998).

Vogler, R. A., *Graphic Works of George Cruikshank* (New York: Dover 1979).

Walkowitz, Judith, *City of Dreadful Delight: Narratives of Sexual Danger in Late Victorian London* (Chicago: University of Chicago Press 1992).

Ward, Philip, *Cambridge Street Literature* (Cambridge: Oleander Press 1978).

Whalley, Joyce, *Cobwebs to Catch Flies – Illustrated Books for the Nursery or Schoolroom 1700–1900* (London: Elek 1974).

Wood, Marcus, *Radical Satire and Print Culture 1790–1822* (Oxford: Oxford University Press 1994).

# Index